Walsenburg
CROSSROADS TOWN

A HISTORY BY
Dorothy Rose Ree

COMPLETE AND UNABRIDGED

Available from

The Walsenburg Mining Museum
Post Office Box 134
Walsenburg, Colorado 81089

miningmuseum@rocketmail.com

or online at www.lulu.com/rodeowriter

Printed in The United States Of America on acid-free paper.

The *RodeoWriter Brand* and *Nocturn Lunar Cat's-Eye* colophons
are trademarks of **Nocturn Independent Publishing**.

Cover photographs provided by Carolyn Newman.
Book Design by William J. Bechaver

Front Cover Photo: Walsenburg Mining Museum coal miner statue.

COPYRIGHT © 2006
Dorothy Anne Rose Ree

ISBN: 978-0-9846572-1-6

First Edition
Third Printing Published April 2012 By

Nocturn Independent Publishing
William J. Bechaver, Publisher
Post Office Box 87
Walsenburg, Colorado 81089
Voice or Text 719-989-1305
rodeowriter@prodigy.net

DEDICATION

To Ben Ree, the love of my life and my lifelong companion, without whose support and encouragement this writing journey could not have been completed, and to Carolyn Newman, extraordinary friend, who pushed, prodded, and encouraged me all the way,

I dedicate this book.

Dorothy Rose Ree

Acknowledgments

Dr. M. Edmund Vallejo for his generous sharing of the materials of his mother, Frances Nelson Vallejo, and his own article on the 1913-14 coal strike.

Jay Crook, editor and publisher of the *Huerfano World*, for lending the bound volumes of old newspapers and allowing me to take them home.

The city clerks, Marilyn Gale Rynhart and John Zgut, for their help in using the minutes of the City Council and the Ordinance Books of Walsenburg.

John Irwin, Western History Department, Denver Public Library.

My relatives, David, Daniel, and Debbie Niles, for their unfailing support in this effort, including getting me into downtown Denver to do research.

Jan and Steve Perkins for opening their home to us, and to Jan, especially, for using her time to take us to downtown Denver to the library and to the Colorado Historical Society to do the research.

The staff of the Stephen H. Hart Library for their assistance in providing documents for my research.

Karen Cordova of California.

The Walsenburg All-School Class Reunion, the Dorothy Ree Memorial Fund and Jeanette Mall.

Mrs. Maria Elvera Cordova, great-granddaughter of John Albert.

Chuck and Nancy Hutchinson. He is the great-grandson of Cornelius Hendren.

Norma Lou Brunelli Murr. Interview about early and mid-20th century Walsenburg.

Monica Kirby [Birrer], John Thomas and the staff of the Spanish Peaks Library.

Gerry Sporleder, interview given to Carolyn Newman and me, in October 2005. We discussed her family and growing up in Walsenburg in the 20s and 30s.

Dan Unfug Summers, interview concerning his family, Jan. 30, 2006.

Richard and Betty Ridge for interview concerning the Cotarco fiasco.

Ben Ree and Carolyn Newman for their work in editing and correcting the text. William J. Bechaver, *Nocturn Independent Publishing*, for his assistance.

Albert Tomsic for loaning me his file of newspapers featuring Cotarco.

Marian Tressell for an interview about her family and for agreeing to lend pictures.

Glenn Davis for an interview about Peakview School and for allowing the use of historic photos.

Maurice Brau for interview on the proposed water park.

Margaret Gleisberg for interview on the Save Our School project.

Dan Harper for service above and beyond the call of duty in getting my computer up and running.

John and Jaye Thomas for various kinds of assistance.

To Marti Henderson for interview concerning her new business and La Plaza B & B and her interest in revitalizing Main Street.

To Municipal Judge Paula Sterk Conder, formerly City Clerk, for her help in accessing the early Ordinance Books of Walsenburg, and to Cathy DeHerrera Pineda, Richard Ridge, Debbie Bustos Hurtado and Vernie Smallwood for their work years ago in transferring the handwritten ordinances into a typed version.

Toni Brgoch and Rhonda Hribar for their help in making copies of historic photographs and documents.

Dr. David Gray, incoming superintendent of Re-1 schools, for being the third reader of the manuscript.

Larry Crosson for lending materials and a photograph of John Mall.

Carol Glorioso, who provided a portrait of John Mall.

Members of the Book Committee: Ben Ree, Carolyn Newman, Margaret Gleisberg, Carol Glorioso, and Suellen Levy.

TABLE OF CONTENTS

Chapter One

LA PLAZA DE LOS LEONES

It is nine o'clock in the morning at the corner of Main Street and Seventh Street in Walsenburg, Colorado, in the year 2006. So much traffic comes into town from the west on Highway 160, turning north to reach Interstate 25, that the state recently added a left-turn arrow to the traffic light. The light is one of only two in all of Huerfano County.

The cars turning left may be just on their way through town, but two doors west of the intersection Editor Jay Crook and his staff are about to put this week's edition of the Huerfano World to bed. The Art Deco marquee of the Fox Theatre announces the newest first-run movie to be shown starting Friday. The recently refurbished gasoline station on the corner is open for business and across from it the Black Diamond Art Gallery is offering a new exhibit. Star Drug will be opening at any moment and people are waiting to go inside to have prescriptions filled at the only pharmacy in town. Across the street Carl's Jr. stands ready to meet the hamburger needs of townspeople and tourists with its bright signs showing all the possibilities for juicy, thick hamburgers and sandwiches. It is just another day in a small, rural town in a western state, but this spot in Colorado was not always like this. Go back in time almost 147 years ago and the picture changes. Look south toward the Cucharas River. It is the year 1859 and mist is rising from the river in the early morning air and smoke curls gently up from the adobe houses near by.

In the home of Don Miguel Leon, Dona Cruzita stirs the fire so that breakfast can be prepared. In the corrals and pens the lowing of cattle and the gentle baaing of the sheep are heard as they wait for the boys and girls of La Plaza de los Leones to take them to the lush green pastures nearby.

Near the river Uncle John Albert lifts himself slowly out of bed. He's getting old now and his eventful life is behind him. He just wants to sit with his friends by the Sporleder Hotel and reminisce about more exciting days in the past.

All around this small village the day is beginning. Soon the families will eat their meager breakfasts of beans, tortillas and mutton stew. Doors open and the boys start the small herds of sheep, cattle and goats down the old Indian trail that serves this community as a street.

Throughout the day the women of La Plaza go about the tasks of making the home. They spin wool, weave cloth, clean the houses, wash clothes in the river, gather fruits and berries and cook the food for the evening meal. The men work at their own tasks – sharpening tools and making new ones, trading animals and goods with each other and with the occasional travelers who come down the trail. Traps are prepared for the winter trapping season. They go to nearby fields to tend their small crops of grain and the plots of pumpkins and squash that nestle among the trees.

Those children too young to herd the animals play along the river like young animals themselves. They wander in and out of the lush growth of wild plums and chokecherries, climb the great cottonwood by the riverbank to pick the grapes from the vine which twines among its branches.

When evening comes the herds come home with tired children trailing behind. Mothers call their families to evening prayers and the evening meal. People go to bed early because another day of toil and survival in the wilderness of the lovely Cucharas Valley will come soon, and the pattern will be repeated.

For hundreds of years this gentle valley saw only herds of wild animals and the occasional passing of Native Americans living their nomadic lives. Then came Miguel Leon and his family and several families named Atencio. They looked upon the valley and found it good. Perhaps they felt the winters would be less severe than winters in the San Luis Valley to the west where they had previously lived.

The Leones established homes beside the Indian trail near the river. The Atencio families chose a hill a mile or two to the west. Their settlement came to be known as Tequisquite while the settlement near the river became La Plaza de los Leones.

The settlements were established about the year 1859 and for several years they existed exclusively as Spanish settlements. There were two other small plazas, one of which was called Los Germanes, west of La Plaza and south of the river.

The first homes built by all of these settlers were called in Spanish *jacales*. They were made of logs set upright in a trench and the crevices were chinked with mud. Floors were of dirt and windows, if any, were small. Within a few years these somewhat primitive houses were replaced with houses built of adobe bricks, sun dried, and able to withstand all kinds of weather. The walls were thick and the houses had sod roofs and dirt floors.[1]

Of this small community, Helen Hunt Jackson in her book, ***Bits of Travel at Home*** (1878), wrote:

> *Walsenburg is an old Mexican town. There are perhaps fifty houses in it, and more than half of these are the same Mexican huts – mud floor, mud wall, mud roof; if there had been any way of baking mud till you could see through it, they would have had mud windows as well. As there were not, they compromised on windows, and have but one to a room, and many rooms without a window at all. These houses are not as uncomfortable as one would suppose and by no means as ugly. The baked mud is of a good color, and the gaudy Roman Catholic prints and effigies and shrines with which the walls are often adorned stand out well on the rich brown. The mud floors are hard and for the most part clean and smooth. Gay blankets and shawls are thrown down upon them in the better class of houses; chairs are rare. The houses remind one more of bee hives than anything else, they do swarm at their one small entrance; women and girls are there by the dozens and scores, all wearing bright shawls thrown over their heads in*

an indescribably graceful way. Even toddlers of six and seven have their brilliant shawls thrown over their heads and trailing in the dust behind; I am not sure that they are not born in them. The little boys are not so much clothed, in fact many of them are not clothed at all… All the women's voices are low and sweet; their eyes are dark and soft as the eyes of a deer, and their unfailing courtesy was touching.[2]

To the west where the Atencio clan established Tequisquite, the people also first built *jacales* and later replaced them with more substantial adobe homes. The hills to the south provided excellent pasture for cattle, sheep, and goats. Across the way was an encampment of Ute Indians, and these peaceful people, and the people of Tequisquite, visited back and forth and helped each other when needed.[3]

In La Plaza Miguel Leon lived with his wife in a well-built adobe home. Sons or perhaps brothers of Miguel were Tomas and Bernardo Leon. Tomas lived in a house just north of the home of Miguel. The two houses were connected by corrals. In fact, most of the houses had corrals connected to the homes for the sheltering of their small herds at night.

Other families included John Albert, Carmel Martinez, Jose Dolores Esquibel, Tomas Sproul and, by about 1870, Henry W. Jones, August Sporleder and Fred Walsen.[4]

The quiet, peaceful aspect of La Plaza de los Leones was not destined to last forever. Other settlers found the Cucharas Valley to be a desirable place to settle. Trappers and traders moved up and down the trail that would become Main Street, and other settlers began to establish farms and ranches along the Huerfano River and in the established area of Fort Francisco in the present town of La Veta.

About 1870 major events occurred in the Cucharas Valley, which in just a few years, would change the peaceful village of La Plaza de los Leones into a thriving, striving community dominated by German immigrants. A change in name would come about as well.

Settlers from the south who came to be known as the Georgia Colony had been arriving in the area some years before the Civil War under the leadership of Green Russell. Many settled in the La Veta area, but one group arriving in 1870 had among them Robert A. Quillian and Asbury Quillian. The two men were related, but the exact relationship is not clear.

Robert was a lawyer. He located a small cabin near the river and opened his law practice. Asbury, an ordained Methodist minister, promptly set about founding churches in the area.

In 1869 Bishop Machebeuf established the parish of *Nuestra Señora de los Siete Dolores* (Our Lady of the Seven Sorrows) in the Plaza and sent Father Joseph Percevault as the pastor. Father Percevault built a *jacal* church on the northwest corner of Main and Seventh Streets. It was not large but it would do for the small parish.[5]

Cornelius Downing Hendren arrived with his Spanish wife, Damiana Camareno, and settled on a small ranch east of La Plaza.

August Sporleder arrived in the valley about 1873 and established a small hotel. More and more travelers were going through La Plaza on the old Indian trail, and a stopping place was needed. His nephew, Louis B. Sporleder, Sr., described the inn and his uncle:

> There he became known as an inn keeper of unrivaled reputation. In the old adobe structure on the banks of the Cucharas River, usually termed the Sporleder Hotel, the "Governor" administered graciously to his many and varied guests. One dined well in those days at the inn, not so much on a variety of food, but on quality. Such heaping platefuls of lamb or mutton, done to an absolute finish! Such wonderful biscuits and pies, deep and flaky!
>
> The heart of the hotel was a long, big room (the lobby), with a Mexican fireplace and a portal in front with benches where guests could loiter and observe the beautiful trees which then covered all the river bottom. The writer recalls the large round table in the

center of the room, a lamp with a green shade, bunks along the walls, covered with buffalo robes.

A pitch-pine fire burned during the long nights of winter, a few guests reclining on bunks or chairs – topic of conversation drifted mostly to buffaloes, Indians, railroad building and trail blazing. The uniqueness and strangeness of the hotel and the beauty of the surroundings in summer days, the romantic old crossing, bordered by giant cottonwoods, the fragrance of blossoms and flowers, the shadowing recesses in the wood, the soft tinkle of bells, when herds and flocks were passing – all helped to give the place an indescribable charm which words can never express... Notable men stopped at the hotel frequently; among them General Palmer, Governor Hunt, Judge Hallett, Colonel Francisco, Colonel Boone and many others. With all of them the old innkeeper would convene and converse on a basis of equality, for he was a reader of books and his knowledge embraced many subjects.[6]

Others came to La Plaza de los Leones, notably Fred Walsen and Alexander Levy, and with all of the new arrivals came a desire for a more permanent government than was provided by the little Spanish plaza. The county seat of Huerfano County was then in Badito on the Huerfano River, and Fred Walsen and others began a campaign to have it moved to La Plaza. Incorporation then became a goal and the town was platted and named Walsenburg in honor of the energetic businessman, Fred Walsen. One account says that the name was suggested by an early Pueblo newspaperman. At any rate the little village name of La Plaza de los Leones passed into history. Soon the lovely valley could no longer be described as it had once been.

The Cucharas Valley, in which the Plaza de Los Leones rested, could be taken in at a glance. It was like a picture in its frame. In viewing the scene, as I often did in the old days, the impression on my mind was always one of intense pleasure. Life was fresh and young, all nature – forms saturated with the unimpaired vigor and beauty of an unsullied natural existence. Cold and clear ran the water of the river, its banks bordered by a vegetation of tropical richness. Trees grew straight and tall from the rich black soil, and wild fruit of every kind hung low on little trees and gleamed in varied colors from lesser bushes.

One tree with a huge grapevine entwined through its branches, I remember particularly. This monarch measured no less than four feet in diameter, and the vine stem at its base as thick as a man's thigh. Somewhat isolated from groves and forests, these two plant-forms had attained the limit of earthly perfection. Tubs full of grapes were picked from the vine every year.

The character of the landscape was altogether pastoral. An idyllic simplicity rested over the valley; peace and repose mingled with the manifold voices of Nature. The men and women who lived here in that remote period appreciated the beauty of the valley, perhaps unconsciously only, for they were a simple people, most of whom were illiterate.

They made no attempt to clear the land and the natural beauty of the valley remained unimpaired. Only what Nature offered in arable land was used. Natural opening and deep indentations into the forest were cultivated, mostly to pumpkin and corn patches. Small grain was planted on the higher levels.

The forest bordering both sides of the river was never disturbed, but was left to serve as shelter to the domestic creatures in winter. The great trees and the bushes and vines suffered destruction later by the more "civilized" species of men – followed by most disastrous results.[7]

Chapter Two

THE PIONEERS

Into the lovely valley of the Cucharas River came the early settlers. Trappers and perhaps a few traders had come to the valley in earlier years to trade with the Native Americans of the region and to search for the wealth available through trapping. But by the middle of the 19th century, groups of families came from the San Luis Valley to make their homes in the milder climate of the Cucharas Valley. Among the first families were the Leon and Atencio families. The patriarch of the Leon family was Don Miguel Antonio de Leon. Don Miguel was born about 1799. He traveled widely as a young man. He trapped with the Challifou brothers in New Mexico. Together they went on a trading expedition to the mouth of the Columbia River on the Pacific coast.

He was an old man when he came to the valley and established his home. Others came with him or followed soon after to La Plaza de los Leones, the forerunner of Walsenburg. Don Miguel was a quiet man who was not given to talking about himself. He watched life in his village and was prepared to offer assistance to all who might need it.[1]

Miguel Leon was twice married. His first wife was Isadora Vigil. His second wife was Maria de la Cruz Mestas, whom he married on August 19, 1872. It was she who came to be known as Cruzita. She was known to travelers for her hospitality and to other villagers for her skill as a midwife. Just how many children were born to these two unions cannot be verified; some of his children were probably adults by the time Don Miguel settled in the Cucharas River valley.

By the few accounts available, Miguel Leon wanted only a quiet, pastoral existence in the valley to which he came. He built an adobe home in typical Mexican style, on the east side of the trail, with closed outer walls and a patio or garden inside. Nearby Tomas Leon, a son or other relative, built a similar house and the spaces between were filled with walled pens or corrals for the stock.

Don Miguel was noted for his wisdom and just approach to all problems. He was the *alcalde,* a combination of mayor and judge. One story was told of a tragedy which might have caused another tragedy had it not been for the intervention of Miguel Leon.

> *At times there was unjust and unrighteous persecution. In one instance lightning had stricken a lad and left him horribly crippled. The blame, in some way, became attached to "Polonia", an inoffensive but rather queer old woman. At a midnight meeting an assembly of men decided to drive her forcibly away which meant sure starvation, a succumbing to the elements or to the wild beasts. Old Don Miguel protested, at first without apparent results, for the wild and blood-lusty crowd yelled "revenge."*
>
> *Soft-spoken words do more good sometimes than vociferous shouting. Don Miguel argued, slowly, mildly with the conviction of one who knows he is right. "Do you believe, you men here assembled, that God would permit lightning's power to be placed in the hands of an ignorant and feeble old woman? Do you really believe lightning obeyed her and that she directed the bolt which struck Francisquito's body? Were this so, then she is more powerful than God and henceforth we must direct our prayers to her - and not to our "Tata Dios". Much commotion and clamor followed, but when the hubbub ceased, Don Miguel had gained his point, the old woman remained in the Plaza and was not further molested.*[2]

Miguel Leon was buried in South St. Mary Cemetery in Walsenburg on June 24, 1884, according to parish records.[3]

The patriarch of the Atencio clan who settled in Tequisquite, west of La Plaza on the south side of the Cucharas River, was

Miguel Antonio Atencio. He was born in New Mexico in 1810, according to the 1870 census records, and was buried on June 21, 1885. His wife, Rumalda Martinez Atencio, also born in New Mexico in 1830, was buried on May 15, 1905. There are discrepancies in the birth and death records of the census and St. Mary Church in Walsenburg so determining their exact ages is not possible.

There is no record of when they were married. The family legends say that Atencio was much older than Rumalda, that she was only eleven when she was married and that she still played with her dolls.

The couple had seven children – Encarnacion, Luis, Rosario, Juan, Presciliana, Francisco and Antonio Cleto. At least two of these children went on to play a significant part in the history of Walsenburg.

Like the residents of La Plaza de los Leones, the people of Tequisquite first built *jacales* and later replaced them with more substantial adobe homes. Their nearest neighbors, the Utes, who lived on a hill north of the settlement, were peaceful and the people visited back and forth and helped each other when needed.[4]

Another of these interesting early settlers was John David Albert, who was known to the residents of the La Plaza as Uncle John.

Before Albert's birth his father had helped to found a colony of German and Dutch Quakers in Germantown, Pennsylvania. The family later moved to Hagerstown, Maryland, where John David was born in 1806. His father was killed in the Battle of New Orleans in 1811, and his mother died shortly thereafter, leaving him an orphan at the age of six.

Exactly how the boy lived and managed until his teens is not recorded, but he survived and came west to the Mississippi River in his teens. He worked up and down the Ohio and Missouri Rivers on flat-bottom boats until he finally stopped in St. Louis.

From there he moved further west into the Rocky Mountains. In some accounts he is said to have trapped on the Cucharas in

1834, but this doesn't seem possible since he came west with John A. Turpin in 1834. This party wintered north of where Denver is now located. Probably it was a year or two later that Albert ventured south to the Cucharas River.

After further wanderings in southern Colorado and northern New Mexico, he settled in the Taos Valley. It was his intent to live a quiet life as a farmer and to give up the trapping of his earlier days.

His plans were changed, however, by the turmoil in New Mexico that led to the uprising of 1847. Governor Bent and many others were murdered in Taos. On the day of the uprising John Albert was in Arroyo Hondo, a village seven miles north of Taos.

Word came that the marauders of Taos were heading toward Arroyo Hondo. John Albert and nineteen others took refuge in a large building known as Turley's Mill. Among the defenders of the mill were the owner, Turley, and the well-known mountain man, Tom Tobin.

The besiegers demanded unconditional surrender and promised that no one would be killed. Having already heard of the carnage in Taos, the defenders of the mill chose to fight. First blood was evidently drawn by John Albert, who shot an Indian who had been dancing in full view and taunting the defenders. Infuriated by this shooting, the attackers charged the mill. They were soon inside and the mill was set on fire. Amid the chaos of the fighting, Tom Tobin and John Albert managed to escape.

Tobin went to his home across the arroyo where his wife and children waited, but John Albert had no home to go to.

After barely escaping from his foes in the mill, he reached the outside world minus his coat and hat. Even with a foot of snow on the ground, he knew that his only hope was to go north. His goal was Fort Pueblo (where the current city of Pueblo stands) some 140 miles north.

During the night he met two men, one of whom was Antonio Sotelo Pino. Albert hoped to get information or assistance from them but was unable to do so. One account speculates that he killed one or both of them and obtained a horse.

He continued on, passing the site of the present town of Questa, New Mexico, and arrived at Costilla, which straddles the Colorado and New Mexico border, many hours later. He pushed on to the foot of the Sangre de Cristo Mountains. He had covered ninety miles in twenty-four hours.

He was still lacking in warm clothing and food, but he had managed to keep rifle, powder and lead safe and dry. A deer appeared within easy rifle distance and, despite his weak condition, Albert shot the animal. He ate a piece of raw liver which he had done many other times, but this time, probably because he had been without food for so long, the meat made him deathly ill. When he recovered, he skinned the animal. Wearing the fur side of the skin next to him and placing the head of the deer on his head, he went on his way.

At last he reached a party of Mormons near El Pueblo. They carried him to the Fort where he was restored to health. He told his story and a message was dispatched to Bent's Fort to William Bent, the brother of the murdered governor.[5] John Albert stayed on in the area and eventually settled in La Plaza de los Leones. He erected a fort on the banks of the Cucharas River for the protection of the settlers and built his home near by. At first the unnamed settlement was known as John's Town. Albert was the first postmaster and chose the name Carson for the post office, in honor of his friend Kit Carson.[6]

He claimed to have been married twice, although a third marriage in New Mexico is possible. Albert stated that he had fathered twenty-six children and at least fourteen children have been verified by researchers looking into the records.

Louis B. Sporleder, Sr. wrote of his long friendship with John Albert:

> Uncle John, as he was familiarly known, and old "Governor" (August) Sporleder, called thus because of his great dignity, were on the most intimate terms of an enduring friendship. Every evening in pleasant summer days Uncle John took his place on the bench beneath the arcade which fronted the old Inn and long

conversations ensued. Many thrilling tales were told to the few guests, some of whom, in later years, gathered riches and fame. It was the privilege of the writer to attend these discourses from which he gathered a large store of facts.

During the long years of my friendship with this unusual man (although not an educated man) he greatly influenced my life with his good common sense and his strong and original traits of character. He visited me often and on one occasion brought with him the snow-white pelt of a beaver which he trapped where the city of Walsenburg now stands. Very rare are albino beavers and Uncle John was elated over his "streak of luck". But he gained nothing from his lucky catch for he found no buyer for the freak pelt and finally presented it to my cousin, Emilie Sporleder Walsen.[7]

It was John Albert's custom upon the death of his wife to divide his property and money among his children by that wife. He would then start again. Because he may have had twenty-six children, John Albert was finally left with little more than his small home by the river. But by all accounts he was a contented man as long as he could sit and reminisce with his friends.

Because of his many children, John Albert has numerous descendants, some of whom still live in Walsenburg. One of his great-granddaughters, Mrs. Elvera Cordova, lived in a three-room miner's cottage on East Seventh Street.[8]

One of the first Anglo settlers in La Plaza was Henry W. Jones, who was born in 1818 in Westminster, Maryland. He arrived in 1865 and first settled on the Francisco-Daigre ranch near La Veta. The next year he moved to the Cucharas River and built a house just west of what is now Walsenburg's Main Street.

Jones established a ranch and, according to Sporleder, the boundaries extended from a point near the present United Methodist Church at the corner of Walsen Avenue and Kansas Avenue, south to somewhere across the river, west to an old railroad water tank, north to what is now Wyoming Street and back to the beginning.[9]

Jones and his wife, Eliza Yantes Jones, had the first Anglo baby born in La Plaza. The midwife was Cruzita Leon, the wife of Don Miguel Leon. Although Mrs. Jones spoke no Spanish and often felt out of place in La Plaza, she became friends with Cruzita thanks to her successful midwifery. The baby, named Fanny, became the darling of the community and when the Jones family moved away, it was with great sadness that women of the community said farewell to the little Anglo girl who was so different from their own beautiful, dark-haired, dark-eyed children.

Because of the language barrier and, perhaps, a gentler upbringing, Mrs. Jones was not happy in La Plaza. A letter written by her to the Pioneer Association in the early 1920's relates her feelings:

A request of the Pioneer's Association that I give a little sketch of my life in the early days of Walsenburg, which is now a flourishing and prosperous town of five or six thousand inhabitants.

To say the least – my life was neither a happy nor a prosperous one. Isolated from all civilization, our house of adobe, with dirt floor and roof which leaked in storm of rain or snow, without comfort or convenience of any kind. Even the water we used, had to be carried a block from the Cucharas River. Not a white neighbor among several hundred Mexican families, excepting a once Lieutenant in the U. S. Army, who had a pretty Mexican wife and little girl. She could speak a little English and I a little Spanish. We managed to understand each other and visited occasionally.

My heart ached many times when I thought of my little children – innocent of all civilization, growing up without any associates or schooling. No excitement of any kind except occasionally a rumor of hostile Indians in the valley – which was far from a pleasant excitement. Only a rough and unpolished life of the early pioneer. I wonder how I ever lived through it.

The only redeeming feature is – we were never sick. I recall a conversation. A man from the "States", as we termed it then, chanced to stop overnight with us. Asked what we did for a doctor when we got sick, I replied – we were never sick. He looked amazed. I suppose it was the first family he had ever seen who were never sick.[10]

From the tone of her letter it seems clear that Mrs. Jones was not cut out to be a pioneer in a Mexican settlement although she was a descendent of Daniel Boone. In 1869 Jones moved from La Plaza to Las Animas where he served as judge and clerk. Later the family moved to Pueblo where he served as city clerk for two terms. He died October 5, 1885. Mrs. Jones apparently outlived her husband by many years and the much-loved Fanny, born in La Plaza de los Leones, also lived to a great age.

The first of the Sporleder clan to make the Cucharas Valley a permanent home was "Governor" August Sporleder. No one seems quite sure where the title originated although it may have been the handsome old man's dignified appearance.

The Sporleder Hotel was near the river (the northeast corner of what is now Eighth and Main Streets) and remained there for several years. Later August built another hotel which was located at the northeast corner of Main and Fifth, the Unfug Hardware store site.

The "Governor" was proud of the family traditions handed down from generation to generation: transmitting beliefs supported by the facts of history which date to the Thirteenth century. According to this continuing, unwritten story, all Sporleders are lineal descendants of a clan in North Germany which flourished from the year 1300 A. D. to the time of the Thirty Years War. It was a mounted military organization, with the titles of its members not hereditary, but conferred only for unusual deeds of valor.

These cavalry men were known in the ancient days as the Freiherrn von Spornleder, a term when translated into English means the "Knights of Freemen of the Spur". Literally, the word Sporleder means spur-leather or spur-strap. The men of the various troops were mercenaries, serving dukes and princes for pay or the privilege of looting camps of the enemy.[11]

Eventually these troops of mercenaries were disbanded and the members went their separate ways. August, who was born on a little estate in Brunswick in the early nineteenth century, came to America at the request of two older brothers who had already made the journey.

He established a business in Westport on the Missouri River but transferred his movable property to St. Louis during the troubled times that led to the Civil War. He stayed in St. Louis until coming to Walsenburg in 1873.[12]

It may have been in St. Louis that August married and became the father of two daughters, Emilia and Lillie, both of whom married men prominent in the history of Walsenburg.

Captain Cornelius Downing Hendren was an early settler who took up land about two miles east of La Plaza de los Leones, probably along the river.

Hendren was born February 6, 1829, at Norfolk, Norfolk County, Virginia. He was a West Point man who accepted a commission as lieutenant in the 3rd U. S. Infantry April 3, 1857. Apparently an advance in rank occurred along the way since it was as Captain Hendren that he traveled to New Mexico to join his regiment on November 19, 1857. He saw service at both Fort Massachusetts and Fort Garland and received an honorable discharge on June 30, 1860. It seems likely that he remained at Fort Garland or in its neighborhood for several years since the records show that he married Damiana Camareno, a widow, on May 20, 1863, at the fort.[13]

After his marriage he and his wife moved to a small ranch east of La Plaza. They built a home and started their family which eventually included five children: Fred, Syrus, Bella, Virgie and Gertrude. It was during this time that Mrs. Hendren became friends with the unhappy Eliza Yantes Jones, the mother of the first Anglo baby born in La Plaza.

Later Hendren and his family moved to land near the Spanish Peaks, probably along the Santa Clara Creek near the Sporleder ranch. Hendren and Louis B. Sporleder became acquainted when Louis was able to repair a rifle for him.

Sporleder wrote of his friend:

> *The captain was a Spanish scholar of distinction. He frequently acted as an interpreter in the district court, and what his delivery lacked in speed, his aggregation of words far exceeded even that of Joseph Bourcy, the official interpreter in Huerfano County for many years.*
>
> *Aside from his law books (he dabbled a little in the practice of law), Captain Hendren possessed a small but well selected library, chiefly historical works, and books pertaining to Ethnology.*
>
> *His penetrating intellect readily observed business propositions, but owing to a dearth of ready cash, and too proud to ask, and not gifted with the talent to persuade and induce others to advance the necessary capital, he contented himself by figuring out those propositions theoretically.*
>
> *Years before the idea of creating reservoirs in Huerfano County took form, he had in mind located the most promising site: among others, the big lake west of Walsenburg (Martin Lake) from which the Fruth and Autry ranch was irrigated.*
>
> *One project which he had in mind, even before Colorado became a state, was the development of the group of small, natural lakes, situated between the head of Bear Creek and the Story branch of the Santa Clara. A body of clear and intensely blue water was to be found in the largest of the lakes. A shore of green sward, dotted with innumerable flowers and giant trees, created a beautiful setting.*
>
> *The Captain's plan was to bring water from Bear Creek to these lakes and raise the level of the water high enough to connect the group into one large reservoir of very irregular outline – but not for irrigation purposes – only for the culture of fish.*[14]

Later Captain Hendren moved his family to Walsenburg in order that his children might receive a good education.

His son, Fred, was at one time the official lamplighter in Walsenburg when the streets were lit with gas lights. Fred married Margaret Wiehl and they had three children: Arna Josephine, twins Alfred Charles and Freddie, Jr. The boy Freddie died in infancy.

The founder of this early pioneer family, Cornelius Hendren, died in Walsenburg on November 17, 1894, following an accident when his team ran away en route to Cucharas Junction. Like many of the early pioneers, a street in Walsenburg is named for him.[15]

Another remarkable early settler was Jose Anastacio de Jesus Valdes who wrote of himself that he and his family and other Spanish settlers came into the Cucharas Valley in 1862 to spend the winter. They grouped themselves together as a means of protecting their stock and themselves from the Plains Indians who roamed the area. As the valley was not yet settled, these families continued to come only to winter here.

In March of 1867 J. A. J. Valdes and his father established residence in Germanes {or spelled Hermanes} Plaza, which lay west of La Plaza de los Leones and north of today's U.S. 160 before the highway starts up the hill to Lathrop. Among these settlers were Evaristo Gonzales, Antonio Jose Vallejos, Juan M. Chavez, Jose Antonio Martinez, Eulojio Martinez and others.[16]

Jose Anastasio de Jesus Valdes was born in Questa, New Mexico, April 27, 1847. His father, Jose Mariano J. Valdes, a farmer of Taos, New Mexico, removed to San Pablo, Costilla County, Colorado, in 1861, where his son was engaged in herding sheep. In 1867, Mr. Valdez, now twenty years old, came to Huerfano County.

Always anxious to better himself he went to Pueblo where he attended the school of the Rev. Samuel Edwards. In exchange he instructed Rev. Edwards in Spanish and gave Spanish lessons to others.

Mr. Valdes was a member of the Territorial Legislature in 1874 at which time he framed a bill imposing punishment for malicious damage to property. The bill passed and became law.

He studied law with the Hon. Robert A. Quillian in Walsenburg and was admitted to the bar in 1890. He served as judge one term, 1881 to 1884, and as County Clerk in 1869 and 1870.

On February 12, 1873, Judge Valdes married Maria Silvenia Salazar of Las Animas County. After her death in 1882, the Judge married Victoria Sanchez of Walsenburg. She passed away in 1886. Two children, Eloy and Magdalene, were born to them. In 1885 Mr. Valdes furnished valuable aid in obtaining information for the State census. He visited every part of the County obtaining facts, concerning crops, stock, poultry as well as details about the villages and towns. He served one term as Mayor of Walsenburg.

During the years 1906-1912 Judge Valdes edited and published a Spanish newspaper, La Opinion Publica, which proved a factor in the intellectual life of this growing community.[17]

Benton Canon was an early Walsenburg settler who lived here for a relatively short number of years, but nevertheless had a profound effect on one aspect of the history of Huerfano County.

Canon arrived in Denver in June of 1865 after a career in railroading and other activities. He came to Huerfano County in 1866 and raised a crop of corn on the Huerfano River, which he sold to Kit Carson, commander of Ft. Garland. The price of the corn was twelve cents per pound.

In 1872 Canon went into the mercantile business in Walsenburg. He served as the first treasurer of Huerfano County and held that post for ten years.

After living in La Veta for a number of years, he moved to Grand Junction but never forgot his beginnings in Huerfano County.

He began to think of putting all of his memories into a history and in that interest he sent a form letter to his Huerfano County friends.

A message to my Pioneer Friends of Huerfano County:
In 1880 the late Robert A Quillian, Charles O. Unfug and myself decided that we would lay the foundation for the future

history of Huerfano County by collecting biographical details relating to the oldest settlers and other information about the county, past and present. We set about gathering material in the hope that therefrom a connected narrative might be made subsequently. We each contributed $100 toward a fund for necessary expenses. We employed the late Judge Daniel J. Hayden to do the work and he accumulated a mass of reminiscences from the oldest pioneers and papers of inestimable value, but unfortunately interest in the undertaking waned. Judge Hayden lost his manuscript, and my two old-time associates crossed the Great Divide without seeing the fruits of their endeavors preserved on the printed page.

Realizing that time was flying and the ranks of the pioneers were getting thin, I made a visit from Grand Junction to Walsenburg for the purpose of discussing with old friends the propriety of reorganizing our Pioneer Association. The result was a meeting of old-timers held at La Veta, November 10, 1915 and the Huerfano County Pioneer Association was organized. Those present mutually agreed that it was desirable to go ahead with our original undertaking. Thereupon the following officers and directors of the association were duly elected.

Hiram W. Vasquez, President; Louis B. Sporleder, First Vice President; J. K. Kincaid, Second Vice President; W. T. Sharp, Third Vice President; Samuel J. Capps, Secretary; and James G. Hamilton, Treasurer. Directors: Alexander Levy, Louis B. Sporleder, Charles Mazzone, Samuel J. Capps, Hiram W. Vasquez, J. K. Kincaid, James G. Hamilton, Fred G. Walsen, Samuel Jacks, W. T. Sharp, T. M. Hudson, Benton Canon and Mary E. Hayden. Benton Canon was elected historian for the Association.[18]

Unfortunately the plans of this association to create a history of Huerfano County came to nothing, but the writings of Benton Canon came into the hands of Louis B. Sporleder. There is little doubt that Canon inspired Sporleder's desire to write his biographical sketches which are priceless in the current writing.

Robert A. Quillian was born in Dahlonega, Georgia, in 1842. He was educated at the Home Academy run by a Colonel Boyd and later studied law with Boyd. Like other southerners he enlisted as a private at the onset of the Civil War. He must have been a capable soldier as he received several promotions, and at the end of the war he was the Regimental Adjutant.

Quillian found the idea of going west desirable in the aftermath of the terrible war. He joined one of Green Russell's wagon trains and started out with his brother and sister and another relative, the renowned preacher, Asbury Quillian.

He began his law practice in a small cabin on the Cucharas river in Walsenburg and for a time lodged in a boarding house managed by Thomas A. Rivero.

Robert married Isabell J. Campbell of Walsenburg on Thanksgiving Day, November 25, 1875. The couple had four children, George, Mabel, Robert and Helen.

Quillian was chosen as a delegate to the Colorado Constitutional Convention in 1875 and helped write the document which brought Colorado into the Union on August 1, 1876, as the 38th state. He went on to serve one term in the legislature but then returned home to spend his time with his family.

An active citizen, Robert Quillian was one of four charter members of the Methodist Church, helped found one of the two Masonic Lodges, and later served as Grand Master of his lodge.

Quillian was at one time the County Attorney and also the District Attorney for Huerfano and Las Animas Counties.

Quillian died December 8, 1892, and many of the most notable citizens of Walsenburg including J. A. J. Valdes, who had studied law with him, Alexander Levy, Fred and C. O. Unfug, Dr. T. D. Baird and others were his pallbearers. It was said of him that he never refused a case in which he believed just because the client might not be able to pay him.[19]

In 1874 a remarkable man arrived in Huerfano County from Cincinnati, Ohio. His name was Charles Mazzone and he first worked for his brother-in-law, Herman Duhme, on his ranch in the Santa Clara Valley.

Ranch life didn't suit the young man and he decided to go into business in Walsenburg. Sporleder tells us his story in the following:

As a good business man, he saw that there was an opening for the dispensation of wines and liquors, all of which, up to that time, had been handled only by the traders and merchants. Walsen and Levy, Benton Canon and other storekeepers of the county, each carried a stock of wet goods – but it was sold wholesale only, and not by the glass or drink.

It must be remembered that the selling of liquors was a perfectly legitimate business then, requiring only a so-called government grocery-license to dispense it to the people.

The saloon which Mr. Mazzone opened, undoubtedly, improved conditions greatly - and assisted in regulating the traffic in the stronger drinks. At the trading posts and stores the article was sold by the gallon or quart - sometimes tempting the purchaser to drink more than was good for him. Mazzone sold whiskey by the glass - a small glass at that; further, he introduced beer, theretofore an unknown beverage among the natives. Beer and wine, largely, took the place of the strong, burning "aguardiente" - to which the natives and the old westerners were accustomed.

The establishment Mr. Mazzone opened was one of the cleanest, best-managed concerns of its kind in Colorado. There was no rowdyism or drunkenness; the law pertaining to the sale of intoxicating beverages to the Indians, minors, and habitual drunkards was religiously observed.

Mr. Mazzone first located north of the old adobe Masonic Hall. From there he moved to the two-story brick building, known for many years as the Opera House. During all the long years the "lobby" was open to the public - it served as a sort of meeting place for the most prominent men of Walsenburg and Huerfano County.

Charley took pride in his establishment. There were round tables and comfortable chairs where one could sit down for hours - to dream, meditate, or read the newspapers. The big room conveyed a sense of home-like comfort, and a spirit of "camarade-

rie" prevailed among the frequenters that is never quite approached in the present so-called clubs.

Immaculate in dress was Charley always - well-groomed and tidy as a woman. Decanters and glasses gleamed like diamonds. Pretzels or an appetizing lunch stood on the bar invitingly. Beer and wine were perfectly cooled - and what is more important - they had been properly made and aged...

Not alone were spirituous liquors, wholesome wine and beer of the best quality dispensed, but one could get a glass of real seltzer, mineral water, a mug of beef tea, clam juice or buttermilk - just as readily. Many teetotalers, pledged to total abstinence, patronized Mazzone's saloon.[20]

Charles Mazzone married Caroline Lagomarsino in 1877 and their children were prominent in the history of the town. Mazzone also served as county treasurer and as mayor and alderman of Walsenburg. Some of his descendants still live in the area although there is no more named Mazzone.[21]

Another early resident of the area was Charles Otto Unfug. Born in Bielefeld, Westphalia, Germany, July 3, 1846, he was a member of a large and well-off family. He came to this country in the early sixties, settling in St. Louis for a time as did so many of the newcomers. He was employed by the large firm of F. W. Posthoff and Co. He joined an ox-drawn caravan as a bull-whacker. Not being used to this kind of work, the young man soon found himself in real difficulty. Fortunately a Mexican worker, Francisco Martinez, a freighter, took pity on him and helped him work out a plan whereby he could ride part of the time in a wagon.

Unfug remained with the firm for four years, learning the business and learning Spanish.

In 1869 he was in Badito, which was then the county seat of Huerfano County. Ferdinand Meyer measured his worth and placed him in charge of his Badito Store.

Sporleder wrote of him:

Clerking or running a trading establishment in the early days of the country was not an easy task. It required a certain type of man, not alone possessing a large amount of courage and business ability, but also the virtue of a well-balanced mind and a pleasing personality. It was not long until he entered the political field of Huerfano County, then centered at the old Plaza de Los Leones, now Walsenburg. The young politician's influence and power increased and he was soon elected to public office.[22]

Unfug served as county clerk and recorder and was later elected clerk of the county and district courts. He was nominated for the office of Secretary of State on the Democratic ticket in 1880, but his party went down to defeat. He again was nominated for this office in 1884 and again failed to be elected.

Thereafter he devoted himself to his mercantile business. Several of his brothers also came to this county and the name Unfug was prominent in many aspects of community and business life for many years. The hardware store which was a fixture on the northeast corner of Main and Fifth Streets bore the name Unfug Hardware until 2006 even though there were many other owners over the years.[23]

In 1870 the first of two remarkable men arrived in La Plaza de los Leones. Heinrich Anton Frederick Walsen was born in Petersagen, Germany, June 14, 1841. At age eighteen he emigrated to America, landing in New Orleans. Like so many others his next stop was St. Louis. He enlisted in the Union Army in 1861 after first serving with the Missouri Volunteers. After his discharge he joined the Missouri National Guard with the rank of sergeant.

Following this service Walsen went to Fort Garland, Colorado, where he was employed as a clerk with Ferdinand Meyer and Co. After a few years of this he came to La Plaza in 1870 and opened the first trading post in a room of the building known as the Sporleder Hotel.

In 1871 the second of these two men arrived in the Cucharas Valley. Alexander Levy, who was born in Austria to Jewish parents, came to the United States in 1866.

Like so many other Jewish pioneers in the west, Levy entered into trade. He worked in New Mexico for several years as a wagon boss for Wedeles Brothers in Mora, New Mexico, and as a clerk in the mercantile house of Ilfeld in Las Vegas.

In 1875 he entered a partnership with Fred Walsen in the general mercantile business. In 1883 Levy bought Walsen's interest in the business and carried it forward in his own name for many years. An early volume of Colorado biographies said of him:

Immediately after coming here, Mr. Levy opened a general mercantile store, but in December of the same year he sold out his business. He then engaged in his brother's business in Trinidad, remaining in that city until 1875, when he returned to Walsenburg and here he has resided continuously since that time. In 1875 he entered into partnership with Fred Walsen in the general mercantile business, but in 1883 he bought his partner's interest, and has since carried on the business alone, having through his energy and reliable dealings built up a trade that extends through all the surrounding country. In 1875 he became interested in railroad contracting, which he carried on, in addition to his other business. He had contracts in Colorado and New Mexico, and built sections of the Denver & Rio Grande, the Santa Fe, and the Rio Grande Southern railroads. Up to the present time he has continued to take contracts. He also owns a fine ranch and has stock interests in Huerfano County, besides real estate in Walsenburg.

As an adherent of the Democratic party, Mr. Levy has taken an active part in local politics and is a leading man of his party in the county. Both in 1880-1882 and 1890-1892 he served as county treasurer. He also held the position of town treasurer and member of the city council. Actively interested in the cause of education, he has promoted the interest of the local schools through his efficient service as a member of the board of school directors, of which he has served ably as president. In this position it has been his aim to do all within his power to promote the standard of scholarship and benefit the schools, in order that the children may have all the advantages which a thorough education affords.

Fraternally he is connected with the blue lodge of Masonry and has been its master; he is also identified with Walsenburg Chapter R. A. M. {Royal Arch Masons}. *His marriage took place in 1880 and united him with Lillie Sporleder, by whom he has four children, Archie, Ralph, Walter and Earl.*[24]

The names of both of these men and their wives loom large in the history of Walsenburg and more will be heard of them later. Their influence cannot be overestimated. No descendants of Fred Walsen remain in the city which bears his name, but many descendants of Alexander Levy are still important figures in our modern town.

Chapter Three

LA PLAZA BECOMES WALSENBURG

The lovely village called La Plaza de los Leones could not long remain merely a peaceful Spanish town. By the time Fred Walsen opened his first trading post, the country was already changing.

Cornelius Hendren, Herman Duhme, Louis B. Sporleder Sr. and others had established ranches in the Santa Clara Valley near the Spanish Peaks. The land there was fertile and plenty of water was available for stock and people.

The settlement known then as Francisco Plaza or Francisco Fort in 1863 was well established with pioneers such as Colonel John Francisco, Henry Daigre, Hiram Vasquez and others starting businesses and taking up land in the area.[1]

Two pioneers near Walsenburg were William Green Russell and Joseph Decatur Patterson, childhood friends from Georgia. Russell had first prospected in the Pikes Peak country on his way to California in 1849 and again in 1852 on his way home. In 1858 and 1859 his friend, "Kate" Patterson, came with him on a mining expedition to the area around Pikes Peak.

Finding the country desirable, they went home to Georgia and persuaded a number of people to move west. Among the members of this first group were Dr. Levi J. Russell and J. Oliver Russell, brothers of Green Russell, and a cousin, James H. Pierce. Others were Samuel Bates, Isaac G. Roberts, William and John Wisher, Robert Field, John Glass and the Joshua P. Potts family.

During the Civil War these people attempted to return to the south to aid the cause of the Confederacy. They were pursued and captured by military forces from Denver and taken to Fort Union, New Mexico, to be held as prisoners of war. They were told that they would find it almost impossible to make their way through Indian country to return to their Georgia homes.

While at Fort Union, Kate Patterson met many of the famous men of the Rocky Mountains: Ceran St. Vrain, Richens "Uncle Dick" Wooten, Lucian B. Maxwell, Kit Carson, Governor A. C. Hunt, Governor Gilpin and others. Through their influence the Georgians were released. St. Vrain urged Patterson to take the colony and settle in the Huerfano Valley. This they did and thereby brought a new influx of settlers to the area near La Plaza de los Leones. Patterson and his bride settled near the home of John W. Brown. By the 1870s a considerable number of southerners had come west to form what is known as the Georgia Colony. Among its members were John Alexander, John Brown, Albert Chastain and other members of his family, Dr. John Gribble, Robert Julia, Perry T. Kimbrel, James and Joseph Kincaid, Isaac Prater, Robert A. Quillian and his brother and sister, Green Russell and his family, and the remarkable Asbury H. Quillian and family. [2]

New settlers were coming from many other areas as well. Along the Huerfano River near the "Orphan" Butte, a group of Frenchmen took up land and began a new settlement. One of these newcomers was Antoine LaBrie.

Like many other settlers, LaBrie's American story begins in St. Louis. He came from Canada and after a time he and several other young men were engaged by Colonel Bent to come west with one of his wagon trains. The arduous journey by wagon train eventually brought them to Bent's Fort, where they stayed for some time and learned more about the country.

When he left Bent's Fort, LaBrie established a ranch on the Huerfano River with a stage station and store at the Huerfano crossing of the stage line between Denver and Santa Fe. It was known as the Butte Valley station and was located about two miles east of Huerfano Butte. [3]

Some accounts of the time said that LaBrie left the Huerfano Valley years later, but the truth is somewhat different. He married Merry Leon Strange, the daughter of Henry Strange, who opposed the marriage, and moved to the area now known as Pryor. His niece tells the story:

> *Some historians have written that the Frenchmen then left the Huerfano never to return but this was not true of Antoine LaBrie. He was at Butte Valley when the Strange family arrived there in 1868, and on September 9, 1869, he and Merry Leon Strange were married in Trinidad, Colorado. For several years, they lived on a ranch on the Santa Clara River, or creek as it is known today, where the Pryor Brothers had located after the Civil War and the place became known as "Pryor". Antoine built a log house there and Aunt Leon was fortunate to have "help" with the housework. Even then, coal was near the surface of the ground and was used to keep the log house warm and comfortable. An item in a local newspaper stated, "Antoine Labrie, owner of a fine farm where Pryor is situated, conceived the idea of cutting and curing the high prairie grass to sell to the Stage Companies and traders at the villages of Walsenburg and Cucharas." A canyon north of the Santa Clara, and running into that creek at Pryor, is still known as "Antoine Canyon."*[4]

Other French-Canadians also settled along the Huerfano River near LaBrie and these people also were part of the growing number of ranchers and farmers who were taking up land along the Huerfano and Cucharas Rivers, the Santa Clara Creek and the many other waterways that crisscrossed the territory.

During this time, La Plaza de los Leones was undergoing change. Gone was the placid Spanish plaza where the way of life was one of serenity and leisure. The travel up and down the trail and the influx of new settlers required businesses to serve their needs. Fred Walsen, Alexander Levy, the Unfug brothers and others came west to fulfill those needs.

Walsen arrived in 1870 after having been at Badito for several years in the employ of Ferdinand Meyer. In La Plaza he established a trading post in part of the building which was the first Sporleder Hotel. Alexander Levy came the following year and soon the two formed a partnership. They built a new trading post, believed to have been on the southwest corner of Seventh and Main, which they operated along with their other business interests for two or three years after which the partnership was dissolved, and Levy went into business for himself.

The two men had chosen the two daughters of innkeeper August Sporleder of St. Louis as their brides. Walsen married Emilie Sporleder, the older of the two sisters and Levy married Lillie Sporleder. Levy and Lillie were married in the Sporleder Hotel run by the bride's father. Both of these marriages produced several children. The Walsen family later moved to Denver, but Alexander and Lillie Levy lived their entire lives in the town where they were married.

As the town grew, its residents began to desire a more permanent identity. The Leon family donated more than three hundred acres to be the center of the town.

There are several stories about how the name, Walsenburg, was chosen, but it seems likely that the name came from a Pueblo newspaper whose editor suggested that, due to Fred Walsen's many activities in support of the growing community, the city should be named Walsenburg in his honor, and, for a time, was spelled in the German way with the letter h at the end – Walsenburgh. The name Walsenburg, however, was formally adopted and the name La Plaza de los Leones faded slowly into history.[5]

The actual establishment of the town was accomplished in 1873 with the following order:

ORDER TO INCORPORATE
THE TOWN OF WALSENBURG
Whereas, a petition has been presented to this Board signed by two-thirds (2/3) of the residents of the Town of Walsenburg in Huerfano County, asking that the Said town be incorporated.

It is hereby ordered that the Said Town of Walsenburg be and it is hereby incorporated, and that the inhabitants within the following described metes and bounds shall be a body politic and corporate by the name of the Town of Walsenburg. To Wit: The South-east quarter (1/4) of the South-east quarter (1/4) of Section

Four (4); and the East half (1/2) of the South-east quarter (1/4) of Section Nine (9); and the West half (1/2) of the North-west quarter (1/4) and the South-west quarter (1/4) of the South-west quarter (1/4) of Section ten (10) township twenty-eight (28) South of Range Sixty-six (66), west of the Sixth (6) municipal meridian.

Corrected to read as follows, viz
The South-east quarter (1/4) and the South half (1/2) of the North-east Quarter (1/4), and the East half (1/2) of the South-west quarter (1/4) of Section nine (9) in Township Twenty-eight (28) South of Range sixty-six 66) West of the Sixth municipal meridian.

The following named persons were appointed Trustees, for the time required by law, of the aforesaid Town of Walsenburg, viz:
    s/ Fred Walsen   *s/ Joseph Bourcy*
    s/ John Albert   *s/ Jose Rafael Esquibel*
    s/ Carmel Martin [6]

It is not clear from the documents just how long these men remained as the sole governing body of Walsenburg or when the decision was made to begin electing a mayor, city clerk and other officials.

Next the enterprising businessmen of the newly named community set their sights on making their town the county seat.

Huerfano county, as originally organized in 1861, comprised the area which now constitutes the counties of Huerfano and Las Animas, together with that part of Bent lying south of the Arkansas river, and that part of Pueblo lying south of the same stream and east of the St. Charles river. The county was so inconveniently large that as its settlement progressed, it was, with the common consent of the people, divided by an act of the Territorial Legislature in 1867, when the present limits were established. The organization of the county as a political entity in those first years was little more than a figure of speech. Because the distances were so immense and towns did not exist, official proceedings presented a real problem. It is doubtful if the first county judge ever held court, and the commissioners met only once during their term of office. After the division it was the good fortune of the county to inherit about an equal portion of plain and mountain.[7]

To bring the county seat to Walsenburg took major effort and all of the leading citizens, including Fred Walsen, were involved in it. Badito had been the county seat for some years. It had a courthouse, other businesses, and homes and, not surprisingly, wished to continue in its position as the seat of county government. Walsenburg, however, was the growing community and its situation along a main avenue of commerce and its position on the Cucharas River made it a natural, at least to Walsen and his allies.

In order to change the location, an election was necessary. The first efforts were unsuccessful due to the fact that each community in the county voted for itself as the best location for the county seat. It is said that in order to accomplish his goal, Fred Walsen went to Denver and engineered a change in the law so that a simple majority of voters in the county could effect the change. Since Walsenburg had the largest population, the vote promptly brought about the desired relocation of the county seat.

This was accomplished about 1872, but it took several months, possibly a year or two, before the last of the records were moved from Badito to Walsenburg. On the day of the final transfer, a celebration took place as the records were transported by wagon accompanied by a parade which included banners, a band and lots of celebratory noise.

The first courthouse in Walsenburg was a simple wooden building located on Lot 2, Block 52 (on the east side of Main Street between Seventh and Eighth). A few years later a second building was built, which in later years, was known as Ben Arnold's Carpenter Shop.

During the next few years the city continued its growth as new businesses came into being. The Unfug brothers had arrived and had started what would eventually be a variety of business activities, but their principal work was in hardware.

Fred Walsen and Alexander Levy built a new trading post in 1881 which was described as follows by Editor J. B. King in the *La Veta Herald* as quoted by Henry Nardine *In the Shadow of the Spanish Peaks*:

> It was our pleasure on Saturday last to take a look through the handsome new store just erected and opened in Walsenburg by Messrs. Walsen and Levy, the enterprising merchants of that city. This building during its construction has been of more than usual interest throughout the area.
>
> The new building is 28 × 106 feet in dimensions, 14 feet to ceiling. In front of each side of the large double doors are handsome, elegant show windows protected by wire screen upon which the painter was just putting the finishing touches. The reader is invited to take an imaginary stroll with us through the immense establishment... The shelves on either side are crowded to their utmost capacity with goods of variegated colors that harmonize and captivate the eye, blending in harmony with the furniture of the room. The neat, elegant counter handsomely grained with top and base walnut finish...
>
> On the right, as we stand at the entrance we note in the first department fine dress goods, such as plaids, ginghams, suitings, merinos, alpacas, etc. in great variety and latest patterns. On the opposite side calicos, flannels, jeans, toweling, shawls, bed-tickings, etc. in a great variety and style. Returning we undertake the rounds of the room in regular order. Passing the first department we reach that of gentleman's furnishing goods, hosiery and clothing. In this department alone a stock of about $2,000 is constantly carried. Their sales from this department have always been great, but this winter it is more than usually good. A fine line of California goods has been quite enticing to their many patrons.
>
> Then comes the boot and shoe department, an array of footware that would be a credit to an exclusive establishment. Eighty cases have just been received and opened. It seems that

every style, size, and quality of goods that could be desired can here be found...

Re-entering the main building and proceeding upon our tour we strike first the hat and cap department. This stock is all new and just large enough to be in keeping with the other full lines on hand...

Next come stationery, blank-books, school books, cards, envelopes, and everything in the paper line that would or could be called for, including an immense stock of notions. Just at this time the counters are fairly groaning under their load of Holiday goods. Kris Kringle has evidently been here in person and Fred has got away with his whole outfit...

Last, but not least, is the department devoted to patent medicines – as crowded and neat a department as could be found in the whole establishment. Taste and mature judgment is noticeable in the neat and systematic arrangement of the business from first to last.[8]

This enthusiastic editor then takes his readers through the old store which was used to display dishes, glassware and groceries.

In another room heating and cooking stoves were found along with an immense stock of liquor.

An outside enclosure led one to the two-story wool house. Other rooms held barrels of salt, dipping tobacco and sulphur. Another room contained bins filled with wheat, oats, corn and other grain, and one room was filled with thousands of pounds of beans. Beans, of course, constituted a large part of the diet of the citizens of the new town.

A large barn held tons of hay with the lower floor divided into stalls for horses and a harness room.

Concluding, the editor writes:

The stock just opened was purchased in the East under Gen. Walsen's personal supervision and is the most complete general stock ever brought to Southern Colorado. Upwards of $50,000 are invested in the establishment, which perhaps will give the reader a more general idea of the immense business done. The *improvement is the most extensive one of its kind ever made in Huerfano County, if not in Southern Colorado.*

It is a credit to us as a people and a fitting monument of the enterprise, public spirit and liberality of our wide-awake merchants Messrs. Walsen and Levy.[9]

Following the incorporation of the town, things began to change rapidly. Fred Walsen was elected the town's first mayor (actually called then "head trustee") and held that post for years. He built a spacious home on Main Street between Fifth and Sixth Streets. Both the Walsen and Levy families were prominent in the growing society of the newly minted Walsenburg, and Emilie Sporleder Walsen and Lillie Sporleder Levy were active members of it. Lillie Levy was especially noted for her "coffees" which featured her famous coffee cakes.

The girls' father, August Sporleder, continued to run the first Sporleder hotel until it and other buildings were destroyed in the flood of 1878. After that, another hotel was built on the northeast corner of Main and Fifth, where the building which was once the Unfug Hardware Store later stood.

Charles Mazzone moved into town and built the Mazzone Building which stood where the school district bus garage was later located between Seventh and Eighth on the east side. This building was built in 1875 and 1876. Downstairs was a saloon and skating rink. In later years the saloon and opera house were moved to a building on the southwest corner of Main and Sixth where the Black and White Grocery once stood. In fact, the Black and White building was actually the first floor of the once proud Mazzone Saloon and Opera House.

Herman Duhme built a livery stable where Star Drug now stands on the northeast corner of Seventh and Main. The livery stable was operated by George Anderson. Duhme had brought Kentucky-bred horses to Walsenburg. His principal business was his ranch on the Santa Clara Creek.

As the town progressed through the 1870s all of these changes altered forever the pastoral nature of the village which had been

La Plaza de los Leones. Bit by bit over many years, the other plazas such as Los Germanes and Tequisquite died away. Behind the location of the new Walsen-Levy store, a large corral stood for many years, covering the rest of that block. This block now contains the offices of the weekly newspaper, the *Huerfano World*. Along the south side of Seventh Street toward the west are a series of small business locations including a cell phone store, a dry-cleaners and some empty buildings. At the end of the block is the nursing home, located in what was once the Lamme Brothers hospital. At the time of the new name for the town, however, only the corral was there and beyond that acres of vegetation – chokecherries, wild plums and others.

Old Don Miguel Leon continued to live in his house until his death. In 1873 the Catholic parish purchased a piece of land from him along the Cucharas River for the purpose of building a church to replace the *jacal* on the corner of Main and Seventh, which had burned just three years after its construction.

The property transaction for the new church reads as follows:

> *This Indenture, made and entered into this twenty-first day of August, in the year of our Lord, One Thousand, eight hundred and seventy-three, Between Miguel Leon, and party of the first part and Louis Merles and Joseph Percevault, the parties of the second part, (all of Huerfano County, Colorado Territory) Witnesseth, that for and in consideration of the sum of One Hundred (100) Dollars, the receipt of which is hereby acknowledged, the said party of the first part has bargained, sold, conveyed, and granted by these presents does, grant, bargain, sell and convey unto said parties of the second part all of the following lot, piece or parcel of land situate, lying and being in the County of Huerfano, Territory of Colorado, and particularly described as follows towit: Commencing at the corner of the house now occupied by John Albert, and running thence about one hundred and eighty yards to the house now occupied by Cruz Mestes (in front of the door of said house); thence about 240 yards in an Easterly direction to the lands claimed by Francisco Atencio;*

thence Southerly along the said Atencio's line to the Cucharas River; thence to the point of beginning, containing about twelve acres of land more or less..." [10]

However inexact the land description may sound, the Catholic parish now had property on which to build a church.

The people of the parish began construction of the church in 1873, but it was several more years before the church was ready for occupancy. The Reverend Howard L. Delaney wrote in his booklet *All Our Yesterdays* in the 1940s:

> *Father Merles had planned to have a church cruciform in shape, but lack of sufficient money forced him to simplify it for the time being at least. Work was begun on the building in the summer of 1873. The people were poor but willing. Some few contributed money; others gave the stone for the foundation; some made adobes for the walls; still others gave cattle, sheep and horses to be sold and the proceeds used. The more well-to-do, that is, those who were the owners of team and wagon, hauled lumber. In the end, all this amounted to a building seventy-five feet long, thirty feet wide and sixteen feet high. It made no pretensions to any style of church architecture, except, perhaps to that popular American style known as "Four walls and a roof."*
>
> *Two years after the beginning the church was opened for religious services. There were no interior furnishings. The congregation either had to stand or else bring their own chairs. In October of 1876 when a new pastor arrived, he found the place still without vestry, altar railing or pews, and the bell which had been donated by Fred Walsen was still resting on the ground because there was no tower in which to hang it.* [11]

Father Merles had more ambitious plans for the church which he hoped to execute as the years went on, but an accident occurred two years later when Father Merles was thrown from the spring wagon in which he was riding and suffered a broken neck. His driver escaped with minor injuries, but since the town had no doctor at the time, nothing could be done for Father Merles. He died without regaining consciousness.

An adobe schoolhouse (now a parking lot) on West Sixth Street just behind the Mazzone Opera Hall served all Protestant worshipers together until the Presbyterians built a church in 1883. This church was located on Main Street. That building, which still exists, is now a part of the Neece Family Medical Clinic (northwest corner of Main and Fourth).

The energetic newcomers soon dominated most of the town business, but the Spanish settlers continued to have a role. The Atencio clan and the Leon clan all had prominent members of the community. J. A. J. Valdes, a resident of Los Germanes, became a lawyer and judge and served the community in several different capacities in the early years. The first sheriff of the county was John Berrard, but for several years thereafter this position was filled by Spanish-Americans including the unfortunate Juan Dolores Esquibel who was murdered on the streets of Walsenburg.

The little town grew and trade increased, but a monumental change in the economic and social aspects of the town was about to happen.

From the beginning of the settlement, residents had dug coal from deposits that lay on the surface of the hills to the west, but in 1876, Fred Walsen leased the land where the first coal mine, later known as Walsen, was located and the character of the tiny town of Walsenburg changed forever.

Chapter Four

COAL

A story told in the Atencio family about the land west of Walsenburg, just at the end of Seventh Street, says that one of the Atencio clan sold a number of acres of land to Fred Walsen for a wagon, a team of mules and $100 in cash.[1]

The truth of this story cannot be determined over one hundred years later, but what is known is that Fred Walsen, however he acquired it, leased that land to two men who then opened the first coal mine in Huerfano County.

The existence of coal had been known for many years. Some seams extruded into the open and families had dug coal and hauled it home for use in their homes. Now it would be mined commercially with the arrival of the railroad, and the character of the pastoral village of Walsenburg would change forever.

The first mine, known as Walsen Mine, opened sometime in 1876. It was a crude affair, little more than tunnels into which miners crawled. The first miners were principally English, Scottish and Mexican, but in later years many men of many nationalities would come to work in the mines.[2]

The coming of the railroads cannot be overestimated in their importance to the town. The existence of the coal fields in Huerfano and Las Animas counties became more widely known, and the economic impact of such resources was not lost on the builders of railroads.

Both the Santa Fe and the Denver and Rio Grande railroads were actively seeking areas where they could build new rail lines. The focus of the Santa Fe was on the eastern plains beginning at the Kansas border and continuing west toward Pueblo. The Denver and Rio Grande, on the other hand, seemed more interested in laying track south from Pueblo toward the coal fields. Engineers began to lay out the grade from the Huerfano River to Cucharas, which was then a small community about six miles east of Walsenburg. Building was also going on from the southern part of the state north. A new town named El Moro sprang up where the lines would pass. Plans also were in mind for running a line west from Cucharas toward La Veta Pass. As Griswold wrote in his book, ***Rio Grande: Along the Rio Grande***:

> Six miles west of Cucharas was the seventeen-year-old Plaza de Los Leones which was a delightful settlement of adobe homes, perhaps not the most beautiful plaza, but definitely one of the most peaceful. Don Miguel Leon and his wife, Cruzita, had a fine plum orchard behind their home and corral, and the other residents engaged in farming and stock raising so that the plaza was practically self-sufficient. Just a few years before the railroad built to the area, Fred Walsen along with other German families settled in the area. By the time the railroad started building west from Cucharas, the settlement had taken Fred's name rather than Don Miguel's. The town of Walsenburg made a deal with the Denver and Rio Grande to deed the railroad one-half of all the town lots if the railroad built a depot within five miles. The railroad agreed to the deal, and so by the end of May 1876 the Denver and Rio Grande was completed as far as Walsenburg.[3]

The arrival of the Denver and Rio Grande Railroad line in Walsenburg in 1876 was soon followed by the Colorado and Southern. Both of these lines had their own train depots and freight outlets. Rail lines crisscrossed the town. As the coal industry grew, so did the rail lines. One branch line known as the Loma Branch ran north of town toward the mines, ending at the Alamo Mine. Even passenger service could be had on this line and some high school students regularly rode the trains to reach their school in Walsenburg. The railroads were also vital to the mining industry as the means of hauling timbers and ties for the mines and railroads.

With the coming of industry and the railroads, the town grew even larger. New businesses sprang up over the years between the incorporation of Walsenburg in 1873 and the end of the century. One of the most notable of these businesses was the Mazzone Saloon and Opera House.

The first floor of the building housed the saloon, which became a gathering place for the men of the town. All manner of liquid refreshment could be had including many non-alcoholic drinks. Free lunch and snacks were always available. Many businessmen made it their daily habit to spend some time in the congenial atmosphere of the saloon. One could read the papers, talk with friends, and, probably, transact business at the tables in the large bar.

The second floor of the building held the opera house. This included a large hall which offered all kinds of performances. Many of the well-known names of the time – singers, actors, speakers – performed at the Mazzone Opera House.

One of the more unusual features of the Opera House was a two-story outhouse. Indoor plumbing in Walsenburg was still a thing of the future, but the needs of citizens had to be met. A walkway connected the upstairs of the Opera House to the second story of the outhouse. The two-story facility was intended to make it unnecessary for ladies attending a performance to descend to and through the saloon.[4]

A weekly newspaper was established. Either the *Walsenburg Cactus* or the *Walsenburg World* was the first. Over many years Huerfano County would have as many as fifty newspapers, most of which did not last long.

As previously noted, the town was incorporated in 1873 with the name changed from La Plaza de los Leones to Walsenburg. The county seat was moved from Badito to Walsenburg in 1874 and the first trustees were Fred Walsen, John Albert, Joseph Bourcy, Jose Rafael Esquibel and Carmel Martinez.

Many sources list Fred Walsen as the first mayor of the town and state that he held the post for many years. The ordinance books of the town do not bear out this story; apparently he was named head of the trustees. The town operated for several years by the actions of the board of trustees. The first mayor to sign an ordinance was Charles Mazzone. Other sources list J. A. J. Valdes and Cornelius D. Hendren as mayors before Mazzone, but while Fred Walsen may have been the dominant force in town activities, he apparently was never formally elected as mayor.

The first sheriff of Huerfano County was John Berrard, who was probably one of the French settlers along the Huerfano River near the butte.

The Spanish community members in Walsenburg continued to live in the adobe houses they had built before the arrival of other settlers and went on with their work of stock raising and farming. Much of the control of Walsenburg passed to the more aggressive newcomers, but the Spanish inhabitants also held important posts.

The Leon family seems to have died out after the death of Don Miguel Leon, or some of them may have returned to the San Luis Valley, but the larger Atencio clan remained prominent in the community for many years. The patriarch of the clan was Miguel Antonio Atencio who came with his wife, Rumalda Martinez Atencio, from New Mexico to settle in Tequisquite. Most of their children were born in New Mexico and came with them to the new settlement. Three of them – Preciliana, Juan and Antonio Cleto – were born in Colorado.[5]

Of these three, Preciliana, also called Maria, became a well-known and much loved citizen of Walsenburg. She married a Scottish miner named John Neilson. As they were not able to have children, they prevailed upon her brother, Antonio Cleto, to allow them to raise one of his children, a little girl named Francisca. They also raised a son of another sibling whose mother had died. The little boy's name was Moses. This was not an uncommon thing in the Spanish community where children were often seen as belonging to everyone. The little girl, Francisca, grew up to be a major figure in the history of Walsenburg and Huerfano County. She would later be known as Frances Nelson Vallejo, long-time county superintendent of schools and amateur historian whose writings are invaluable to the researcher.[6]

Mrs. Nelson Vallejo wrote of Preciliana:

> *Mother Preciliana loved to sing at weddings and mingled with friendly Ute Indians living in the hill opposite of Tequisquite. The path from Tequisquite to the early settlers in La Plaza de Los Leones was overgrown with groves of trees, choke-cherries, wild plums and numerous bushes of various kinds and there was only a footpath when Preciliana left her home to work every morning.*[7]

Preciliana also became noted for her baking, and many residents regularly visited her home to buy her breads and pastries.

Eventually she and her husband built a home on West Seventh Street, on the southwest corner of Seventh and Leon, which became not only a home, but also a boarding house for miners who worked at the nearby Walsen Mine. This house was important during the dark days of the coal war in the first third of the 20th century, and it still stands just east of the administration building of the Huerfano Re-1 School District. John Neilson also owned and operated a general merchandise store, probably on Seventh Street, around 1907. This would have been before he and his wife built the boarding house.

The Walsen Mine did not remain the only mine for very long. Other veins were opened north, south and west of Walsenburg. Some of these were the Toltec, Pictou, Maitland, Alamo No. 1 and No. 2, Robinson, Cameron, Solar, Rouse, Pryor and others. In time Walsenburg would be known as "The City Built on Coal."

With more and more mines, of course, came more and more miners. For the most part the miners lived in housing built at the mines. These houses in the early days were little more than shacks, with no indoor plumbing, and often the families had to carry their water from nearby streams.

All of the industrial activity coming from the mines brought changes to the town. Businesses opened, livery stables were built, cattle and sheep raising prospered. The Sporleder Selling

Company did business all up and down the coal range and out into the ranching areas.

Fred Walsen and a man named Wheeler went into the banking business.

Other banking services also came into being and medical care arrived when several doctors set up their practices in Walsenburg.

The coming of many miners to the community also brought about a surge in businesses of another kind. There were as many as forty saloons during the coal mining days and also numerous establishments offering the favors of prostitutes. Gambling was a thriving industry.

With all of this activity came an increase in crime and the county decided that the tiny rock jail which had served the community for some years was not enough. A larger and more substantial facility at the northwest corner of Main and Fifth Street would be built and several meetings of the county commissioners were devoted to the planning of this new jail. The completed jail served the needs of Walsenburg until another still larger jail was built on Fifth Street in 1896. This handsome building of gray sandstone at 112 West Fifth Street still stands and is the home of the Walsenburg Mining Museum.[8]

During all of this time the people of Walsenburg had high expectations for their town. This optimism included an unshakable belief that Walsenburg would be one of the largest cities in Colorado, along with Denver, Colorado Springs and Pueblo. In 1889 an article in the **Colorado Exchange** expressed this optimism.

> *Wonderful Walsenburg! The county seat of Huerfano county, located south west of Pueblo and south of Fremont county, in one of the richest agricultural, mining, and coal-producing districts in Colorado, is attracting unusual attention this year. Heretofore this portion of the State had been practically or almost wholly ignored, as but little was known of the vast area of agricultural lands capable of giving sustenance to thousands of additional families. Why it is so much attention has been given to the northern portion of the State in this branch of industry while*

Southern Colorado has been considered almost useless as a grain-producing country baffles all understanding.

Northern Colorado contains a very limited area of grain and fruit land in comparison to the southern portion of the State, while its supply of water is meager to that with which the latter is blessed. Numerous large rivers and streams intersect the broad valleys, which renders it comparatively easy to adopt a complete system of irrigation to assure a constant supply of water for that purpose. Southern Colorado possesses many advantages in various ways that no other portion of the State enjoys. It contains the largest coal fields in the West and a product of superior quality. Its mountain ranges are rich with various precious metals. It abounds with mineral and hot springs, all kinds of game peculiar to the Rocky Mountain region are to be found in great abundance and its rivers and streams are alive with various species of fish. Taken altogether it is bound to become the objective point in the future to which the eyes of capitalists and manufacturers must be turned, as every opportunity for the manufacturing industry is offered in all its diversified forms. No part of the west affords greater inducements than does Walsenburg.

Perhaps no city or town in the State today displays more visible signs of developments in the way of buildings and public improvements than this thriving town, so justly termed "Wonderful" by its pushing and enterprising newspapers. The following, from the Walsenburg World, is an accurate description of Walsenburg and Huerfano county:

'Along the eastern base of the Rocky Mountains there are five cities which are found to be the largest cities in the State of Colorado for all time to come. They are Denver, Colorado Springs, Pueblo, Walsenburg, and Trinidad. The superior natural advantages of these places warrant this belief. I know that natural advantages alone never did and never will create a city of importance, but those backed by enterprise and liberality always did and always will. I use the word "liberality" in this connection, meaning sly, for illiberality on the part of real estate owners often

retards the growth of cities and in many instances has proved fatal.

'*With the exception of Denver, perhaps, there is not a city along the line that has a brighter future than Walsenburg, in Huerfano county. "Ah, indeed," says one, "if your city of Walsenburg has such a bright future, why have we not heard more of it than we have heard? Why has it been slumbering in obscurity?" I will tell you, my friend. It is the heart of the finest coal region in the State, and five large railroad and coal companies have long known this, but have kept this information to themselves until they could complete arrangements for mining and transportation facilities. As two of these companies have already reached here and three others will be here with their roads inside of a year from date, they are now willing that all the world should know what they are coming here for. Again, the first business men who located here in Walsenburg happened to be shrewd, far sighted businessmen, who had experienced the results which have followed premature booms, that is efforts to call in strangers faster than the active resources of a city would warrant. They said to the other cities who were booming themselves beyond all reason and judgment, "You just go ahead with your booming and we will abide our time and in the end come out ahead." This policy has characterized this city. It has only welcomed a steady growth, and to-day it has the most healthy growth of any city in Colorado. Thanks to its building judgment, and right here I will state than in less than a quarter of a century Walsenburg will become the largest city in this state, Denver alone excepted, if she continues the policy she inaugurated in the out-set and has cause to prevail ever since.*'[9]

It is clear from the enthusiasm expressed in this piece that the business community of Walsenburg expected nothing less than spectacular growth and prosperity, and for many years growth and prosperity did occur.

More and more mines opened until at the high point of coal production there were at least fifty separate mines in Huerfano County. The Walsen Mine lay directly west of Walsenburg, beginning at the very end of Seventh Street and extending some distance west and north. At the height of its existence Walsen Camp had two schools, the company store, a YMCA (Young Men's Christian Association), rows and rows of company housing, as well as all of the structures necessary to the operation of a huge coal mine.

Other mines in the area were Robinson One and Two, Cameron, Maitland, Pictou, Alamo One and Two, Ideal, Raven-wood and many others.

Coal operators brought in miners from all parts of the world – Great Britain, the Balkan countries, Greece, Italy, Mexico and Asia. Most of these miners came to America seeking to earn money for their families in the old countries. When they came, many had no real plans to stay in America. Their intent was to earn enough money to allow them to return to their native countries and live more comfortably than they would have otherwise. They spoke many languages. At one time it is said that as many as twenty-seven languages could be heard on the streets of Walsenburg.

The work of the miners was unbelievably difficult. They worked in "rooms", where the coal face had been exposed, and were expected to load coal cars, place a brass tag on the car which identified the miner to whom the load should be credited. A "room" was sometimes not more than four or five feet high, forcing the miners to work on hands and knees or even lying down for long periods of time. A miner and his partner might fill several cars in the course of a shift which consisted of at least ten hours. A good account of a miner's work is found in the book, **Buried Unsung**, written by Zeese Papanikolas.

Papadakis ended up at the Victor-American camp of Hastings. They sent him over to the company store to get outfitted: pick and shovel, hand of fuse, electric lamp, roll of waxed paper to wrap the charge in. He signed up for a can of double F black powder. He was already well in debt to the store. The next day he went up to the mine and got the numbered brass checks he would attach to the coal cars for weighing. If there was an accident, it would be the check that would identify his burned or mangled body.

He went to work with an old timer, a black man named Dave. Dave kept a wad of tobacco in his cheek, spat, showed the Greek the ropes. He showed him how to test the roof of the room with the blade of a pick, listening for the clean ring of metal against stone that meant it was solid. He showed him how to set a prop. It didn't take many words between them, the old timer and the green foreigner. Dave pointed his finger above his head at the treacherous roof and the Greek kid didn't need a translation. They set to work loading the first of the day's cars, shoveling the loose coal until it rose over the car's sides, sometimes using their picks to break the pieces that were too big to handle. They trimmed the cars with the heavy chunks of coal, wrestling the slabs into the car against their knees. Together they could load seven or eight cars on a good day. They were paid fifty cents a ton.

When the loose coal was loaded, they dressed the face of the room, undercut the bottom of the coal seam with their picks, then set to work, drilling the holes for the next round of charges. Four along the roof, two on each side, four on the bottom with a thread bar and box. Twelve turns to the inch, six feet for each charge. It could take both of them, using all their strength, to turn the bar. Then they placed the charges and stuck in the clay-filled dummies for the shot firers to tamp. They drove each room two hundred fifty feet, then had to quit, for the air was bad at Hastings. Every time they moved they had to scavenge the mine for old rails, rip them up and set them again, since the Victor-American Company did not allow them to use new rails. They were not paid for this. They were moving sixteen-pound rails, five or six hundred feet of them. Every time they'd move a rail they would sit down and curse.[10]

This passage gives some idea of the deadly difficulties faced each day by coal miners. The mine called Hastings, which was mentioned in this story was in Las Animas County near Ludlow, but the conditions under which miners worked were the same throughout the coal field. Only the coal that arrived at the mouth of the mine with their tags on the cars brought wages to the miners. Often a car that a miner believed had 4,000 pounds in it would be weighed at 3,600 pounds. There was no way for a miner to dispute the word of the company weigh men.

They were not paid for all kinds of "dead work". This included timbering a room in order to make it safer, clearing away shale or other forms of rock that were not coal, and all other forms of work besides piling coal into the endless stream of coal cars.

Accidents and death in the mines were frequent. The most common cause of death was a "fall of rock", in which a miner was crushed by the collapse of the ceiling of the room in which he worked. Explosions from the build-up of gasses and runaway coal cars were other forms of sudden death. Invariably coroner's juries found that the accident was due to the miner's own carelessness and his wife and children were fortunate if they were offered a few dollars for funeral expenses. The idea of a pension was unheard of.

Not surprisingly with the kind of working conditions imposed on miners plus the wide variety of backgrounds from which these men and their families came, and the many languages that were spoken, there was little communication between those who worked in the mines and those who lived in the community of Walsenburg.

The coming of the mines brought increased prosperity to the community. More and more businesses opened, more and more fine homes were built, but this prosperity did not extend to those who dug the coal that made it all possible.

Fred Walsen did not remain in mining or in his other local businesses for very long. In 1882 he was elected state treasurer and following this unexpected political victory, Fred Walsen moved his wife, Emilia Sporleder Walsen, and their children to Denver. He served only one term as state treasurer, but the family remained in Denver and Walsen went on to engage in other lucrative businesses.

Alexander Levy stayed in Walsenburg and continued his many business activities. The store prospered as did his sheep and cattle holdings, and he also had many contracts for railroad work. In time his company would supply most of the ties and timbers for the railroads and mines.

From the beginning of the coal mining era, strikes were a periodic occurrence. The miners made so little, and the working conditions were so dangerous, that it is not too surprising that they made frequent efforts to secure better working conditions. The strike was the only weapon they had since there was no recognized union or other bargaining agent.

The first major strike occurred in 1893 but it was quickly put down. The miners had little choice but to return to work in whatever manner they could.

Another strike occurred in 1903-1904, and this was a more serious strike. It brought the first efforts to unionize miners and marked the first appearance of the union organizer, Mary Harris Jones, known to the miners and to posterity as Mother Jones. This strike, too, led to defeat and a return to the coal pits for the miners.

It is not surprising that there was little interaction between miners and the other citizens of Walsenburg. Workers had little choice but to buy their necessities at the company stores since they were paid in company-issued scrip, which could be used only at the company store. So it was that the community saw the miners principally as customers for the saloons and other establishments dispensing liquor.

Paul Krier, son of an early merchant, wrote about life in Walsenburg in the late 19th century.

I was born just off Main Street on West 8th Street. It was a tough neighborhood – gamblers, tin-horns, gunmen and what have you. Bob Ford, the man who supposedly killed Jesse James, was a frequent visitor in the neighborhood. Ford ran gambling games in the Charles Mazzone saloon. He also had his own saloon and dance hall. It was located on 7th Street, south and just east of the C. & S. Railroad. Saloon and gambling were on the lower floor, with dance hall and scarlet women on the top floor.

After a short stay on W. 8th St., the family moved to West 6th St. where the Otero Savings stands {now the First National Bank of Trinidad}.

Dad was a shoemaker. He not only repaired shoes, he made them. His first shop was a part of the home we lived in. He accumulated a few dollars over the years, bought the building, now Caywoods. At that time it was one story and only 60 feet in depth. This building was shared by Henry Blickhahn, father of Judge George Blickhahn of Alamosa and Mrs. Edna Levy, and Mr. Johnson, father-in-law of Fred Walsen, Jr. Dad was the shoemaker, Blickhahn, the harness maker, and Johnson, the watchmaker. All three men prospered and each needed more room. Mr. Walsen, whom Walsenburg was named after, put up a building now the Western Café, for Dad and Dad added ready-made shoes, men's furnishings, and clothing to his stock. He also, after a couple years, hired a shoemaker in order to give himself more time to sell his wares. Dad worked hard at the store, 7:30 a.m. to 8 p.m. daily and half-day on Sunday. These same hours were observed by all the merchants. Walsenburg was a prosperous town. Miners went to the mines early and returned late, consequently they had to do their shopping evenings.[11]

The town prospered as the mines prospered and it would seem that some business came the way of merchants other than the sellers of liquor and the favors of women. Mr. Krier's story continues:

As a ten year old, I worked in a combination confectionery-bakery store for ten cents a day. The bakery room was an old adobe, no plastering inside and just a plain dirt floor with a horse barn about 30 feet away. No sanitation whatever. I also worked shooing flies while the blacksmith was shoeing horses. For this I received 10 cents a horse. There were two blacksmith shops within 100 feet of our home. Still later, as a 14 year old, I worked for a Chinese laundry, our next door neighbor. We had no water system in town, so all the water had to come from wells. I pumped and carried water to barrels about 75 feet away and received ten cents for each 50-gallon barrel. The pay was good for I usually filled six barrels. Ying Lee, the man I worked for, was a kind man and one of Walsenburg's best known citizens; everyone liked him. Most Chinese have a yen for gambling and Ying was no exception. He would gamble away his weekly earnings but he never failed to pay his bills. He had Chinese lilies, Chinese candy, and Chinese nuts shipped to him every year and he would always give them away to his many friends.

Walsenburg was a tough place to live, but a very prosperous community. It was nothing to see prostitutes on our streets or to see them at night soliciting the men from lower Main Street. Most saloons had a rear room and entrance for these prostitutes. Most every day one could see our town police club someone over the head with a billy. It was hard to see this brutality and hold your tongue. If you dared to protest you would get a taste of this club. Gambling took place in most every saloon and the games were stacked against the player. Our ministers and priests fought this kind of life but it took patience and a lot of courage and years to eradicate these evils. Houses for prostitutes were located on the second block of W. 8th Street. Father Lefebre, who succeeded Father Ussel after his death, was especially prominent in the fight against the city bads, crooked politicians, gamblers, etc. Harassment in many different forms was dealt out to him for being so active in his fight for decency and better community living. It was often said, Father Lefebre's death, at the age of 39 was hastened because of his activities.[12]

So life continued in the growing town of Walsenburg. Businesses were established and prospered. More mines opened bringing in more and more miners and more wealth and prosperity to the town and, especially, to the coal operators.

Unfortunately since all of this wealth didn't extend to the miners and their families, these households struggled. Miners were paid fifty cents a ton or less for the coal they dug.

Their wives raised gardens and wove rag rugs on homemade looms to supplement the family income as best they could. Some mine couples such as John Neilson and his wife, Preciliana, turned their homes into boarding houses for single miners.

By the turn of the century conditions were so poor for the miners that labor troubles were inevitable and the first major strike came in 1903 at the beginning of the century that would bring so much turmoil and struggle to the little town of Walsenburg and to the rest of the world.

Chapter Five

THE KING OF HUERFANO COUNTY

The coal mines changed the nature of Walsenburg and Huerfano County forever. The dependence on raising livestock and trading with Indians and other travelers grew less. More people arrived to establish new businesses to serve the mines and the community. Two railroads came in and within a few years had extended their lines to serve the many coal camps.

All of this did not automatically mean prosperity for everyone. Coal must be dug from the ground and the people who did the digging came from all over the world. Suddenly the peaceful town, which had been populated primarily by Mexican farmers and German businessmen, saw an influx of people who came from Italy, England, Scotland, Wales, Greece, the Balkan states and Asia.

Many came with no intention of staying. It was the hope of these men to earn money in the mines and then return to their country of origin. Even those who came with wives and families did not quickly assimilate into the community, and the coal operators for whom they worked did not encourage assimilation.

The rash of new businesses included an increased number of saloons. No longer was the community-oriented Mazzone Opera House and Saloon the only place where spirits could be bought by the drink.

Ladies of the evening and gambling were also quickly provided to the miners for their Saturday-night pleasure.

Bob Ford, known to history as the man who killed Jesse James, came to Walsenburg. Ford owned a home at 320 West Seventh and a saloon, probably on the corner, and is said to have run the gambling games in Mazzone's saloon as well. Many of the prostitutes may also have been under Ford's control.

Ford did not stay in Walsenburg long, but apparently he was a well-known and powerful figure in the community. Not all memories of him are bad. When Victor Mazzone was a small boy, he shined shoes in a local barber shop. One day Bob Ford was in the shop while little Victor was shining the shoes of a man passing through town. When the shoe shine was completed, the man refused to pay. Ford asked the man why he wouldn't pay. The man replied that he didn't like the shine. Ford said he would shine the man's shoes and proceeded to give a few swipes to the already shined shoes. When he finished, he said: "Now pay the boy." The traveling man, having heard Bob Ford's name mentioned, promptly paid little Victor for the shoe shine. To the end of his long life, Victor Mazzone remembered this and always refused to believe that Bob Ford had killed Jesse James.

The upstairs part of the building which currently houses the Eagles Lodge was occupied by prostitutes, and another story has more of these women living in the upstairs part of what is now the Fox Theatre.

Movies also had come to Walsenburg in the early part of the century and there were at least two movie houses available. Uncertainty existed on the part of some citizens about the newfangled moving picture shows, and they insisted that steps be taken to assure that movies would not pose any moral threat to the youngsters of Walsenburg.

The Walsenburg power structure was ruled by its sheriff, Jefferson B. Farr, who was whole-heartedly the tool of the coal industry. He was known far and wide as "The King of Huerfano County" or "Czar Farr." As the coal mining industry grew, the need to control the miners also grew, and Jeff Farr was just the man to handle the job. George McGovern, in his book *The Great Coalfield War*, wrote:

> *Unknown outside Colorado, no particular name to conjure*
> *with in Denver, Farr comported himself around Walsenburg and*

vicinity with despotic self-assurance, safe in the knowledge that when necessary for the ratification of his questionable tenure and tactics, he could draw upon both political influence in the capitol and some of the wealth of Wall Street. Farr's interests were indistinguishable from those of the CFI and the county Republican organization. Local businessmen and lawyers opposed them at professional and physical risk. Under Farr's domain district attorneys were impotent. "His word was a command to voters," one attorney testified. "In criminal cases where he took an interest I have never known one where the verdict was not in accordance with his wishes. If he desired a man convicted, there was no lawyer powerful enough to acquit. I have never known or read of any man who had such complete and absolute control over the destinies of the people where their rights and liberties were involved as had Sheriff Jefferson Farr of Huerfano County."

Jeff Farr was one of three sons who left their native Texas to become the biggest cattle dealers in southern Colorado. At the height of their prosperity Edwin Farr was elected sheriff of Huerfano County and was into his second term when, in July 1899, a train robbers' syndicate formed by ex-members of two notorious outlaw bands, Black Jack Ketchum's and Butch Cassidy's, held up a Colorado and Southern train near Folsom, New Mexico. Posses mustered at Walsenburg and Trinidad, crossed the mountains, cornered the bandits near Cimarron, and in the ensuing gun battle Sheriff Ed Farr was shot dead. Jefferson Farr succeeded his late brother as sheriff, swearing vengeance against evildoers, and as his subsequent career made plain, these he was quick to identify as union organizers, labor agitators, and all foes of the county Republican Party. During the course of three successive terms the political machines Farr created ran elections and law courts for the benefit of the Party and the Colorado Fuel and Iron Company. To his cattle interests he added real estate and wholesale liquor, thereby gaining control of saloons and brothels. A prominent citizen of Walsenburg whose sheer survival as a critic of the Farr machine owed much to his advanced age and distinguished Civil War service charged that virtually all of the county's forty-five saloons belonged to the Spanish Peaks Mercan-tile Company of which Jeff Farr was president.[1]

One writer of the period was Barron Beshoar whose biography of union organizer, John Lawson, provides valuable information about Jeff Farr and the coal strike era. Beshoar says of Farr:

> *According to his own lights, Jeff Farr was a pretty decent citizen. He had the 100 per cent American's contempt for the uneducated foreigners who toiled in the mines, and a respect that was akin to reverence for the mine owners. Jeff saw, too, the vices of the workers, their brutality and baseness. He never bothered about their redeeming qualities nor wondered if the operating methods of the coal barons might be in some measure responsible for the condition of the miners and their families. Jeff's philosophy was built around the belief that "coal has got to be dug and by God somebody has got to dig it." It cannot be denied that Jeff had his admirers. Many Colorado residents, and some of them were the very best people, saw in him a stalwart personification of law and order, a Horatius who could be counted on to stand fast when the status quo in the coal fields was subject to assault.*[2]

Determining how the original inhabitants of Walsenburg felt about all of the new residents of the town and the coal camps surrounding is not an easy matter, but one can speculate that their feelings were mixed. The many coal camps and the men who labored there brought new money into the community. Other workers made a living in cutting and hauling the timber used for mine props. The miners themselves had little choice but to do their shopping at the company stores which existed in the camps, but the operators of these stores bought their supplies from Walsenburg businesses. Certainly the saloons profited mightily from the Saturday night activities of the weary miners.

Farmers raised crops that could be sold to the mine families, and some of the miners' wives raised gardens with which they could supplement the diets of their large families of children. No doubt seed was bought in Walsenburg by these industrious women.

Over the years, schools were established in the coal camps, and some of the local ministers provided church services once or twice a month to inhabitants of the various camps. There is little evidence that the mine families ever attended the churches in town.

Wages were poor for the miners and the work extremely dangerous. Miners were paid only for the actual coal that was dug from the coal seams. These seams were sometimes only four or five feet thick so the rooms in which miners worked were only a few feet high. Since water regularly seeped into the mines from underground rivers, the workers often spent their days in cold, dirty water. There was little light except the feeble flame provided by the carbide lamps on their helmets.

Miners were required to buy their own tools, boots, black powder and anything else they might need. The miner was in debt to the company store before he ever set foot inside the mine and he rarely, if ever, was able to get out of that debt.

That labor unrest was a part of the mining scene in Huerfano County almost from the moment the first mine was opened was undeniable.

During the period of coal mining in the county there were two weekly newspapers, one Republican and one Democratic. It could not always be determined by the political bent of the paper which party the coal operators favored. It often depended on who was running for which office.

This excerpt from the *Cactus* of May 8, 1884, gives an idea of where this particular editor stood on the matter of the first coal strike:

Let the miners stand firm for yet a few days.

Uncle John boasts that he will break the coal miners combination in a very few days. We think he will in his mind.

Why should the miners be compelled to pay one dollar a month each into a "fund" from which they receive no benefits?

It is an easy matter to find an excuse for discharging a miner, especially when the boss has a particular spite to vent on him.

Several of our merchants and citizens have made very liberal donations of money and provisions to the families of needy miners.

The most insignificant, cold-blooded and tyrannical creature connected with the C. C. I. Co. is "Uncle John Cameron" the general superintendent.

If coal companies cannot afford to pay their employees fair living wages, let them charge more for their coal. The public can stand it better than the poor laboring man.

The managers of C. C. & I. have more gall than judgment. The people of Colorado are growing heartily sick of their way of killing business by their pig-headed way of bull-dozing honest working men.[3]

(The term C. C. & I. stood for Colorado Coal and Iron Co., the forerunner of Colorado Fuel and Iron, which would replace it within a few years.)

This strike did not last very long, and the miners went back to the miserable conditions in which they worked in order to feed their families, and their wives continued to bear their children and do their part to make decent homes in the drafty, company-owned shacks in which they lived.

The next major strike came in 1903 when again the union attempted to organize. Some names of great importance in the coal field struggles first appear in Walsenburg at this time. One of the principal union organizers was John Lawson. Another avid union man was Mike Livoda, and Mary Harris Jones, the fiery little Irish woman known to the miners as Mother Jones, first came to Walsenburg at this time.

Another new arrival in Walsenburg in the new century was Archibald Allison, a mining engineer and a well-educated man. Allison was born in Scotland and later traveled to Indonesia and lived there for some years working in various mines.

He came to Huerfano County in the early 20th century and worked in the Robinson Mine, not as an engineer, but as an

ordinary miner. He became active in union affairs and participated in both the 1903-04 strike and the larger, more violent
strike of 1913-1914. Allison kept a diary, writing in pencil in small
notebooks of his day-to-day activities as a miner and as a coal strike
activist.

Some excerpts from Allison's diary offer a look at the circum-
stances of the 1903-04 strike.

> *Wed. Nov. 4 - Heard Mother Jones speak at Mazone's (sic)*
> *Hall. She is a clever impressive speaker and seemed to be an*
> *earnest American patriot.*
>
> *Sat. Nov. 7th - Some armed men arrived at the mines in*
> *connection with some agitation generated among the miners and*
> *other workmen, who, I understand, wants an 8 hour-day {work-*
> ing day}, *better ventilation in the mines and some other just and*
> *reasonable laws established in the State of Colorado and sur-*
> *rounding states.*
>
> *Thurs., 19th - Went to Pictou and heard Mother Jones and*
> *W. Bujoni, an atillian (sic) visitor address a meeting of the*
> *miners. Meeting orderly, men advised to pull together, get*
> *organized, get unionized. Hold out for 8-hour day and better*
> *conditions of ventilation or union demands.*
>
> *Jan. 4, 1914 - Meeting at U. R. {Union Restaurant}*
> *when several motions were passed. I thought the one about the*
> *employment out of order, but I voted to petition the government or*
> *Governor Peabody. To grant a measure of free speach (sic) and*
> *was instructed to draft a heading for petition... There was an*
> *incident when the train arrived at noon. Several black men*
> *arrived to work in the mines and when at the station the union*
> *secretary Mr. Braten said, "boys you are going into a big strike"*
> *Sheriff Far (sic) then hit Braten on the face with his hand, and on*
> *Braten saying he had no reason to do that, the sheriff drew a*
> *revolver and holding it to him, said he was to say no more or he*
> *would give him that.*
>
> *There were some things said about the duties of the officers of*
> *the law, and then they separated. (sic)*[4]

Many of the demands of the miners were so basic that it seems strange to people of our day that they even had to be asked for. The matter of ventilation was vitally important in the coal mines as there was a constant buildup of coal dust in the mines, and pockets of methane gas were frequently encountered. Either of these could cause devastating explosions. Black powder was used for blasting the coal seams and this, too, was dangerous. The coal operators preferred black powder to dynamite because it broke up the large chunks of coal less. Many miners died in the mine explosions. Especially notable was the Hastings Mine explosion in Las Animas county in which 121 miners lost their lives.

Miners' families could not hope for any compensation for the death of a father or son. Sometimes the coal company would provide a small sum for the burial of the dead miner, but then the widow and her children were on their own.

Through all of this growth and strife in Huerfano County, Sheriff Jeff Farr considered it his personal goal to keep the miners in what he deemed to be their place. He was first and foremost a company man. What the mine operators wanted, Jeff Farr was more than happy to give them.

In due time the old Colorado Coal and Iron Co. became the Colorado Fuel and Iron Co. Its principal stockholder was John D. Rockefeller, Sr., and the property was supposed to be under the supervision of John D. Rockefeller, Jr.

The mines were under the direct supervision of managers and executives like Jesse Welborn and LaMont Montgomery Bowers, who reported on conditions to Rockefeller at his New York office. Their reports invariably said that the miners were all happy in their work situation and with their wages. All labor unrest was attributed to the efforts of the United Mine Workers to organize the workers.

Rockefeller trusted his coal mine operators implicitly. He had never visited his western properties and saw no reason to do so. The word of his management team that all was well and that the miners were satisfied workers was enough for him. The very idea of a union which would represent the interests of the miners and which would require collective bargaining was anathema to him. In his view each miner should be free to make his own choices of where he would work and under what conditions. That the miners were desperate for work and were quite unable to argue about wages and working conditions with the stern men who controlled them never seemed to occur to Rockefeller. To the end of his life, even after the desperate violence of the coal strikes, he opposed labor unions.

In April of 1913 a union meeting was held in Trinidad to authorize a strike. In a last attempt to reach agreement with the coal operators, the miners issued a list of their demands. Archibald Allison reports those demands:

> *Memo of Trinidad Demands*
> 1. *We first ask recognition of the union.*
> 2. *A 10 cent advance in wages on tonnage and rates and day wage scale.*
> 3. *Eight hour day for all classes of labor in or around the mines.*
> 4. *We ask pay for all narrow and dead work which includes brushing, timbering, removing falls, handling impurities, etc.*
> 5. *We ask checkweighman at all mines to be elected by the miners without interference by company officials in said election.*
> 6. *We ask the right to trade in any store we please and the right to choose our own boarding house places, and our own doctor (state law).*
> 7. *We ask the inforcement (sic) of the Colorado Mining laws and the abolition of notorious guards.*[5]

A few efforts were made to reach some sort of agreement between management and the workers, but the basic demands outlined by the miners were rejected. Some of their demands such as the eight-hour working day were already law in Colorado, but the laws were rarely enforced. At length the miners saw no alternative but to walk out of the company houses in the coal camps and strike.

The strike began on Sept. 23, 1913, in the midst of a blinding snowstorm. All up and down the canyons of the mines, miners and their families left their flimsy shacks and moved into the tent cities supplied by the United Mine Workers. In some instances the tents had not arrived, and the cold and miserable wives and children huddled near their carts. They had no idea what lay ahead and could only hope that by taking this drastic step, their lives would improve.

A total of twelve tent cities were set up from Walsenburg to Trinidad, including Cameron, Lester and Rugby as well as in Walsenburg. The most famous of these would be the Forbes colony and the Ludlow colony as the events of the strike unfolded over more than a year.

Walsenburg apparently had three or four tent cities, some for miners and their families and some for the militia. One for miners was located on the property where Washington School now stands. These tent camps housed miners from many of the nearby mine camps, but some of the people who worked at Walsen Mine, which was located just at the end of Seventh Street on the west side of Walsenburg, either owned or rented homes on Seventh Street and the miners walked the few blocks to work. This created problems for those workers who chose not to join the strike.

Daily, as these men went to work, the wives and children of the strikers gathered to jeer at them. Threats were made on both sides, and the situation grew more and more tense.

One family which felt this tension was that of John and Preciliana Nelson. Their name had been spelled Neilson when John first arrived in Walsenburg from Scotland, but somewhere along the line the spelling changed. John's wife, Preciliana, was a member of the noted Atencio family. John built a brick home on West Seventh Street just east of the Seventh Street Primary School. Other members of the Atencio clan lived in houses to the west of the school building.

In their brick home the Nelsons ran a boarding house for single miners who preferred Preciliana's cooking to that available at the Walsen Camp boarding house. Union men and Mother Jones often stayed at the Nelson home when they could find no other business to rent rooms or serve meals to them. With the coming of the strike, however, the miners were no longer able to afford the boarding house, and most of them moved out.

John Nelson worked at Walsen Mine as a fire boss. This position required him to be the first man into the mine each morning to inspect the mine for gas and to determine whether or not it was safe to work. Nelson did not feel he could abandon those miners still at work so he remained on the job.

Whether or not this made him a "scab" in the usual sense could probably be debated, but in the eyes of the strikers there was no doubt. Life became harder for the Nelsons until John finally chose to stop walking the several blocks from his home on Seventh Street to the mine at Walsen each day. He moved to a boarding house at the mine in the hope that life would be a little easier for his family. His adopted daughter, Frances, was instructed to take a different route home from St. Mary School to avoid the taunts of the striker children.

Violence came quickly all up and down the coal fields in this strike. Colorado Fuel and Iron Company hired the Baldwin-Felts Detective agency to guard the mines. Sheriffs in both Huerfano and Las Animas counties hired deputies and both counties sought to have the governor call out the state militia. Gov. Elias Ammons decided against this. Edmund Vallejo wrote in **The 7th Street Massacre**, his family's account of events:

> *Events in Walsenburg, however, soon caused Governor Ammons to reconsider. The day after he took the train from Walsenburg to Denver, tragedy struck in the west part of town in what is now referred to as the "7th St. Massacre." This incident occurred, on October 24, 1913, at the Wahlmeier home, immediately east of the Antonio Atencio residence and a few doors away from the Nelson Boarding House.*
>
> *Mrs. Wahlmeier was alone because her husband, like John Nelson, had boarded at the Walsen Camp to avoid the taunts of striking miners as he walked to work each day. On the morning of October 24, she found a note pinned to her door reading, "If you don't move out of this neighborhood within twenty-four hours, we*

will blow you out. Your husband is scabbing. We mean business."
After telephoning the mine superintendent, she was promised three
wagons with an escort of deputized mine guards to collect her
furniture so she could join her husband at the mine. When the
wagons and mounted guards arrived, the wagons were parked in
the alley behind the Wahlmeier house.

Before the wagons could be loaded, however, a crowd of
strikers and their wives and children, many of whom had just
come onto the scene from the Seventh Street Primary School two
doors away, harassed and jeered at Mrs. Wahlmeier and the
guards. The guards moved onto West 7th St. in front of the house
and began to threaten and curse the crowd; however, the crowd
started up with a new chant: "Scab Herders! Scab Herders!" As
the crowd thickened, several children scooped up dirt from the
unpaved street and threw it at the guards.

From her vantage point at the house next to the scene, Ana
Atencio, eldest daughter of Antonio and Elisa Atencio, observed
a striker crouched behind the fence under the rear window with a
rifle raised. Up to that point, no shots had been fired by either
side, but when the first wagon was being loaded, the gunman
under the Atencio window took aim and fired, hitting a guard in
the ear.

At that point, the guards opened fire into the crowd on the
street, and the demonstrators scattered. In five minutes, it was
over. Two miners were dead where they lay, one of them directly
in the street in front of the Nelson Boarding House. Miner Kris
Kokich lay draped over the fence in front of the Atencio home with
a mortal neck wound. He was rushed into the Atencio home and
laid on the bed until help could be summoned for him. Kokich died
at midnight in a Walsenburg hospital.

Meanwhile, Frances Nelson, who was coming home from St.
Mary School, seven blocks from the scene, was shocked by the sight
of a dead man in front of her home. She ran for the protection of
her brick house, which had been riddled on the west side with stray
bullets. Her sister, Ana, had taken refuge behind a table and
didn't venture out until a group of men rushed in with the

wounded Kokich. Tircio Valdez, who was a mine guard at the Walsen Mine and uncle to Frances and Ana, rushed out to the Atencio farm to notify Antonio and Elisa Atencio about the incident and to bring them back to care for their children at their home in Walsenburg.[6]

This was the first blood shed in Walsenburg during the great coal strike, but it would not be the last. The strike went on, and more and more miners joined the union in spite of the efforts of the coal operators to portray the strike as representing only a few of the miners.

Jeff Farr continued his harassment of striking miners and other citizens whose sympathies lay with the workers. His deputies, too, showed great brutality toward the strikers. One of these deputies was "Shorty" Martinez, so named because of his height of 6'4" and his penchant for tall, cowboy hats which made him even taller. Shorty Martinez would survive the turbulence of the coal strike years and continue in law enforcement in Huerfano County for many years.

One incident of brutality was related by Archibald Allison and others. A man named John L. East, an attorney sympathetic to the miners and who would later be district attorney, was severely beaten at the railroad station by Deputy Lew Miller, who seemed to take particular pride in beating up people. Archibald Allison relates:

> *Leaving the hall I went and asked the Mayor if he intended fulfilling his promise and carrying out the saloon closing ordinance. He said "Yes, why do you ask?" "Are you aware that John East was beaten up at the Depot and Marc Bird on the street yesterday?"*
>
> *He said, "No, I did not hear of it."*
>
> *"Well it happened and it was Deputy Sheriff Miller did it," I said.*[7]

The incident seems typical of the blind eye which many prominent people turned to the offenses of the sheriff's department.

As the strike wore on, many of the National Guardsmen went home and were soon replaced by men who had been the mine guards before the strike began. Gen. John Chase, a Denver doctor, continued as the militia commander. His views were that strikers had no right at all to strike, and that the strike should be put down by whatever means necessary.

Soon many of the tent cities were ringed with mine guards, some with machine guns overlooking the camps. Especially under the gun were the camps at Forbes and Ludlow near Trinidad.

Trinidad saw many marches, some led by Mother Jones, who was particularly effective in stirring up the women of the mining camps to support the strike.

Mother Jones was arrested in Trinidad and imprisoned under guard in a room at Mount San Rafael Hospital. She was held there for more than a month with no opportunity to communicate with the outside world. She was not charged with any crime. The mine operators simply wanted her to go away.

One march in particular occurred during the time of her imprisonment. The women and children of the nearby camps gathered in Trinidad and began a march up the principal street of the town. General Chase believed that the women were marching to the hospital with the intention of freeing Mother Jones. He ordered mounted cavalry men to confront them. During the confusion Chase struck out at a young girl. She fell against his horse and caused the horse to rear. Chase was thrown from the saddle.

Infuriated at this and jeered at by the girl, Chase cried out: "Ride down the women!" His mounted militia obliged and several women and children were injured in the melee. Chase ordered the arrest of several of the women, and they were shoved into the filthy Las Animas County jail along with their children. One woman in particular, drove the guards mad with her constant leading of the singing of union songs. Eventually the women were freed.[8]

On October 28, 1913, Companies C, D, F, I, & I of the 1st Infantry, Troop D, 1st Squad Cavalry and the Boulder Department of the Medical Corps left Denver. They were joined by Company K of the 2nd Infantry in Colorado Springs and detachments of Companies from other parts of the state at Pueblo. These troops were under the command of Colonel Edward Verdeckburg, of the 1st Infantry and were deployed to Walsenburg.

In a report to Brig. Gen. John Chase, Verdeckburg wrote:

> *The work of detraining began about 7:00 a.m. after a cordial reception by Major P. P. Lester, who, because of his residence in the city and his great familiarity with all available and strategic sites, had chosen for us the location between the two railroads and almost within the center of the city. The wisdom of his choice has been apparent every day in the quick movement and transfer of troops. Through the Major's activity and influence the camp was early provided with water by the extentions (sic) of the city mains into the camp streets and cook houses, a fact which went far to keep the men in good spirits. Heard of outbreak at Aguilar and sent Major P. J. Hamrock, 1st Infantry. Attempting to disarm everybody from mine guards to ranchers to miners. An attempt was made to import "strike-breakers" which action only served to inflame the feelings of the labor forces."* [9]

The presence of Dr. Lester in the establishing of the military encampment in Walsenburg is significant. Dr. Pliny P. Lester was an established member of the community and a well-respected physician who enjoyed a wide practice among the townspeople and at the mines. He was also a member of the militia and reportedly was concerned about his membership when the strike began and the militia was called out. He is said to have considered resigning his commission, but then changed his mind and participated in militia activities throughout the strike. His assistance in setting up the militia encampment is the first mention of his activities.

In a report to The 'Surgeon General, Major Lester gave the following account of his activities on behalf of the militia.

On October 28, 1913, I became advised of the coming to this district of a detachment of the National Guard for strike duty. I immediately went over the ground adjacent to the town of Walsenburg and picked out a suitable camp ground, ascertained what could be done in the way of water supply, electric lights, and telephone accommodations.

On the morning of the 29th I met the train bearing that portion of the troops that were to be stationed here under command of Colonel Edward Verdeckburg, and showed to him the ground that I had selected as the tract of land most desired and he directed that camp be made immediately in that track of land lying within the limits of the town between the D. & R. G. and C & S. tracks near the D. & R. G. Depot. Camp was begun about 8:30 a.m. and was all in shape, including the Regimental Infirmary before darkness of this first day in Camp.

There came with the Medical Corps, Captains Osborn, Luzell, and Peck and Lieutenant Wescott and the men of the Hospital Corps.

Water was obtained by the laying of some 1500 feet of water pipe and the placing of three hydrants for use of the Camp, Cook tents and one for the horse corral which has given us a very good quality of water for all purposes.

On account of the flat condition of the ground selected as a camp site, slag and sand from nearby was hauled to make paths and to fill in the low places in the ground. Straddle trenches were dug for the use of the men temporarily and latrines were constructed together with boxes for same the second day and the trenches were filled and covered with quick lime. These latrines have been burned out with crude oil and hay or straw every two days since that time and the condition has been very satisfactory. Recently I have had quick lime placed in the vaults on account of there having been a slight odor even after the vaults have been burned out. We have been very fortunate so far in not having to contend with flies and the garbage has been hauled away regularly by parties who wished it for hogs and from this source have had no trouble since the first week or ten days.[10]

Dr. Lester seems to have been preoccupied with his duties as a militiaman and there is no mention of whether or not he was able to carry on his regular practice as a doctor at this time.

Verdeckburg continued his activities in connection with the strike. He saw himself as trying to be fair to both sides and sent Hamrock to arrest any strike-breakers and bring them to camp. He sent Capt. Charles G. Swopes to La Veta following the deadly attack on mine guards at Oakdale. He transferred some of his troops to other stations such as sending Co. F, 1st Infantry to Walsen west of Walsenburg on December 13, 1913. The cold weather caused difficulties as the troops lacked enough blankets and overcoats and therefore suffered somewhat from the cold.

At the same time it is apparent from one item in Verdeckburg's report that the troops enjoyed the support of much of the community. He wrote:

> *At frequent intervals during the entire tour of duty, a number of pleasant social affairs, with varied programs were arranged to which the citizens of Walsenburg and vicinity were urged to come. They responded with most generous attendance and hearty enjoyment of the entertainment provided all of which went far to dispel the suspicious and misunderstanding which usually attends the troops upon such service in a community.*[11]

Concern on the parts of some of the citizens for the well being of the strikers and their families did exist. Efforts were made to supply food, and presents for the children were distributed at Christmas in 1913.

For the most part the strike went on fairly quietly. Sheriff Jeff Farr had prepared for the strike by deputizing 258 men and later reported that he did not know or particularly care whether or not some of them were criminals.

At the turn of the New Year, events in the strike began to move toward more violence. Many of the regular National Guardsmen had gone home. Some may have finished their tour of duty, but some simply left. They were quickly replaced by mine guards and some of the Baldwin-Felts detectives. With this change in the makeup of the militia, what had been fairly civilized relationships between the troops and the strikers, began to deteriorate.

When Mother Jones was released from her incarceration at the hospital in Trinidad, she was put on a train to Denver with instructions not to return to the southern coal fields. After a few days in Denver, she caught a train back south intending to return to Trinidad, but word went ahead of her and she was taken off the train at Walsenburg and placed under arrest. Colonel Verdeck-burg describes Mother Jones and her arrest:

> *Perhaps the most widely known character among the labor leaders is Mrs. Mary Jones familiarly known as "Mother" Jones. She came among the miners in the colonies or wherever an assemblage might be held and her speeches were of a character as to be deemed inimicable to law and order. After her incarceration at Trinidad she insisted upon a return to the district and under orders from the District Commander I directed her arrest upon receipt of intelligence that she was on a certain train. On the early morning of Mar. 23, 1914, she was apprehended by Capt. Nickerson and Lt. Hawkesworth and placed in the city jail at Walsenburg. She was held "incommunicado" awaiting disposition of a certain civil process which was being prosecuted in the higher courts. Every consideration has been shown her while under my care consistent with her status as a military prisoner."*[12]

The city jail was in the basement of the courthouse, and the cell where Mother Jones was held later became the office of the county extension agent.

In Mother Jones' account of her incarcerations, she described a cold, damp cell with a window which allowed her to see only the feet of people passing by, and she told of having to fight off sewer rats at night.

Whatever the conditions of her imprisonment, it is a fact that Mother Jones was charged with no crime and no hearing was ever held concerning her arrest. She was released after twenty-six days. If Verdeckburg's account of the day of her arrest is correct, she still would have been in jail in Walsenburg at the time of the infamous Ludlow Massacre in Las Animas County on April 20, 1914. As she is said to have gone to Washington to testify before Congress after her release, it is likely that this is true.

The **Walsenburg World** carried the following account of her release:

> *Mother Jones the aged strike leader was released from the cellar under the court house, Thursday morning, between 9 and 10 o'clock and went immediately to the Union headquarters, where she was warmly received by the men and women who had gathered there when it was known that she was to be given her freedom by the Operator's Militia. Mother Jones had very little to say against the treatment accorded her by the Military Authorities here and appears to have had very little trouble with any of them except Dr. Lester whom she characterized as a "dirty little sewer rat" saying that she was forced to ask Colonel Verdeckburg to stop him from annoying her. Like many citizens of the county of Huerfano, Mother Jones referred to Colonel Verdeckburg as a gentleman.*
>
> *The Colonel is the one man in the Militia, who has been in the southern field, at whom the finger of scorn will not be pointed for his malicious conduct toward the miners in the interests of the operators.*
>
> *Mother Jones was taken to the train in an automobile, escorted by the Independent Band and several hundred men and women. She left for Denver where she will rest for a week, returning to Walsenburg and Trinidad where she will address the miners.*[13]

The incident known as the Ludlow Massacre occurred on the day after the Greek New Year when the colony had been celebrating with a softball game, among other entertainments. The following day the colonists were alarmed to see the militia setting up machine guns on Water Tank Hill, which was located to the south of the tent city and the buildings of the little town of Ludlow. The tension continued through the morning. Some of the women and children fled from the colony and took refuge in a large arroyo north of the tents. Eventually someone fired the first shot and the battle was on. Other women and children fled to a large railroad well which contained steps down into its tank, and the women and children huddled on the steps. Still others sought refuge in the long pits which had been dug under the tents for extra storage or perhaps for warmth during the long, cold winter.

Sometime in the afternoon one of the tents was set afire. It is disputed as to how the fire occurred, with the mine operators claiming that a stove had overturned, and the miners insisting that the tent had been deliberately set afire by the militia. At any rate, the fire started, and the entire colony was soon in flames.

In the aftermath of this burning of the tent city, the bodies of eleven children and two women were discovered in one of the pits, dead of smoke inhalation. Two women who had been near the top survived, but their stories were never sought in the investigations which took place afterward. Others among the dead included a fourteen-year-old boy who had been bringing water to his mother and two miners – Louis Tikas, the Greek camp leader, and James Fyler, the paymaster. Their bodies were left lying in the open for three days. When the bodies were finally examined, it was found that Tikas had been shot three times in the back, and Fyler had died from a gunshot wound to the head.

The violence at Ludlow set off a ten-day wave of violence all up and down the southern Colorado coal fields.

In Walsenburg the militia set up at Walsen Camp at the end of Seventh Street on a hill overlooking the street which was occupied largely by miners and their families and several small businesses. Two small cannon which were said to have been cast in Pueblo were brought to Walsen Camp by the militia along with one or two machine guns. Flood lights were also put in place and kept burning all night. During the next few days the militia periodically sprayed Seventh Street with gunfire. Some of the militia were deployed north of Walsen Camp near a water tank.

The striking miners were deployed along the hogback, a rocky ridge at the northern end of town. The miners had rifles but no machine guns. Fighting was sporadic for the next few days.

Gunfire seems to have been indiscriminate, and it was not always possible to determine who was doing the firing when someone was killed. A young boy, Mike Lenzini, was killed in front of his family business on Seventh Street. Another young man, a blacksmith named Henry Floyd, was shot off his motorcycle as he journeyed toward Pueblo with his girl friend riding behind him. A miner, George Bouck, was killed as he sat at his dining room table in his home on Seventh Street by a stray bullet coming through the house. Another account said that Bouck was killed by a shot in the back of the head fired through the door of his home on Seventh Street. Bouck left a wife and six children. It is said that the west wall of the Seventh Street Primary School was scarred by bullets and, given its proximity to the Nelson boarding house and the homes of two members of the Atencio clan, it is certainly likely.

Verdeckburg describes his arrival:

> We arrived at Walsenburg Court House where we detrained at 7:30 a.m. I reported our arrival to General Chase at Louisville, and informed him that a battle between mine guards and strikers was then going on at the Walsen Mine, that the buildings on the McNally Mine property were on fire and that before we left Ludlow we could hear firing at Forbes, that I was unable to go to their assistance because my orders were to go to Walsenburg, and that I had been unable to get The General by telephone before I left Ludlow to report these facts to him, and that I was now awaiting further orders. My orders were to clear the hills of all strikers at once. I immediately proceeded with my command to the Walsen Mine, where I found a battle in progress. The Companies were assigned to quarters and Captain Marshall in the meantime was obliged to get more commissary supplies in Walsenburg so as to be able to serve breakfast to the officers and men. In the meantime, Company H, 1st Infantry at the Court House having had their breakfast, I ordered Captain Dowling to report to me with his Company at once at the Walsen Mine, where I had established my Headquarters. In the meantime at 9:00 a.m. I detailed 1st Lieut. Morrison with six troopers of Troop "D" as a patrol to get information for me on or near the Pueblo road near

the hog back where the strikers were intrenched and 1800 yards from a ridge directly in front of the Walsen property where the mine guards were engaged in battle with the strikers. Two hundred yards back of this ridge is where I established Headquarters. Directly in front of me was situated Water Tank Hill. This is where the water supply for the Walsen Mine property is stored and where a powerful searchlight was located. This is the point which the strikers seemed anxious to capture.[14]

The fighting was not long in beginning. The strikers were arrayed along the hogback while the mine guards were stationed at Walsen Camp. Other militiamen under Verdeckburg's command eventually found their way onto Capitol Hill where they shot in the general direction of the miners.

Fighting was carried on along the hogback toward Walsen Camp throughout the afternoon and evening. Major Lester, the Walsenburg doctor who was a member of the militia, was killed during this battle. He was said to have been tending a wounded militiaman although others claimed he was leading a charge. The exact truth of the matter is probably not provable. That he was tending a wounded man seems likely, but that he sided with the militiamen and not with the miners and people of Walsenburg is also not in dispute.

While the fighting was going on, efforts to bring about a cease-fire were also underway. Talks were going on in Denver between elements of both sides and Verdeckburg at last reported the following:

At 1:30 p.m., I received a telephone message from Mr. Hawkins in Denver stating that I would probably receive an order from General Chase to cease firing and that he, Hawkins, had a talk with Don McGregor and he would see what could be done in regard to the strikers laying down their arms. In the meantime I had issued instructions that the mine guards were to replace our troops in the immediate front which consisted of Companies A, B, F and H, so that I would be able to reinforce the right and left flanks. At 1:45 p.m., I received the following instructions from General Chase in Denver:

> *"That all firing was to cease for one hour, and to meet and arrange with Don McGregor the leader of the strikers, the laying down of all arms in the Possession of the strikers, and report."* [15]

Various negotiations continued for some time. Problems arose with the miners who were unwilling to lay down their arms without the militia doing likewise. Verdeckburg stated that if the strikers did not disarm within a short period of time, the fighting would be resumed. Efforts were made by the militia to retrieve Major Lester's body. This took more negotiating, and when the body was finally retrieved, the claim was made of his having been shot twice after death, of mutilation of the body and theft of personal articles. It is uncertain just how many of these claims were true, but there can be no doubt that the miners felt considerable animosity toward Dr. Lester due to his siding with the militia.

Efforts were also made for the miners to retrieve their dead, but Mr. Ball, the assistant manager of Walsen and McNally mines, refused permission until daylight. Verdeckburg asked McGregor to withdraw his men that night and to get the bodies the following day. McGregor complied with this request.

The wave of violence which followed the Ludlow Massacre at last persuaded President Woodrow Wilson to intervene and send in federal troops.

Major Williams, Captain Dorn and 1st Lieutenant Hawksworth arrived in Walsenburg on the afternoon of April 30, 1914, just ten days after Ludlow.

Verdeckburg reported on this arrival:

> *I reported the last conference to General Chase who directed me to turn over all details to Captain Smith, who commanded the Federal troops who would arrive in Walsenburg on that day and take charge, and that our troops were to be withdrawn upon their arrival. Captain Smith and one troop of cavalry consisting of 70*

men arrived at Walsenburg at 4:15 p.m. I met Captain Smith at the depot when the special carrying the United States troops arrived. I conferred with him and gave him all the details in reference to the situation and conditions in the Walsenburg District. I also requested him to receive Major Lester's effects from Don McGregor as they had not been turned over to me at that time.[16]

With the arrival of the federal troops, the violence and the strike came to an end. Gradually the miners went back to work. The horror of the Ludlow Massacre and the subsequent battles in the following ten days aroused the nation to the plight of the working man, and many weeks and months of hearings on both state and national levels were conducted. Accusations of murder were lodged against various union men including John Lawson, who was convicted of a murder he could not possibly have committed. He was later exonerated and released.

What of the town during all of this strife? The city council continued to meet and discuss various local problems throughout. In April of 1914 the council appointed Dr. P. P. Lester as the city health officer. In May they reported that, due to the death of Dr. Lester, he would be replaced with Dr. Chapman in that position. Not a word was recorded in the minutes as to how Dr. Lester had died.

The saloons had all been closed in April by order of the town council and remained closed until November of that year. This caused a substantial loss of revenue for the town and, at length, the council petitioned the state for permission to raise taxes to cover the losses. They simply observed that due to the "turmoil" the saloons had been closed since April. Throughout all of 1913 and 1914, the city council went about its deliberations without ever using the word "strike" in the minutes of their meetings. Surely the councilmen were deeply concerned with the effects of this monumental labor dispute, but they never saw fit to mention it in the official record of their deliberations.[17]

The redoubtable Sheriff Farr and his deputies were apparently holed up in the courthouse with their machine gun during all of this violence. There does not appear to be much evidence that he and his men took part in the three days of fighting, but during the months of the strike, he had been very much in evidence, intimidating strikers and other innocent people, causing or participating in beatings and generally throwing his weight around.

Within a relatively short time after the strike the novelist, Upton Sinclair, wrote a novel entitled **King Coal**. While Sinclair insisted that the town in his novel was not intended to represent a particular coal town, it seems reasonable that Walsenburg served as a model for the town in his novel as he mentions Sheriff Farr in his postscript. Sinclair wrote in this postscript just how extensive the investigation of the strike was:

> There was never a strike more investigated than the Colorado coal-strike. The material about it in the writer's possession cannot be less than eight million words, the greater part of it sworn testimony taken under government supervision. There is, first the report of the Congressional Committee, a government document of three thousand closely printed pages, about two millions words; an equal amount of testimony given before the U. S. Commission on Industrial Relations, also a government document; a special report on the Colorado strike, prepared for the same commission, a book of 189 pages, supporting every contention of this story; about four hundred thousand words of testimony given before a committee appointed at the suggestion of the Governor of Colorado; a report made by the Rev. Henry A. Atkinson, who investigated the strike as representative of the Federal Council of the Churches of Christ in America, and of the Social Service Commission of the Congregational Churches the report of an elaborate investigation by the Colorado State militia; the bulletins issued by both sides during the controversy; the testimony given at various coroners' inquests ...[18]

The aftermath of the coal strike held a number of disturbing activities for all of the southern Colorado coal fields. Various indictments were brought against both sides. Accusations against National Guardsmen and the guards of the coal companies were quickly set aside through investigations carried out by the military itself.

Four Walsenburg coal miners, Enoch Mair, Fred Garcia, Arthur Quinn, and Michael Savage, were indicted for the murder of Dr. P. P. Lester. This trial was held in Castle Rock in 1915 and was extensively covered by the two Walsenburg newspapers. Eventually the four were found not guilty due to conflicting testimony and the inability of anyone to have seen clearly what was going on that night. Had the trial been held in Walsenburg, the outcome might have been much different.

The Huerfano County election was hotly contested, as usual, between the two parties designated as the Taxpayers Party and the Independent Party. In reality the Taxpayers Party was the Republican Party and the Independent was the Democratic Party. These names rather than the national designations had been in use for some years.

The Republican candidates for county office included Jeff Farr for sheriff, Antonio D. Valdez for county commissioner, Jose Sanchez for assessor, and W. H. Freeland for clerk and recorder. The Democratic slate offered E. L. Neelley for sheriff, Robert Young for county commissioner, Charles H. Sanchez for assessor and J. G. Archuleta for clerk and recorder.

Apparently the Republican county commissioners were uneasy about the possible outcome of the election. Prior to the election they changed the boundaries of seven precincts so that they were fully enclosed on coal company property. The seven coal camps were Cameron, Rouse, Pryor, Oakview, Walsen, Ravenwood and Niggerhead. Some of these were completely surrounded by fencing and all were controlled by armed guards.

No one was allowed on company property without a pass from one of the mine officials or, significantly, Sheriff Jeff Farr. Advocates of the Democratic ticket were unable to enter the premises of these precincts and were denied access to the voting rolls in order to determine the eligibility of those on the rolls.

When the election was held in 1914, the winners were Jeff Farr by a margin of 329 votes, and the other Republican candidates by 173 votes, 233 and 90 votes.[19]

Without the pluralities received in the seven closed precincts, these candidates would have been defeated. It would seem that the general population of Huerfano County was finally tiring of the rule of Farr.

E. L. Neelley and the other Democratic candidates immediately challenged the election results and the case began its long trip through the courts. As might be expected, the two newspapers, *The Walsenburg World* and the *Independent*, continued their war of words on the subject.

The case was heard before Judge Henry Blickhahn of the county court. The contestors were represented by Philip Hornbien, chief counsel, and Attorneys John L. East and Romilly E. Foote of Walsenburg.

Testimony was offered by Robert S. Mitchell, chairman of the County Democratic Party, about the difficulties he encountered during the election of 1914 in attempting to enter the closed precincts to make a canvass of the voters to determine if they were truly qualified.

E. L. Neelley gave similar testimony as to the above mentioned camps; that one, Wetmore, a mine guard, and one Williams, a tipple boss, were election judges at Walsen; that he and Mr. East watchers, were escorted to Walsen by a detachment of U. S. troops; that Joe Ball, assistant general supt. Of the C. F. & I. Co., and two nephews of J. B. Farr were near the polls helping bring in votes and talking to voters.

Wm. Jardine and Mrs. Lucille Hoffamier each testified that prior to election they were excluded from Walsen camp and prevented from distributing democratic literature by mine guards. Mrs. Hoffamier said that at the last general election she had been politically identified with the democratic party and that recently she had been accosted by Joe Hill, a deputy sheriff who was working for Farr, and told that he would make her leave town;

that "Shorty" Martinez, another deputy, had told her that she was indicted in connection with the hogback fight and that she had better leave town.[20]

Judge Blickhahn eventually ruled in favor of the Republican winners and the case was immediately appealed to the Colorado Supreme Court.

The Supreme Court heard the case early in 1916 and eventually handed down its 10,000-word opinion. The lengthy opinion offers much more evidence about how politics was carried on in Huerfano County at this time. In the opening pages of the opinion, the justices wrote:

> *The principal industry of Huerfano County is coal mining, the mines being operated by certain corporations. In 1913 a strike of the miners, members of a certain union, occurred, and many disorders and acts of violence ensued. Federal troops were finally summoned to restore order. No rioting occurred after their appearance, but the agitation engendered by the strike and its attendant disorders still divided the community. The coal companies in the election of 1914 supported the ticket presented by the Republican Party, while the opposite faction gave its support to that presented by the Democrats. The county commissioners, being Republicans, at the instance or with the connivance of the coal mining companies in July, 1914, changed the boundaries of certain election precincts so as to constitute the private properties of seven of the coal mining companies, an election precinct, surrounded by a fence in some instances, and protected by armed guards in all, so that each of these precincts was under the private control of the corporation. Every resident within these precincts was an employee of the corporations, or of their allied companies, with a single exception; the polling places were everywhere upon these private grounds, and the registration lists for the election were kept in the offices of the companies, and treated as their private property. During the months succeeding the establishment of these precincts the public of every class were excluded therefrom.*[21]

The opinion goes on to describe the entire situation which had prevailed in Huerfano County for many years. The rights of people to enter the camps, even on ordinary business, was also discussed and the testimony of one witness was included.

The undisputed testimony of witness Newkirk is fairly illustrative of the system of espionage and exclusion by the coal companies, of citizens of the county from the closed election precincts during the political campaign. This witness testified in substance as follows:

"*He resides in Walsenburg and is employed by McIntire in the furniture business. He went to Walsen camp sometime before the election to deliver furniture. Was stopped at the gate, was informed that he could not deliver in there. Was stopped again after he got into the camp, and told he would be arrested and thrown in jail if he was caught in the camp again. On another occasion he was stopped at the gate with a load of stuff that he had to take up. Was told by a guard that if he wanted to deliver goods up there he would have to get a pass from Jeff Farr. His employer, McIntire, has run a business in Walsenburg for some time, and when witness could not deliver the goods he came back and went up the next morning and entered the camp where the fence was cut, up by the schoolhouse, but he never went back any more. The guard at the camp showed witness a list of names of people who were barred from the camp. Witness' name was not on the list nor was that of his employer. Krier's store was on the list. Krier is a merchant in Walsenburg, and witness thinks Krier is affiliated with the Democratic party. The C. O. D. Store and the Sporleder Selling Company were on the list. Mr. Tim Hudson, clerk of the District Court, was on the list. He is affiliated with the Democratic party. Neelley is connected with Neelley & Caldwell, and was a candidate for sheriff on the Democratic ticket last fall. M. A. Sanchez, who runs a store in Walsenburg, was on the list. Dr. Adbun-nur, a physician, and Mr. East, an attorney, and Mr. Robert S. Mitchell, connected with the Independent paper, and chairman of the Democratic party, were on that list. On cross examination the witness testified that he did not know the guard's name. He was not a military man. The same man that showed witness the list told him about getting the pass from Jeff Farr. This occurred the latter part of 1914, and just before the election."* [22]

Control of the coal camps was so rigid that several accounts relate an occasion when the governor of the state and his adjutant, while on official business, were denied entry into one of the closed camps.

One witness told of being allowed to hold a political meeting at one of the camps. Upon his arrival he was told to wait in a certain place. As he waited he observed several miners approaching the building where the meeting was to be held. In each instance mine officials stopped the miners, spoke with them, and then the miners went back the way they had come. The Democrat told the few who had come with him that it appeared they would not have the opportunity to hold the meeting and they left.

The argument of the coal operators in justifying these actions is interesting. The court opinion offers this item.

Counsel contend that the closed precincts were an "industrial necessity," and for such reason the conduct of the coal companies during the campaign was justified. However such conduct may be viewed when confined to the private property of such corporations in their private operation, the fact remains that there is no justification when they were dealing with such territory, after it had been dedicated to a public use, and particularly involving the right of the people to exercise their duties and powers as electors in a popular government. [23]

In a later portion of the opinion, the justices reveal just how voting in the precincts was conducted.

> *It appears from the testimony that in those closed precincts many of those who voted were unable to speak or read the English language, and that in numerous instances, the election judges assisted such, by marking the ballots for them in violation of the law. Again, it appears that the ballots were printed so that the first letter of the name of each political party was printed in unusually large type. The coal company employees provided voters not familiar with the English language, a card upon which was printed a large capital R corresponding with the letter R on the ballot in the word "Republican," and the testimony in relation to the use of this kind of card by such voters is as follows:*
>
>> *"This card could be slipped right down the ballot until the word R on the card corresponded with the first letter of the word republican and a mark placed right on the top. The card was of the same length as the column on the ballot having the names of the candidates, and their political designation, and the R was so arranged that if the card was placed lengthwise it would meet the R in the word Republican. These cards were distributed quite frequently during the day."*
>
> *Just how many votes were cast in this way in the several closed precincts does not appear, but it is plain that it was a system. One of these cards in evidence shows the letter R to have been printed and not written. Thus such voters were not choosing candidates, but, under the direction of the companies, were simply placing the cross where they found the particular letter R on the ballot, so that the ballot was not an expression of opinion or judgment, not an intelligent exercise of suffrage, but plainly a dictated coal company vote, as much so as if the agents of these companies had marked the ballots without the intervention of the voter. No more*

fraudulent and infamous prostitution of the ballot is conceivable.[24]

The opinion continues with further evidence and with the court citing numerous court cases in the past dealing with the subjects of elections. At length the justices of the Colorado Supreme Court in a split vote reached a decision.

For the foregoing reasons the judgment of the court in each case before us, is reversed, and the entire poll in the said precincts of Niggerhead, Ravenwood, Walsen Mine, Oakview, Pryor, Rouse and Cameron, is annulled and held for naught, and the election in each of said precincts is hereby set aside. This leaves a substantial and unquestioned majority for each of the contestors in the county, and which entitles each contestor to be declared elected to the office for which he was a candidate.[25]

Thus after serving almost half of the term, Sheriff Jefferson B. Farr and his fellow Republican candidates were ordered to vacate the offices and turn them over to E. L. Neelley and the other candidates.

The two newspapers had followed the progress of the challenge that Neelley and the others had brought in the election. The **Independent** announced the decision with large headlines and gleeful writing. The **Walsenburg World** reported the decision in a front page column which read in part:

Whatever political beliefs a person may hold, it must appear unfortunate to him and one of the severest arraignments of our system of courts that this decision was strictly along political lines, the decision of the judges being along the lines of their political proclivities. Five democratic judges voted to oust and two republican judges dissented.

The opinion was written by Justice Tully Scott and when boiled down it is found that the only charge the contestors made which the decision upholds is that the precincts which were contested, namely several of the coal camps were what the contestors called closed camps. Those of us who were here during the exciting days of the strike know what the contestors called closed camps. They mean that the strikers were not allowed to do their will to the private property of the C. F. &. I. Co and we all know that it was a matter of self preservation to the company that such was so if true.

The opinion does not recite that any illegal votes were cast in those camps, but simply that the strike agitators which the democratic leaders had turned into political agitators were not allowed to enter the company grounds and stir up strife and destroy property. And justly so, too, for the companies had already suffered from the burning of their property, the killing of their men, and from the inciting to murder, arson and bloodshed.

The decision, then, it would seem, throws out the entire vote of these camps, not because the court found that there were illegal votes cast in these precincts, but because the coal companies, as a matter of self protection, employed guards to protect their property.[26]

Reading the actual opinion might cause a reader to disagree with the conclusions of the **World** about several aspects of the dispute, but every paper is entitled to its editorial view.

Barron Beshoar in his coal strike book, **Out of the Depths**, tells us the final chapter in this legal saga:

Sheriff Farr and his henchmen had ruled over the Kingdom of Huerfano for 20 years. They represented the power of the coal barons and No. 26 Broadway. Jeff and his heavily-armed lieutenants held on to the Walsenburg court house for another week while corporation attorneys sought to carry their case to the U. S. Supreme Court. That tribunal would have none of it, and Jeff Farr abdicated.

He marched out of the court house early in the morning, long before most of the residents of Walsenburg were up and about, with three satellites at his heels – Col. William H. Freeland, county clerk; Jose Sanchez, county assessor, and Antonio Valdez. Jeff paused a moment on the stone steps. The new sheriff, Neelley, who had been elected 18 months before, stood on the sidewalk with

J. G. Archuleta, C. H. Sanchez and Robert Young, waiting to take office. Jeff looked at the new officials and then up and down Walsenburg's main street. A train was just easing into the little depot across the way. Jeff threw out his chest and stuck his thumbs in the armpits of his vest.

"When I die everyone will come to my funeral," Jeff said in a loud voice.

Joe Sanchez was the only one of the dispirited group to ask why.

"Because they'll all want to make sure that old son-of-a-bitch is dead."

With that, Jeff stepped down and walked briskly to the street without so much as a nod to the incoming officials. The Czar was through.[27]

At last the coal strike was truly over, a new sheriff was installed in Huerfano County, and Walsenburg and the county could move on.

Chapter Six

Churches, Schools and Libraries

In many frontier communities the first order of business was business. The men who came to a new location established homes and businesses, and the women worked to do their share providing for the family and helping their husbands in their work. But invariably a time came when the women wanted more, and it was they who set about the task of establishing churches, schools and libraries. Perhaps the first church and school, those of the Catholic parish, were largely the creation of the priests who served them, but there can be little doubt that the job would not have been accomplished as quickly if it had not been for the desires of the devout women of the community.

In the earliest days the village of La Plaza de los Leones had little other than the homes of the residents and the hotel of August Sporleder with Fred Walsen's trading post in one room of it. Most of the residents were of the Roman Catholic faith, but they had no resident priest.

Between 1860 and 1865, the Very Rev. Joseph P. Machebeuf came now and then to minister to the spiritual needs of the populace. He also conducted mass, baptisms, weddings, etc. at other villages such as Badito, St. Mary's, Cucharas and La Veta. The time had not yet come when La Plaza de los Leones was large enough to have its own church.

As the community grew and began to prosper, however, it became clear to the Catholic hierarchy that the time had come when the town could support a parish. In 1869 Bishop Machebeuf established the parish of *Nuestra Señora de los Siete Dolores* (Our Lady of the Seven Sorrows) at Walsenburg and sent Father Joseph Percevault to be its first pastor.[1]

Percevault set out to build a church and bought a lot from Joseph Bourcy for the sum of fifty dollars. The site of this first church was at the northwest corner of Main and Seventh. The site was later Byrne's Hardware Store and is now occupied by a gasoline station.

The first church was a jacal building in which logs were placed upright, side by side and chinked with adobe in between. Many of the houses of the time were built in the same fashion. Doors, windows and roof were added and the entire building plastered with adobe.

The little church was large enough to serve the needs of the congregation at that time. Unfortunately it proved to be even more temporary than the priest had planned. It caught fire three years after its construction and was burned to the ground.[2]

Father Louis Merles became the pastor of the Walsenburg parish in 1871 while the original jacal church was still standing. After the disastrous fire he set about the daunting task of building a new one.

The new church was not built immediately. The bishops, priests and the people chose a lovely spot near the Cucharas River for the new church and purchased the site from Don Miguel Leon. The document describing this purchase states that the price of the land was $100 and the description of the lot was as follows:

> *Commencing at the corner of the house now occupied by John Albert, and running thence about one hundred and eighty yards to the house now occupied by Cruz Mestas (in front of the door of said house); thence about 240 yards in an Easterly direction to the lands claimed by Francisco Atencio; thence Southerly along the said Atencio's line to the Cucharas River' thence to the point of beginning, containing about twelve acres of land more or less..."* [3]

The inexact nature of this description was all too common throughout the sparsely settled West. Such descriptions may have had some bearing on many of the other problems of land description which have plagued Walsenburg and other locations from time to time over the years.

Two years after beginning work on the new Catholic church, a serviceable building was completed. Father Merles had dreamed of a cruciform church, but funds were not available to create this, and when the structure was completed, it was a rectangular building 75 feet long, 30 feet wide and 16 feet high. It had no interior furnishings and the congregation either stood or brought its own chairs. Fred Walsen donated a bell, but it sat outside unused since the building had no bell tower and was probably not strong enough to support a tower. Father Merles also erected a parish house with six rooms and a barn and stable.

The church was dedicated on or about September 29, 1874.[4]

Father Merles did not live to enjoy the new church for very long. In September of 1876, while returning from an errand with his driver, he was thrown from the wagon and suffered a broken neck. There was no trained doctor available, and the priest died the next day.

For the next year or two the Jesuit Fathers of Trinidad served the needs of the church from time to time.

The arrival of the railroad in Walsenburg in 1876 made an enormous economic difference for the town. Coal was just beginning to be mined, and it was expected that the whole area would experience a boom.

The need for a permanent priest for the parish was obvious and filling the post did not take long. In October 1876 Father Gabriel Ussel was appointed as parish priest. He remained until the end of his life, thirty-three years later.

Within two years the church had bought a ten-room house from August Sporleder to be used as a convent for the sisters whom Father Ussel hoped to bring to Walsenburg. His dream, not to be realized in his lifetime, was to open a school.

Unfortunately, the poor choice of site for the church now became apparent. In 1878 after much work had been done to improve the church and rectory and to beautify the grounds, all was lost when the Cucharas River went on one of its periodic rampages. Heavy rain fell steadily for twelve hours, and the river went out of its banks and seriously undermined the adobe church.

It was not swept away in the flood, but was so badly damaged that it fell about a week later.

Father Ussel not only had to postpone his dream of a school but had to turn his attention to securing a new site and new funds to rebuild the church.

The church income was negligible during this time and expenses exceeded income. Bishop Machebeuf helped from his own funds, but it was not until September 1878 that the church was able to purchase five and a fraction lots for $80 from Don Miguel Leon in the center of town.

Many difficulties continued to plague Father Ussel – fundraising, disagreements with contractors, the necessity for cutting back on plans, but finally in 1882 the first part of the planned church was opened for worship.

While Father Ussel never realized his dream of opening a school, he was able to replace the small church, which was built where the rectory now stands, with the more substantial church building in which Catholics of Walsenburg still worship. St. Mary Catholic Church at 121 East Seventh Street was begun in 1892 and dedicated and opened for worship in 1900.

Father Ussel died in 1909 and was succeeded by Father Eugene Lefebrve, who continued to pursue the dream of a school.

Father Lefebrve encountered the same difficulties as Father Ussel had in establishing a parochial school, but at last he succeeded. The school was built during his lifetime but was not opened for classes until after his death in 1912.[5]

The school consisted of the central portion of the building still known as St. Mary School. It is two stories in height with a central entrance up a small flight of steps. The school was opened under the pastorship of Father John B. Liciotti, who arrived in 1913 to serve the parish and remained until 1941. During his time of service, the parish built a new rectory, a convent and two additions to the school.

The Benedictine Sisters of Atchison, Kansas, sent five teachers and a housekeeper. Later two more sisters were sent.[6]

Many, many students earned their education at St. Mary School. In 1926 a high school wing was added to the building, and four years of high school were available.

Over the years, however, it became increasingly difficult for the parish to maintain its school. The high school closed in 1972 and the elementary school closed in 1997. The members of the parish tried hard to keep their school open, but it was not to be. The students who once attended St. Mary School now attend the public schools in Walsenburg. The great brick building stands empty.

While the Catholic community was busy building its various churches and establishing its parish, the Protestant members of Walsenburg were not idle.

> *The first church for Protestant worshipers was an adobe schoolhouse on West Sixth Street in the downtown area. All Protestant groups worshiped together until the Presbyterians built a church in 1883. This church was the first Protestant church building in Walsenburg. The building is now part of the Neece Family Medical Clinic, 100 West Fourth Street, next door to Spanish Peaks Public Library on Main Street.[7]*

In 1884 the Methodists organized their own church with a pastor, William A. Freeman, who served only a month. The church had four charter members: Robert A. Quillian, Fatima Noland, G. P. Noland and Francis Rogers. Over the next few years several pastors briefly served the church, which still met at the Presbyterian Church on Main Street. One of these was Asbury H. Quillian, the legendary circuit rider from Georgia, who established several early churches, including Gardner and Salida, and served them all by visiting them on horseback.

In 1888 Pastor J. E. Squires and the church membership decided it was time to build a church and they did so in 1889, constructing what is still referred to as "the little white church." The building was made possible by the gift of an entire city block to the church from Fred Walsen with the stipulation that it be always used for the ministry and membership of the church. This property was bounded on the west by Walsen Avenue and on the east by Hooper Avenue and lay between Kansas and Pennsylvania Avenues. The church was built on the north end of the property, and a parsonage was built just to the east of the church. The parsonage was later moved to a spot east of the present church and facing Kansas Avenue. In later years parts of the block were sold and today the church owns the part of the block facing Walsen Avenue and includes the church and the 1977 parsonage to the north.

The red brick church was begun in 1928 under the pastorship of R. R. Rose and was dedicated in March of 1929. The beginning of the Great Depression later the same year caused years of financial hardship for the church membership. At one point the church not only was unable to make payments on its debt, but also did not have the funds to pay the paving tax since the city was beginning an ambitious program of street paving in the twenties.

The men of the church began a tradition of Saturday night turkey dinners which were open to the public. The men bought live turkeys, slaughtered, dressed, cooked them and offered turkey dinners for thirty-five cents a plate. This eventually raised enough money to pay the paving tax. The turkey dinners continued for many years, although the women gradually pushed the men out of the kitchen and relegated them to the dishwashing chores.

In 1939 the Rev. C. H. Hatfield was posted to the Walsenburg church with the express instruction to get the church out of debt. His efforts took several years and included a conference with national church officials to reduce the amount the church must repay, but eventually the church debt was paid.

Over the years there were as many as three Presbyterian churches in Walsenburg. One of these was the Spanish Presbyterian Church, which built the brick building at 603 South Leon. This attractive building was the Mennonite Church.

One Presbyterian Church was built on the southwest corner of Kansas and Russell, where the parking lot of the medical building is now. This church later served as the first meeting place of the newly organized Congregational Church in the 1920s. When the

Presbyterian congregation found itself unable to sustain its church, the building was sold to the Congregational Church.

This congregation later added to its property by building a large community building next door. Many activities, especially youth activities, took place in this facility.

The Congregational Church eventually also found itself unable to sustain a viable church and, after many months of negotiations, this church formed a merger with the Methodist Church. The merged church became known as the United Church, although its pastors are supplied by the Methodist Church.

The community building was sold to the county for use as a medical building, and a parking lot was needed so the lovely church was demolished to make room for the parking. Fortunately as many features of the church were saved as possible. One of the stained glass windows was installed in the meeting room of the Walsenburg City Council at City Hall. Two others were placed in the east end of the sanctuary of the United Church above two small doors and lighted from behind. Other items such as the spire, the baptismal font, the pulpit and chairs are now in the possession of the United Church, but no use for them has been found.

A small Episcopal Church once flourished in a building on the corner of Fifth Street and Rito Avenue near Washington School. Among its possessions were an ornate brass altar cross and several brass candlesticks. These altar items moved from the Episcopal Church to the Presbyterian Church, remained with the Congregational Church and now grace the altar of the United Church.

Many other denominations have long had a presence in Walsenburg. One service offered in the 19th century by the Baptist Church was a public reading room, which flourished before the advent of a public library.

Today in addition to those already mentioned there are congregations of the Church of Christ, the Assembly of God, the Jehovah's Witnesses and several other small congregations.

All of these groups struggle financially at all times, but all of them persevere in their missions.

The earliest mention of a public school is of a one-room adobe schoolhouse just off Main Street on West Sixth Street, now a parking lot for Dollar General. This building was used as a place of worship for all Protestants until 1883. It is not known if the building was also used for school while it was being used as a house of worship or if the school had been moved elsewhere.[8]

It is clear, however, that schooling for children was a priority during the 1870s and 1880s wherever school was held.

As the town grew so did its buildings for education. The Seventh Street Primary School at 611 West Seventh Street was erected around 1904 or 1905 with four to six rooms for classes. Hill School was built on a high point at 126 North Polk Avenue. This is a two-story brick building and many residents recall going to school there or teaching there. Due to space and money concerns, the building was used long after it had been condemned. During the 1970s it was also used as the district administrative office. Currently the building is a private home.

During the 1880s the first Washington School was built. This was a two-story brick building, with a bell tower, on the site of the present Washington Intermediate School. Part of the property where this school stood, probably the area where the playground is now, was the site of one of the tent cities which served the striking miners and their families during the coal strike of 1913-1914.

This building was later demolished to allow for the 1936 construction of the yellow brick building with a basement, currently on the site.

In 1892 the first efforts toward a high school were undertaken. There were four students and one teacher, Mr. H. H. Brodie, who also taught seventh and eighth grades. As Irene Elisha wrote in the *Huerfano World*:

> *By 1894 there were eleven high school students and the following year a two-year course of study had been organized. In 1897 three graduates, Mary Campbell, Jessie Snedden, and Maud Wycoff, had completed a three-year course of study and the*

first graduation ceremony was held. The Sporleder orchestra, which consisted of members of the family of Louis B. Sporleder, Sr. and his wife, Louisa Unfug Sporleder, furnished the music for this first graduation in Walsenburg.[10] *Between 1897 and 1901 twenty-one students received diplomas for completing this course of study.*[11]

In 1900 a vote was taken in the county for the organization of a county high school and in 1901, a four-year high school course was adopted.[12]

In 1906 the school was granted a two-mill tax levy and the school became known as Huerfano County High School. The first principal was Dr. W. J. Wagner, who had one assistant. School was held in the Odd Fellows Hall, and by 1907-1908 the faculty had increased to three instructors.[13]

Over the next few years the location of the high school changed frequently since no regular school building had been constructed.

The Elks Club sponsored and supported financially the first basketball team. In recognition of this help, the school adopted the Elks colors of purple and white as their colors. The Armory Building was obtained for basketball practice and games.[14]

The Armory Building at that time was a large brick building located on East Fourth Street behind what was Ludvik's Gasoline Station.

In 1911 both the boys and girls basketball teams, which were called the Panthers, won the state championships.

From 1913 to 1916 the Armory Building was leased for use as a high school building. During this time Chapman Hall was used for basketball. Chapman Hall was evidently located upstairs in a building on West Sixth Street.

Ford Frick, a man who later became the national commissioner of major league baseball, taught English and journalism in Huerfano County High School at this time. During his stay in Walsenburg, he married one of the Cowing girls and he and his wife returned for visits frequently.

While teaching here, Frick also began writing feature stories for area newspapers and then accepted a position with a Colorado Springs newspaper.

He was the author of one of the first fly-over newspaper stories. Frick and another man rented a small plane to fly over Pueblo following the devastating flood of 1921. The resulting story drew the attention of a New York newspaper, and Frick was offered a job as a sports writer. From there his career flourished, and he became an owner in major league baseball, National League President and finally Commissioner of Baseball.[15]

The school in Walsenburg was damaged by fire in the school term of 1917-1918 and part of the high school was held in Hill School and part in Chapman Hall. During World War I the school operated on a six-day week.[16]

The high school committee began to think of a permanent home for the high school operation in 1919, which was the final year of the Chapman Hall lease, although they were able to rent the hall for one more year.

In 1920 plans were made by the committee to construct a building. The location was to be on Walsen Avenue and the well-known firm of Rapp and Rapp were chosen as the architects and Emilio Ghione was given the contract to construct the building.

The result was the three-story red brick building with the twin towers flanking the entrance. Two years later the gymnasium was constructed at the north end of the high school building.

This building provided a complete high school curriculum including basic courses in English, math, and history along with home economics, shop, foreign languages, business courses and others. The library was established on the third floor in a long room on the south end of the building. In later years another room was added to the library by vacating a classroom.[17] Beneath the gymnasium were the wood-working shop, the art room, the cafeteria and the kitchen.

All of these school courses and additions to the building did not come at once but were added over the years as the need arose.

Property just west of the school was donated by Fred Walsen for a football field, but he did not wish the field to be named for him. During the depression a stadium with bleachers set in a foundation of native stone were added in a Works Progress Administration building project.

Like most other small towns in the nation, Walsenburg has always had a passion for sports. In Walsenburg the importance was magnified somewhat by the presence of two high schools – Huerfano County High School and St. Mary's High School. Over the years the rivalry between the public school Panthers and the St. Mary's Crusaders was at times quite intense. An annual city championship was held during the basketball season consisting of a three-game playoff, but in 1931 the deciding game of the series was called off. The first report said the game was cancelled due to scheduling difficulties, but later it was admitted that the cancellation was due to disagreements between the two schools. The coaches could not agree on an official for the game. Tensions had apparently become so great between the two schools that all connections in sports were stopped for years.

In the 1930s one of the outstanding high school athletes was Gaston Santi, son of Mr. and Mrs. Cesare Santi. Following his high school career he attended college at Grinnell College in Grinnell, Iowa, where he was also a standout athlete. Upon graduation he returned to Walsenburg and coached at Huerfano County High School for a number of years. Recently Santi was reported to be living in Denver at the age of 92.

In 1934 a Spanish fiesta was presented by the Spanish classes of HCHS under the direction of Elizabeth Lansdown, Spanish teacher. Songs and dances of various nations and localities in the world were depicted.[18] This program became known as El Fandango and continued to delight the community for many years under a variety of directors, notably Martha King Spock. Currently an effort is underway to revive it and interest among students seems to be growing.

A major headache developed at HCHS in 1938 when the school board chose not to renew the contract of C. Albert Anderson, the principal and superintendent of the high school. There was no unified school district at the time, and the elementary schools and the county high school each had its own school board.

High school students decided to strike to protest the dismissal of the popular Anderson, and some fifty per cent of the student body left school to denounce the board's action. The board offered a contract to John Y. Yost. Yost refused the contract, but the students still wanted Anderson rehired. The school board announced that Anderson had been dismissed for failure to keep discipline and next offered the contract to a former teacher named Paul Nesbit. The students continued their protests for several days, but eventually the school board held a peace meeting and the students agreed to return to school under the principalship of Nesbit.[19] Anderson remained in Walsenburg and opened a successful insurance office.

Presumably calm returned to HCHS until the end of the year. That year eighty-one students graduated on June 1, 1938. The salutatorian was Thelma Davis and the valedictorian was Jane Thompson. The large class also included Raymond Aguirre, June Brunelli, Frances Best, John Calderon, Christina Conder, Lee Crump, Delia Duran, Joe Edward Faris, Eddie George, John Gasparetti, Goldie Hudson, Jewel Krier, Ralph Levy, Jr., Louise Lenzotti, Virginia Laney, Anita Mestas, Floyd Murr, Alfred Newman, Jr., John Pavlich, Virginia Summers, Andrew Schafer, Bessie Skrzynear, Geraldine Sporleder, Jimmie Tesitor, Tom and Betty Lee Thompson, Della Vigil and Clifford Wells.[20] Many of these people remained in Walsenburg and became leading citizens of the town.

In the fall of 1938 the school board adopted a dress code, primarily for girls. Until November 1 and after March 1 the girls of HCHS would wear:

1. *Plain white cotton middy, no belt over it, and having the regulation sailor collar with not more than three straight rows*

*of braid thereon. Sleeves shall be plain with not more than 3
rows of narrow white braid. No further decorations permitted.*

2. *Solid color, black, blue, or red tie of reasonable proportions to
be worn.*

3. *A plain navy blue or black skirt made plain or pleated.*

 *Between Nov. 1 and Mar. 1, the white middy may be replaced
by a navy middy of the same style and regulations as the white
middy. Tie may be blue, black or red.*

 BOYS: No extreme styles will be allowed.[21]

Unfortunately, no explanation of what might constitute
"extreme styles" was given, nor did any comments from the girls
about these requirements make it into the newspaper.

The school remained as Huerfano County High School until
1959 when all of the county schools were consolidated. At this time
the name was changed to Walsenburg High School.

In 1972 a bond issue was floated to construct a new building on
property on Pine Avenue to house science classes since the school
was in danger of losing its North Central Association classification
due to inadequate science labs.

On July 8, 1974, an early morning fire was discovered in the
gymnasium, apparently from arson. The gym, shop, art room and
cafeteria were lost to fire.

The rest of the building suffered smoke damage but was
renovated enough to continue with school there.

Another bond issue was floated in 1974 to build a new high
school. This school was built to the east of the science building and
was named John Mall High School in honor of the long-time
superintendent of schools.

Following the completion of JMHS, the old high school was
turned into Walsenburg Middle School. A new gymnasium was
constructed on the site of the old one destroyed by the fire.

Over the years the Seventh Street Primary School closed and
eventually became the site of the administrative offices. Hill School
also closed, and all elementary school children were taught in
Washington School and Walsenburg Middle School.

In 2002 a new bond issue was passed to construct a science room and a pre-school room at Gardner and to build an early childhood learning center on land just west of the existing two buildings of John Mall High School.

This building was completed and dedicated in 2004. It houses Head Start classes, kindergarten and the first three grades. A full-sized gymnasium, which will provide physical education for the children and also more space for high school sports such as volleyball, girls' basketball and wrestling, is part of this complex.

A contest was held to name the new school, and from among the many entries the Huerfano Re-1 School Board chose the name Peakview.

Due to declining enrollment and with the opening of Peakview School, it was no longer possible to maintain a middle school in the red brick building on Walsen Avenue. Washington Intermediate School housed fourth through the sixth grade. Part of the west building of JMHS was used for most of the classes of the seventh and eighth grades, making JMHS a six-grade school instead of a four-grade one.

It had been the intention of the school board to demolish the former high school, a red brick building, but a coalition of interested citizens formed to try to save the distinguished structure for some other use.

Over the years many people of great ability and integrity have served the schools of Walsenburg. S. M. Andrews and John Mall were two of these.

S. M. Andrews was a longtime principal and teacher in the Walsenburg public schools. At the time of his arrival, he worked mainly in the elementary schools. When the new high school was built on Walsen Avenue, S. M. Andrews became the superintendent of the county high school.

His standing in the community is well illustrated in an article written by Clarence J. Martin in the ***Pueblo Star Journal***.

*During a recent visit to the Walsenburg schools the writer,
who was governed in his school days by the orthodox rule of rod*

and iron, experienced some peculiar emotions as he witnessed in every room the affection of the pupils for the man who represents the acme of discipline to them.

The children did not seem to be afraid. Nobody ducked for cover like a frightened quail fleeing from a hawk when the superintendent unexpectedly entered the room. Instead, as he moved down the aisles, dozens of kiddie hands went up to be held in his own and in a few instances some of the children actually "talked right out loud" to him without suffering even a verbal reprimand. And the superintendent's example is followed by all the twenty-seven teachers in the schools...

Superintendent Andrews of the public schools and Father Liciotti, head of the Ussel Memorial school, each have an efficient corps of teachers, are working together to keep the standard of education in Walsenburg as high as it is anywhere else in the state.

There are in the Walsenburg public schools and three rural schools in District Four, 1056 pupils and in the parochial schools 619. There are 27 teachers in the public schools and 12 in the parochial school.

Prof and Mrs. Lee Saunders are in charge of a night school which is conducted for the benefit of adult foreigners. There are two kindergarten schools with a total attendance of 57 pupils. The enrollment of the high school is 140. No feature of education is neglected. Pupils from both the public schools and the Ussell Memorial school won many prizes at the annual Huerfano county fair held in Walsenburg last September.[22]

Following his retirement as superintendent, S. M. Andrews was granted the title of Superintendent Emeritus and given an office in Washington School, where he continued to work on various school projects.

Unfortunately other problems arose for this dedicated man and on the morning of January 14, 1958, he died in his office at the school, apparently a suicide. He was still breathing when he was found by two sixth grade boys, but died before he could be taken to the hospital. The coroner, Herbert Furphy, found that

Andrews had taken cyanide. Andrews left a number of notes and letters lying on a stack of unpaid bills. The letters were turned over to the sheriff's office, but no finding other than suicide was made.[23]

In later years another remarkable man came to the Walsenburg schools. Beginning as a teacher, John Mall soon was promoted to elementary principal and then to superintendent of schools. This occurred early in World War II when teachers were rapidly being called into the armed forces, and the school needed to secure the services of a superintendent who would not be called away. John Mall remained as superintendent 1955 to 1975 and returned to be interim superintendent on more than one occasion when the school was temporarily without a top executive.

Martha King Spock was another of the many innovative educators who have served the Walsenburg schools. Mrs. Spock was a member of the pioneer King family, who came to the Gardner area very early. Part of her ancestry was Spanish, and she was always greatly interested in Spanish culture.

As part of her teaching service, she developed El Fandango, a Spanish dance group that performed the dances of New Mexico, Colorado, Mexico and Spain for many years and before many audiences. The annual performances were greatly anticipated by the community. Education was also part of the mission of the Spanish Club, and regular trips to Mexico were included. Mrs. Spock made individual trips there to learn new dances to teach to the group.

When Mrs. Spock retired, the organization was carried on for some years by Mary Ann Boyer Pedraza and others, but gradually the numbers of the group grew too few and the activity was dropped.

In recent years El Fandango has been revived as an extra-curricular activity by Gretchen Sporleder Orr and Mary Jo Tesitor. These young women, both former members of Mrs. Spock's group, began with a small group of children and their group has now grown to include high school students and have again reached a high level of performance.

Many other dedicated teachers and aides, administrators, secretaries, coaches, cooks and janitors have served the educational needs of Walsenburg students.

Another facility greatly desired by the women of frontier communities was a public library, and the women of Walsenburg were no exception.

For a time the reading needs of the community were served by the Public Reading Room of the Baptist Chapel on West Sixth Street. This room re-opened in 1904 after having been closed for a time. About 400 books were available to anyone as well as a long list of newspapers and magazines.

A truly public library was also desired, and the group to accomplish this goal was formed in 1896. They called it the Saturday Club, but in about a year the group affiliated with the national organization of Woman's Clubs and the Saturday Club became the Walsenburg Woman's Club.

The public library was their principal dream and they set about making it happen. They saved money by doing without such amenities as printed programs in order to increase their book fund. They offered a series of entertainments featuring performers from Pueblo in 1905-1906 and entertained the performers in their homes in order to save hotel bills. They also required donations of books from their members and solicited donations from others.

In the spring of 1906 the dream was realized with the opening of a public library, which consisted of one locked bookcase in a corner of the courthouse basement. The club members took turns in keeping the library open three hours on two afternoons each week. The key to the library case was kept on a nail in Cowing's Grocery Store.

During the years that the library operated in this manner the collection grew from book donations and purchases and from an occasional donation of money. One donation was somewhat unusual. A large envelope with no return address was received at the Post Office by Walter Hammond. It was addressed to the

Secretary of the Woman's Club who happened to be the wife of Mr. Hammond. He assumed it was another of the many circulars his wife received. When Mrs. Hammond opened it, she found $50.00 in bills and a letter saying that the donation came from the Walsenburg Chapter of the Ku Klux Klan for the benefit of the Walsenburg Library. The Woman's Club accepted the donation and acknowledged it in a letter to the newspaper. Soon after it was noted in the paper that $50.00 in new books had been bought, but there is no record of the books that were acquired.[24]

When a room in the basement of the courthouse became available for use as a library, it was contingent upon the purchase of $500 worth of new books. The board had spent $200 by the time the library and reading room opened.

A new means of raising money was then introduced by the Woman's Club. Tag Day became an annual event in which teams of women and high school students fanned out across town soliciting library memberships and donations. The first such event raised $250, and Tag Day continued on a yearly basis for many years.

The expanded space greatly increased the use of the library, but in 1927 the need arose for another move. The courthouse planned a major renovation of the basement to provide more office space and required the library room for other purposes.

The library moved to a small house on Main Street, next to Heritage Park and next to the office occupied by the Gary Hanisch law office.

The library continued in the little house until 1935 and then made another move to two rooms in the basement of the Elks Home on East Sixth Street.

During its years in the little white house, the library expanded its services. Many books were bought, and books for the blind were obtained. From 80 to 100 books a day were checked out.

At the Elks Home the library had more space, including a reading room which seated twenty persons. The rent for this space was $25 a month. The Civic League, another organization for women, built bookcases for the new location and study tables and chairs were provided.

The Civic League also became a partner with the Woman's Club in running the library. The library board consisted of members from each group, and the librarian was chosen from among them. The combined committee elected the first slate of officers: Mrs. Clyde Pritchard, chairman; Mrs. Ralph Snodgrass, Mrs. Maurice Cowing, Mrs. Annabelle Phipps, Mrs. Leo Stacy, Miss Frances Evans, Miss Louise Queen and Mrs. Rubye Myers. Mrs. Wylie Babbitt was the librarian.

The minutes of the library board over the years reflect both the achievements and the difficulties of maintaining library service for Walsenburg and for outlying communities as well. The depression brought financial problems greater than usual, and the Elks Lodge responded by allowing the library to hold back its rent until county warrants were again available.

Local merchants often donated funds to allow for purchases such as children's chairs and tables and occasional renovations.

A favorite fund-raiser was the Silver Tea, which combined a social occasion and library donations. Tea and cookies would be served and someone would present a book review and perhaps a musical selection or two. One year they had difficulty in selecting a date, and this problem was discussed several times before they finally settled on a date for their tea – December 7, 1941. This was the terrible day that the Japanese air force bombed the United States Naval Base at Pearl Harbor, Hawaii, marking the beginning of World War II. Of course, the tea was postponed. It was held the following week and was well attended.

During World War II the library and the community went all out to collect books for servicemen. Many, many boxes of books were collected and shipped to various locations such as Fitzsimmons Army Hospital in Denver. Community members, school students and others participated in this endeavor.

After the war attention turned to securing a permanent location for the library since the Elks Club needed the space for other purposes.

A new group was formed consisting of representatives of twenty organizations in the town. Efforts were made to secure a lot on Main Street from Miriam Pritchard, a teacher in New York and a member of the prominent Pritchard family in Walsenburg. Another site considered was the county-owned property between the railroad tracks and the courthouse. This site is now the parking lot for the courthouse.

Eventually Miss Pritchard deeded the lot to the library with the stipulation that construction must take place within five years.

Construction of the new library was begun in March of 1952 and was to cost $15,158. The contractor was R. M. Baker and the building supervisor was Walter Wheelock. The library had approximately $9,000 when it began, and a loan of $8,000 was secured from the First State Bank.

The library was ready for occupancy in September. With the help of county trucks, the move began on September 8.

Among the donations made to assist the library in developing its new quarters were memorial donations in memory of the late Miriam Pritchard, who died shortly after deeding the property.

The new officers were Mae Cowing, chairman; Nell Lloyd, vice chairman; and Alvina Luethje, secretary. Board members were Ethel Williams, Sarah Williams, Pauline Sudar, Norma Lou Murr, Ruth Summer and Nina Taylor.

At the time of the move to the permanent library, Mrs. Cora Mockmore was the librarian. She was succeeded several years later by Mrs. Frances King who remained at the post for many years.[25]

In recent years the need for more space grew ever more apparent. A major renovation occurred in the mid-90s when Sylvia Rael was the library director. A grant was obtained which allowed the purchase of a new heating and cooling system on the outside of the building. The old furnace room became a storage and workroom. Both of the basement rooms were renovated for children's services and new carpeting, shelves and computer stations were added upstairs.

This still proved to be not enough room and under the present leadership of Monica Kirby, the library began plans for its first real expansion project since the building was built. A large grant was obtained for use in building an addition, and plans were drawn up for it. Unfortunately problems in the construction of the present building were found which made the proposed new wing difficult if not impossible. After a long struggle the red brick building, which was Walsenburg High School for many years, was purchased by the Economic Development Corporation and the first floor of the building is to become the library if sufficient funds for the necessary renovation can be obtained. It is a daunting task, but through the many years of its existence, Walsenburg citizens have responded to every needed change in the library by somehow making it all come true.

Chapter Seven

WAR AND EPIDEMIC

Much of the activity involved in building the churches, schools, and libraries of the town, went on during the turmoil of the coal mining era.

The bitter coal strike was at last ended. Jeff Farr's re-election in the closed precinct coal camps was contested and by mid-1916 the reign of the King of Huerfano County was over. John D. Rockefeller, Jr., stung by the great volume of criticism that he had received as a result of the strike, paid a visit to the coal camps owned by C. F. & I. He was warmly received by the miners and their families in spite of all their suffering they had endured at the hands of the managers of the Rockefeller properties. Rockefeller promised improvements and, with the help of MacKenzie King of Canada, proposed what amounted to a company union. The miners got some rights of representation and a seat at the table when major decisions were made, but for the most part, they were still at the mercy of their employers. Rockefeller's personal contribution to the improvement in the coal camps consisted of the construction of a few band stands.

Peace returned to the community and its surrounding camps. The saloons were re-opened and business resumed more or less as usual.

Apparently not everything in the community was satisfactory to the city council in the matter of city law enforcement. In May of 1915, the council addressed itself to the duties of the Marshal and Assistant Marshal:

> *It shall be the duty of the marshal, asst. marshal and special police of the town of Walsenburg, Colorado, to enforce the*

*Constitution and Laws of the United States, the Constitution and
Laws of the State of Colorado and the ordinances of the town of
Walsenburg, without fear or favor. And to regularly walk beats
on Main St., meet passenger trains entering and departing from
town, to work for welfare, betterment, protection and peace of
inhabitants.*[1]

The minutes of the council do not specify why they felt it
necessary to issue these instructions, but there is little doubt that
the large number of saloons, possibly as many as forty-five in the
town, caused certain problems. The council further specified that
the officers could be dismissed for entering saloons for the
purpose of drinking, card or pool playing, any unnecessary abuse
of a prisoner, or the failure to enforce laws pertaining to the
carrying of concealed weapons.

At the same meeting the mayor suggested the following to the
council:

*...recommending for the welfare of the town, and for the
handling of tramps, bums, and prisoners in our jail that are
continuously being feed (sic) and cared for; be placed on the Rock
Pile and caused to break up rocks and that the broken rock be used
in the construction of our streets, etc.*[2]

A new Y.M.C.A. building was dedicated at Walsen Camp in
August of 1917. The dedication address was given by J. F. Welborn, president of C. F. & I. and was accepted on behalf of the
workers by C. N. Stark. The building was a two-story affair with
meeting rooms, a large ballroom and other amenities which had
been unavailable to mine workers before. Coal camp buildings
were often constructed alike — the Y.M.C.A. in one camp
resembled the ones in other camps. Churches resembled each
other, and all the houses in the various camps were similar also.

The articles in the **Walsenburg World** at this time on the
activities of the Huerfano County sheriff, E. L. Neelley, and his
deputies very much resemble the articles of the **Independent**
during the time of Jeff Farr. The **World** calls Neelley "the

U.M.W.A. gold star sheriff" and claims that he is surrounded by gunmen who trample on the rights of citizens.

The Chamber of Commerce was organized at this time and this proved to have several beneficial results.

> *The first official meeting to organize a commercial association for the City of Walsenburg was held in the County Court House, March 20, 1916. Several informal meetings were held prior to the one of March 20, and from those meetings the Walsenburg Commercial Club came into being. Mssrs. Charles N. Bissell, Louis B. Sporleder, Sr., Fred C. Sporleder, Edward Slates, H. Chauncy Summers, William R. Shade, and Ralph L. Snodgrass were prominent among those who were instrumental in bringing about the first meeting. John Kirkpatrick was elected Chairman of the meeting. The following committees were appointed: Constitution and By-laws, C. N. Bissell and Dr. A. L. Trout; Membership, Nicholas Agnes, F. C. Sporleder and H. C. Summers; Goodwill Tour to La Veta, Ralph Wayt, Dr. W. N. Hall and Ernest Krier.*
>
> *On March 27 the second meeting of the Walsenburg Commercial Club was held, a large number of public-spirited citizens of Walsenburg being present. They adopted a constitution and by-laws. The Membership Committee reported that 150 members had been obtained. The committee in charge of the "Good-Will Tour" reported that a delegation of almost one hundred visited La Veta the previous Thursday and were received by the Commercial Club of that city. The spirit of the meeting gave evidence of wholehearted co-operation in the joint endeavor to promote the welfare of Huerfano County. These directors were elected: For a three-year term, John Kirkpatrick (President), F. C. Sporleder and Ralph Stanley; for a two year term, R. L. Snodgrass, Ernest Krier and Dr. A. L. Trout; for a one-year term, W. R. Shade, Joseph O'Byrne and Joseph Monnie. A delegation of enthusiastic citizens from the Trinidad Chamber of Commerce attended and expressed the good-will of the people of Las Animas County.*
>
> *Thus the Commercial Club of Walsenburg, Colorado, was launched on its career.*[3]

The number of members of this club are evidence of the confidence that the people of the town had in its future. Between the Commercial Club and the City Council a number of efforts were launched. An industrial magazine was compiled, published and circulated, free delivery of express packages was inaugurated on February 1, 1917, and a reduction in electric light rates was brought about.

The City Council and the Chamber pulled together to bring about free mail delivery in 1917 and to secure a Union Depot, which would unite the train services of both railroads

As early as 1915 the city's newspapers began to be filled with war news from Europe. Story after story told of the gathering war clouds and hope that the United States would not be drawn into the conflict. As time went on, it seemed as if avoiding the conflict would not be easy to attain.

The *Independent* reported the county political news on Jan. 12, 1917.

ALL HUERFANO COUNTY OFFICERS DEMOCRATS
Change Took Place at High Noon Tuesday With Fine Weather and Many Visitors Present in the Court House
   PRESENT COUNTY OFFICERS ARE:
E. l. Neelley, Sheriff
Fred C. Sporleder, Treasurer
Joseph H. Patterson, County Judge
J. G. Archuleta, Clerk and Recorder
Chas. H. Sanchez, Assessor
Robert Young, Walter Hamilton and J. T. Trujillo, County Commissioners
Mrs. Martha Thorne, Superintendent of Schools
R. E. Thornton, Coroner
Ross W. Hornback, Surveyor
   The Huerfano County officers elected at the general election last November, took their seats promptly at Noon Tuesday.

These new officers are all Democrats and for the first time in more than a quarter of a century, every branch of the county government is in the hands of the Democrats.

While there were no formal ceremonies in connection with seating the new officers, and the three re-elected Democratic officials, there was a good sized crowd in the court house to see the change take place. The scenes were all marked by contrast with former "county inauguration days", in that the faces which have attended, and participated in, all former "installations" for more than twenty years were absent.

All of the new officers went to work immediately, as if they were old "war horses". Judge Patterson, who has already had years of experience in court work, began, soon afternoon, the trail (sic) of a divorce case.[4]

New things were happening all over the city in the relative peace which followed the end of the coal strike and the unseating of long-time Sheriff Jeff Farr.

In January the paper announced that work had begun on the new Star Theatre which was expected to be open for business in about ninety days. Paul Krier, manager, announced that the building and equipment would cost about $20,000 and that the building would be made of red, machine-made pressed brick. The new building would face Main Street near Seventh and was just south of the present Fox Theatre. Seating capacity was about 750.

At the same time the Commercial Club announced plans for a Huerfano County hospital. They stated that about $2,000 had been raised and that the proposed building would need about $12,000.[5]

War news continued to dominate the nation and President Woodrow Wilson told Congress that diplomatic relations with Germany had been severed. He cited the efforts that had been made to convince Germany not to molest neutrals in its under-sea warfare and the number of times that Germany had broken its promises.

Within days the United States had demanded that Germany release seventy-five Americans who had been taken from a captured British ship and held in Berlin as prisoners of war. Germany's expected refusal was likely to bring about a declaration of war.[6]

War came to the United States. The **Independent** reported it in a special report on April 6, 1917.

> *Washington, April 6th. War is now on between the United States and the German government.*
>
> *The concurrent resolution, suggested by President Wilson in his address to a joint session of Congress Tuesday night, declaring that a "state of war" now exists between this country and Germany, passed the lower house of Congress at 3 o'clock this morning. This same resolution passed the Senate Wednesday.*
>
> *President Wilson will go to the Capitol building this afternoon to sign this resolution.*
>
> *The vote in the lower house was 373 for to 50 against. Party lines were disregarded. Miss Jeanette Rankin, the first woman to sit in The Congress, walked down the aisle to the front of the Speakers rostrum, when her name was called to vote, and made her maiden speech in the House. She said, "I want to serve my country, but I can not vote for war."*

Newspapers reported that immediate calls would be issued for 2,000,000 volunteers for the army; the whole country would be made a huge war camp within a few days.[7]

Walsenburg made plans to do its share in the war effort. A large patriotic rally was held at Walsen in the club room, beautifully decorated with flags, streamers and bunting. One hundred school children waving flags marched into the room. They moved right and left to circle the room and pledged their allegiance to the flag. A brass band of sixteen pieces furnished the music. Speeches were made and poems were recited and a grand time was had by all.

More importantly, four young men – Walter Arentz, salesman for Agnes Brothers clothiers; Alex Ross of Joe Palisano shoe store,

Andy Judijack and William Moody of Pictou went to Trinidad to join the regular army soon after the rally. More would soon follow.[8]

Congress was spending time debating how to raise the needed army with many members favoring a volunteer plan and avoiding conscription if possible. Again Walsenburg responded, and soon more than eighty Walsenburg and Huerfano county young men had signed the "Roll of Honor" of the cavalry troop being organized by Walter Edwards and Ralph Levy.[9]

Archie Allison, a salesman at the J. W. Smith Dry Goods company's store, went to Denver to enlist in the Colorado Cavalry. He returned on Wednesday as authorized recruiter for the cavalry.[10]

On May 11, 1917, the cavalry troop was mustered in. There were sixty-two men present. From seventy to one hundred were wanted for this troop. The men quickly elected their commissioned officers. Their unanimous choices were Ralph Levy, captain; Walter L. Edwards, first lieutenant; and H. S. Wilson, second lieutenant. Wilson had seen federal service on the Texas-Mexico border. Besides these officers the men mustered in were F. I. Arnold, Paul Beconi, Clarence Baker, Moses Benavidy, J. H. Bennett, R. E. Bludworth, Alfred Bavian, R. H. Brooks, John Burke, D. Catania, Fred Chambers, C. C. Coan, J. R. Coolidge, Sam Costa, Paul Crump, William Dick, Rick Duran, W. L. Farthing, E. F. Furlong, Titus Graham, A. L. Gutiorez, A. B. Harron, F. R. Heckman, W. O. Karst, P. C. Kleppe, Chas. Martin, Albert Martinez, Manuel D. Martinez, Ruben Martinez, William Martinez, Robert Mathieson, D. J. McCarthy, W. B. McCord, Albert Medina, C. Medina, A. C. Miller, S. H. Monnie, J. C. Murray, S. Norojo, E. L. Payne, T. D. Peffer, C. Peno, R. P. Phillips, James Phipps, Eloy Roybal, Joseph Sholtus, G. L. Sessun, E. G. Sheggs, Ben Smith, Orlie Steele, H. G. Stevens, E. M. Stewart, W. A. Story, Emil Thill, Albert Todd, B. L. Valdez, Dule Williams, John Wilson and James Yojecky.[11] These were the first Walsenburg and Huerfano County young men to enlist to fight their country's battles in World War I, but they would not be the last and not all of them would come home again.

The women of Walsenburg had no intention of standing on the sidelines in the war effort. Their first act was to organize to put Walsenburg on the front line in Colorado as a Food Producing Town. They elected officers: Mrs. Ralph Stanley, president; Mrs. C. T. Garnett, secretary; Mrs. W. C. Hunt, vice president; and Mrs. W. N. Hall, secretary pro-tem. A board of control was chosen with Ralph Snodgrass representing the school board, Dr. P. G. Mathews representing the city council, and Carl Sporleder representing the commercial club. The board of control intended to divide the town into districts, and each district would be worked systematically with a supervisor for each. Roy Hill, the city water commissioner, would supervise the water distribution for the entire gardening district.[12] The women of Walsenburg intended to do their share.

Threats or other types of intimidation may have been practiced against the foreign-born residents of Walsenburg after the war began as has so often happened in our country. In any case Sheriff E. L. Neelley felt it necessary to publish the following notice in the town's newspapers. The proclamation was printed in English, Spanish, German and Polish.

Sheriff's Proclamation to Foreign Born Residents

I, E. L. Neelley, Sheriff of Huerfano County, State of Colorado, deem it wise in the present crisis, in this formal proclamation, to assure all residents of foreign birth that even in the event of the United States becoming actively involved in the great European war, no citizen of any foreign power resident of Huerfano County, Colorado, need fear any invasion of his personal property or rights, so long as he goes peaceably about his business and conducts himself in a law-abiding manner.

The United States has never, in any war, confiscated the property of any foreign resident, unless by his own hostile acts he made it necessary.

I take this formal means of declaring to all foreign born residents that they will be protected in the ownership of their property and money and that they will be free from personal molestation, so long as they obey the laws of the State and Nation:

I urgently request that all our people refrain from public discussions of questions involved in the present crisis and that they maintain a calm and considerate attitude toward all, without regard to their nationality.

Let it be understood that every citizen owes undivided allegiance to the American flag, that he is expected to loyally fulfill all obligations which citizenship and residence impose upon him; and that any act, however slight, tending to give aid or comfort to the enemy is treason, for which severe penalties are provided, in addition to that punishment which public opinion inflicts upon the memory of all traitors, in all lands.

E. L. Neelley
Sheriff, Huerfano County, Colorado[13]

The Commercial Club realized that they must accept new duties and challenges, and they co-operated with the various activities of the Red Cross, the Y. M. C. A. and the Liberty Loan Campaigns.

The City Council also expressed its concern over the war effort by passing the following ordinance in August of 1918:

Ordinance
Requiring all able-bodied male persons in the town of Walsenburg between the ages of 18 and 55 years to engage in some useful employment, occupation, business, trade, or profession during the crisis resulting from the present war.[14]

The ordinance made exceptions for students and people on vacation, but included fines or jail time for those caught not working. Clearly, the City Council did not want any slackers in their town.

A County Agriculturist was engaged to assist in the production of food. Farm and city garden clubs were organized, and many men and women gave their services unselfishly.[15]

Agriculture was a growing industry in the area with residents engaged in growing large plots of vegetables. These were used for the family's own table and were also offered for sale to the various mining camps in the area. So many of these gardens were established within the city limits that the Council became concerned about the strains on the city's water system. Recommendations were made about water meters or other measures for determining how much water people could use for the gardens.

Other matters were not neglected during the war years and the *Independent* took time to commend the sheriff and his men for action they took which would ordinarily have been done by the city police.

Town Police and District Attorney Slack

Sheriff's Office Closes "Red Light District" After Waiting Reasonable Length of Time for Proper Town Policing Authorities to Act and After Deputy's Statement that "Nuisance" is "A Necessary Evil."

Last Sunday, the sheriff's office closed the "red light district" and ordered the inmates to leave town immediately [16]

The article goes on to relate the problems of a "red light house' and to detail at length the respective duties of the town police and the sheriff's department and why it had been necessary for the sheriff to act.

This action of the sheriff's office was taken after waiting more than a week for the properly constituted authorities to act, and after it was reported to that office that the deputy district attorney, Mayor Kirkpatrick's Man Friday had stated that "the red light district" is a necessary evil." [17]

While the red light district was officially closed, there is no mention of how many of its inhabitants actually left town or whether or not their services were no longer available.

The most important news of the time, however, continued to be the war in Europe and the departure of many of the city and county's young men to fight in it. On July 13, 1917 the *Independ-*

ent reported that the seventy members of Troop F, First Colorado cavalry would leave Walsenburg and report to Overland Park, in Denver, where they would train until being mustered into federal service in August. There were seventy members in the troop. The commissioned officers were Ralph Levy, captain; Walter Edwards, first lieutenant; Henry S. Wilson, second lieutenant. The non-commissioned officers were Sergeants A. T. Unfug, Jr., Bert McCort and Floyd Heckman; Corporals Orin Karst, John Burk and Albert Medina.

In the meantime life went on in Walsenburg with such exciting tidbits reported as the arrest of Silverio "Shorty" Martinez, now chief of police, and Joe Santistevan, of the Walsenburg night police, on charges of criminal assault on two Trinidad girls who were visiting. They were taken to La Veta where they pleaded not guilty and were released on $2,000 bond each.[18]

The *Independent* in May of 1918 reported a desperate need of the armed forces – socks.

> *America , as every one knows, is now in the war with both feet. She's got to have socks for those feet – thousands of pairs of them.*
>
> *The Red Cross knitters of the mountain division – Colorado, Utah, New Mexico, and Wyoming – must provide immediately, approximately 30,000 pairs of socks. They are for our boys at Camp Cody, Deming, N.M., who shortly will begin a journey incident to the trip across.*
>
> *Edwin H. Brown, Red Cross field director at Camp Cody, has made a requisition on the division warehouse in Denver for 30,000 pairs of socks in addition to the large number already sent to the boys he and his staff serve. Knitters will not have sufficient time between now and the date upon which the boys begin to move to produce the requisite number of socks. But a sufficient number of the foot garments can be supplied if all Red Cross organizations – branches, chapters and auxiliaries – send in, at once all the socks they now have on hand.*[19]

Since organizations in Walsenburg were already busy doing everything they could to help the war effort, it is quite probable that the town was soon hearing the rapid clicks of knitting needles from every house.

As much help as the war effort needed, however, the home front also had its needs and one of these was education. In April of 1917, the papers reported a need to rebuild and enlarge Hill School. Two new rooms would be added to the nine existing rooms and some of the outer walls would be rebuilt. It is believed that high school classes were held at Hill School at this time.[20]

Letters from soldiers overseas appeared in almost every edition of the papers including this one which appeared in the ***Independent*** on June 7, 1918.

Mrs. J. B. Hudson,
Dear Sis: –
I suppose you think that I am pretty good as I have never written to you unless I am thanking you for something you have sent me. But you see that gives me something to write about.

The cigars are very nice and it was very kind and most thoughtful of you to remember me in such a manner. So I wish to thank you very much.

We have been having some very lovely weather for the fowls called ducks. It has been raining for the last three days and nights, not continuously, but almost all the time.

Well Sis, France is a wonderful country. I can't say that I thought very much of it last winter when we were taking on all of those hardships, but as summer comes on and every thing is so beautiful when the sun shines I find myself liking it better every day. I can certainly very plainly see why the French people are so loyal, for they have a country to be proud of. But after all, I suppose it is the people that makes the country and not the country that makes the people. It is certainly too bad that such a war should be forced on to such a nation and I don't believe that there is any punishment too severe for those that have committed such a crime...

We don't get to see much of the real fire works here, sis, but we can hear lots of it. The most of what we see is in the air. That part of it is certainly exciting.

Well, sis, I don't know any thing of interest to write, as no doubt you have realized before getting this far. I never did like to write letters, and I find it much harder since I have been here than ever before. I write mother a few lines once a week and to Irma once in a while, and that is about all the writing I do.

Hoping to hear from you often.

With best wishes to all,

Your Brother,

Leland Thorne

168 F. Hosp. 117 San Tr.

A. E. F., France [21]

The exact number of men from Walsenburg and Huerfano County who served in the armed forces during World War I isn't certain, but the number was extensive. An exact list of those who died has not been possible, but there are listings of the dead in the papers from time to time, although it appears that the loss of life may not have been too great. The first such account of a death in France is recorded in the June 28, 1918, edition of the ***Independent***.

Huerfano County Soldier Dies on French Field

The first Huerfano County boy to die on French soil, so far as we have been able to learn, was reported in the casualty list of June 22.

The Associated Press carried the following report:

Corporal Howard Dickerson, formerly of Walsen, Colo., a member of the engineering corps of the American overseas force, is reported dead from wounds received in action. He enlisted in May, 1917, in Trinidad, and was sent to France for active duty in September.

In a letter received by his cousin, Mrs. J. J. Lynch, of Walsen, sent on May 6, 1918, he said that the "work was hard and warm" but he made no mention of the fighting. This was the last letter received by his friends or relatives. Dickerson came to Walsen two years ago from working in the mines in the southern part of the state. At Walsen he worked as a machinist about the mines until May of last year.

Six years ago he came to Colorado from Kansas, his birthplace. He was born in Pittsburg, Kans., twenty-six years ago, and received his education there.

Mrs. J. J. Lynch, a cousin, is the only relative in Walsen. He has a father, but his whereabouts is unknown

Dickerson was a member of the Masonic order in Walsenburg, and prominent in social circles.[22]

Other such letters and death notices appear in the papers along with the news of all of the town's activities in support of the war effort. Those efforts reached a conclusion when the end of the war was announced on November 11, 1918.

In our current world we are accustomed to instant communication, but this was not always the case during World War I. Death notices continued to appear about the deaths of Walsenburg service men well into 1919.

In 1918 the town had another danger to contend with – the worldwide epidemic of the so-called Spanish flu which appeared in 1918.

The *Independent* of November 22, 1918, carried the following notice on the first page:

SPANISH FLU CLOSES EVERYTHING
The County Board of Health and Council of Defense Held a Meeting Thursday Night, and Ordered "All Schools, Churches, Theaters, Dance Halls and Other Public or Social Gatherings To Be Permanently Closed Till Further Notice."[23]

Obviously the incidence of cases of flu had been growing for some time although not too much mention of it had been made.

This was the epidemic of influenza which struck across the entire world, beginning in Spain and spreading from country to country. It is possible that servicemen returning home to their native countries were partly responsible for the rapid spread of this devastating strain of flu.

In Walsenburg it is difficult to tell just how bad it was. Apparently the authorities did not yet realize the full extent of the epidemic for the first closing of public places lasted only a few days, but was then reinstated. Just seven days later there was another item in the paper.

Walsenburg Under Flu Ban Again Since Friday

The lid was put on again by the health authorities last Friday, all public gatherings, church services and such being prohibited and business places restricted as to closing hours.

It was thought the "flu" had run its course and everything was thrown open for a week, but quite a number of cases appeared and it was thought better to be on the safe side.

There have been three or four deaths in the city and quite a number in the county, but it is thought the plague is on the wane and everyone is hoping it will not be long until it will disappear.

In the meantime it is the duty of all to comply with the regulations and advice of the authorities.[24]

By December of 1918 everything in town was permitted to reopen, but people were urged to be cautious.

Another death was reported in the **Independent** in December of 1918 with the death of Kathryn Lewis. She had been believed to be improving but then died of flu after three months.[25]

Early in 1919 the pastor of the Methodist Church noted in his quarterly report: *We feel encouraged about the General State of the Church in spite of the Flu conditions. The Missionary Society is doing splendid work."*[26]

An exact number of deaths in Walsenburg from the flu epidemic cannot be determined, but it would appear that the epidemic did not strike the community as hard as other parts of the country.

The turbulent decade dragged to a close with a spat between Republicans and Democrats over whether or not to declare Walsenburg a "city of the second class", which was allowed under state law, or to remain a city of the third class as it was. A Supreme Court decision was required to allow the town to move into the new classification, which had been allowable since the 1910 census.

A lawsuit was filed by E. L. Neelley, the Democratic sheriff, and Mr. Archuleta, the Democratic county clerk, against Jeff Farr and Mr. Freeland, the former sheriff and clerk, seeking to have the salaries and fees which had been collected since the 1914 election, which had been declared fraudulent, awarded to the rightful office holders. The lower court decided in favor of the two Democrats, but Farr and Freeland appealed to the State Supreme Court. In due time the Supreme Court handed down its judgment also against Farr and Freeland and awarded all such salaries and fees to the Democrats who had been declared the rightfully elected office holders.[27]

After all the strife, war, sickness and bitter politics in Walsenburg, the people of the town and county at last voted to build a new high school and a drawing of the proposed building appeared in the *Independent*.[28]

Although the bonds had been voted to build the badly needed school, several more years would elapse before it was completed.

No doubt the people of Walsenburg were hoping that the approaching decade of the 1920s would bring a little peace and stability to their town.

Chapter Eight

THE QUIET TWENTIES

After all of the turbulence of the second decade of the twentieth century, the people of Walsenburg were no doubt hoping for a quieter period of time when attention could be given to such matters as water and sewer improvements, paved streets, improved lighting, schools and other such additions to the life of a growing community.

The war had ended, the coal mines were still producing the much-needed fuel, and there was growing interest in the agricultural possibilities of the area.

In March of 1920, an event occurred which must have seemed a sure sign of the changing times.

On March 13, 1920, at one o'clock in the morning, Jefferson B. Farr, aged 57, died. He had been taken ill the day before after having seemed to be in good health. His death was attributed to a weakening of the walls of the heart.[1]

This man had been at the center of so much of the tension and violence of the area for so many years that it must have been a great shock to both sides of the political scene when he was gone so suddenly after having been out of office for fewer than five years.

The *Walsenburg World*, long a supporter of Jeff Farr and the coal companies, took sorrowful note of his death. The funeral was held at the Presbyterian Church, and the service was conducted by Rev. W.B. Fitzhugh, former pastor of the church, and Rev. G. S. Darley, the current pastor.

The list of active and honorary pallbearers was filled with the very top of Walsenburg society. Active pallbearers were C. V. Mazzone, W. N. Houser, Frank S. Mauro, Dr. W. S. Chapman,

Epifanio Martinez, Fred Atencio, Silverio Martinez and Librardo Martinez. The honorary pallbearers were Henry Blickhahn, Charles Hayden, Charles Mazzone, J. J. Pritchard, Baltolo Aragon, J. D. Montez, P. L. Sanchez, A. Levy, Wm. Getchell, Robert Smith, Joe Kincaid, Charles Kaiser, Ricardo Vigil, Alex McDonald, D. T. Wycoff, John McCarthy, George Fruth, James Autrey, Richard Bell, August Unfug, James Baker, John Schwab, J. S. Capps, Parker Wells, F. E. Cowing, and James B. Dick.[2]

The *World* editor wrote a long piece overflowing with praise of the gentleness and uprightness of this man who had ruled Huerfano County as his personal fiefdom. The other paper, which had long been the bitter enemy of the Farr regime, took a strangely conciliatory note in its report, stating merely the facts of his life and death. Perhaps the editor had changed or the paper simply decided that since Farr could no longer run everything, they could afford to be a bit magnanimous in their reporting.

Whatever the point of view, Jefferson B. Farr was gone from the stage of Walsenburg history, and it is history that will have the final say about his reign as sheriff of Huerfano County. The one-time "King of Huerfano County" is buried beside his brother in the Masonic Cemetery of Walsenburg.

Meanwhile the Commercial Club continued its activities in pursuing a wide variety of plans for the community.

One of the chief aims of the club was to secure a union depot to serve the needs of both the Denver and Rio Grande and the Colorado and Southern railroads. It would not be until 1927 before this aim was accomplished, but the club never lost sight of its desire to have it happen.

The necessity for paved streets in the heart of the City of Walsenburg had been talked over again and again, and at the May meeting of the Directors something happened. Chairman Robert Young of the Paving Committee announced that sixty-eight per cent of the property owners on Main Street from Third to Eighth Streets had signed the paving petition.[3]

Street paving and the incorporation of several additions to the town took up a great deal of time during this decade. Among the new areas were Capital Hill addition, Tourist City addition, High School addition, Atencio addition, and others.

Unfortunately in the midst of all of this civic activity, labor troubles again appeared in Huerfano County in 1921. For some reason, the C. F. & I. Corporation decided that it was essential to cut miners wages' by a fairly large sum. Other mines in the area did not follow suit, and a strike of U. M. W. A. workers began. This strike was not uniformly supported by all of the C. F. & I. workers, but a significant number of them chose to walk out. As usual, the company declined to enter into meaningful negotiations with its workers.

The matter was placed before the State Industrial Commission, which handed the matter over to C. F. & I. to make any decision the directors chose in the matter of cutting wages. Before any decision was made, however, the governor of the state chose to send in the Colorado State Rangers to keep order, even though no disorder had occurred or even been threatened. Twenty-five Rangers were dispatched from Grand Junction and Sterling with supplies enough to last for six months.

The November 11, 1921 *Independent* took notice of the event.

> *"We are going down there to preserve order,": said Capt. O. L. Dennis, who is said to be in command of the "rangers."*
>
> *"To preserve order"?*
>
> *From the language used, the uninitiated would immediately imagine that something is likely to happen to destroy order; that the high-ups who are in command of the boys who ride in baby buggies loaded down with artillery and Let's see: On Saturday, three days prior to the above announcement, the state industrial commission handed down a decision turning over the industrial conditions of southern Colorado to the Colorado Fuel & Iron Co. That decision virtually said to the C. F. & I. that they could make any sort of an inside arrangement and cut the wages of the miners as they desired. So far as the public knew, the C. F. & I. had not*

reached any conclusion as to whether or not they would soon attempt to reduce the men's wages.

Just keep in mind that nothing had yet been done by either side, (the company or the men) to indicate that there would be any wage cut, and certainly nothing had been given out that would indicate the probability of a strike. The C. F. & I. officials did not call a meeting till Monday afternoon, and the latest information from that meeting, which continued throughout part of Tuesday, did not state that any cut would be attempted immediately.[4]

Over the next few days the papers were dominated by the news of the strike and the imposition of martial law. The **Independent** took the side of the miners and the **Walsenburg World** sided with C. F. & I. Corporation. The **Independent** was informed that the paper would be censored since the commander of the National Guard was apparently fearful of violence. There is no indication that any violence was contemplated by the striking miners, so it may simply have been that the governor was fearful of the kind of violence which had plagued the southern coal fields in the strike of 1913-1914.

One incident was reported by the **Independent** in which a guardsman attacked the son of the editor of the **Independent**. He next went after the editor, and when another ranger attempted to arrest the first, he found a gun shoved in his face. Next the enraged ranger went after another man named Tony Valdez and forced him to march a block with his hands in the air. Eventually City Marshal Frantz arrived and, with the assistance of Tony Valdez, managed to subdue the ranger and march him off to jail. Other guardsmen denounced their fellow soldier as a drinker and a problem maker.[5]

Although the city was informed that martial law would be in effect for a long time, it actually lasted only a few months. The miners came to a settlement with the company and life went on in Walsenburg and Huerfano County.

In November of 1922, the state of Colorado, Huerfano County and the United States voted Democratic; and the Democratic newspaper lost no time in gloating over it. Even J. F. Coss, editor of the *Independent*, won election to the state senate.

With labor troubles in abeyance for the time being and a new administration in place, Walsenburg was free to consider other matters. The papers announced with pleasure that work would begin the following spring on erecting a Union station for the Colorado and Southern and Denver and Rio Grande Railways. While actually getting it built took until 1927, the project was eventually finished and the present red brick building just off Main Street on Third Street was the result. No longer used as a railroad station, the building was sold for $1 (and conditions) to the city. It now houses the Walsenburg Chamber of Commerce and is a frequent stop for tourists seeking information about the city and county.

The city election of 1923 saw the voters electing a Democratic administration to go along with the county for the first time in thirty years. H. D. Mustain was chosen as mayor and continued in that role for two years.

For most of its history Walsenburg has enjoyed a relatively stable climate with nothing more drastic than an occasional bad wind storm, hail and flooding. Late summer of 1923 brought a more serious problem. The Cucharas River was normally a quiet, gently flowing stream on the south side of the town, but that was suddenly and violently changed.

The *Independent* reported the story.

A terrific electrical storm broke over this city about 9 o'clock Saturday night. The thunder roared, the lightning flashed in lurid gleams and the rain fell in sheets, but no one suspected harm. We thought we were safe. Little did we reckon that the quiet little Cucharas, which usually contains but a small trickle of water, could in so short a time break over its banks, flood almost half the city and carry human beings to their death in its muddy currents a block from its shores.

Superintendent Getchel of the Walsen mine noticed about midnight that the water was rising very rapidly and thinking there might be danger of flooding the lowlands of Walsen and Walsenburg, had the fire whistle blown as a warning and Many heard the whistle blasts and looked for the fire; many others were warned by phone and in a short time the down town streets were alive with people. As soon as the reason for the warning became known the work of aiding those near the river to escape was begun. Men were sent to every house thought to be in the danger zone and the occupants were rushed to the court house and other higher points.[6]

All night the work of rescue went on. People were brought to the courthouse, the Convent, the Maccabee Hall, the Mosco store and the restaurants. Some people resisted leaving their homes and were almost forcibly removed.

The American Legion, the Red Cross officers, the sheriff's force, city police and scores of citizens worked together through the night to save people.

For a time it was thought that loss of life had been avoided, but with the dawn came the news that Mrs. Alfredo Gonzales and her baby had been separated from the rest of the family as they fled their home. The bodies of the woman and infant were found later that day.[7]

Walsenburg could not escape political controversy for long, of course, and in spring of 1924 Mayor H. D. Mustain and Night Chief of Police Charles H. Sanchez were accused of conspiring to violate the Volstead (or Prohibition) Act.

Two trials were held on the matter within a week, the second of which had a jury composed of Pueblo men. It is uncertain why two trials were necessary. Numerous prominent citizens including Ernest Krier, John J. Pritchard, Dr. Walter S. Chapman and Alexander Levy testified to the reputation of the two men as honest and upright citizens. The second trial apparently did not take too long, and the two men were acquitted.

One of the darker chapters of Colorado history concerns the Ku Klux Klan. Just why Colorado should have been the center of so much Klan activity is unclear, but it is known that Denver and Canon City were strongholds of Klan activity and that many prominent people of the time were known or suspected to be Klan members. In the Denver area Klan gatherings were held on a mesa near Golden and streams of cars could be seen going in that direction on meeting nights. Many photographs exist of Klan marches through the city.

Klan activities in Colorado were directed largely at Catholics, Jews, foreigners and law breakers rather than the black people as in the south.

Denver, however, was not alone in Klan activity. Many towns in southern Colorado, including Canon City and Walsenburg, were known to have Klan activity. Just how many members the Walsenburg group may have had is not known, but apparently a number of prominent people were Klansmen. A substantial Walsen Avenue house in Walsenburg is known to have been a gathering place for Klan meetings. Like many houses of the area, it has a long, straight staircase leading from the main floor into the basement, but there is another, shorter set of steps leading from the backyard into the basement. This would enable members to enter the house from the rear without disturbing the people upstairs. One large area of the basement on the street side was designed for Klan meetings.

The east side of this area is 22' 7" in width. There is a concrete slab lined with concrete benches. The benches extend out from either side of the central area to provide additional seating. A table to hold Klan materials could have been placed in the center. The area not covered in concrete is dirt, and no further efforts at finishing this portion of the basement were made. The seating area could probably have accommodated twenty to thirty people.[8]

At least one other location, upstairs in a downtown building, was used for Klan meetings. Members were seen descending to the street in Klan paraphernalia.

The newspapers of the time tell of one Klan march down Main Street with 160 marchers in full regalia. Whether all of the marchers were citizens of Walsenburg is debatable.

The KKK in Colorado was noted for its claims to be a charitable organization interested in education, among other things. An example of their activities in this area include a time in Walsenburg in the 1920s when the women running the city library were raising money for new books in order to move from their one bookcase in the courthouse into a room in the courthouse basement. The Klan gave money to the project.[9]

Another Klan story comes from a local citizen. When her father was a boy, he and a friend were downtown one night, sitting on the curb next to Star Drug, when they heard noises on Main Street. Peering around the corner, the boys were stunned to see the street full of marching figures in white robes and pointed hats. The Klan was on the march. Terrified, the boys shrank back against the building and watched as the Klan marched past them, continued down Main Street for another block or two, then went around the block and marched past St. Mary Church and back to Main Street.[10]

It is also known that the Walsenburg group marched in a parade in Canon City to honor the dead brother of a prominent member of the Denver Klan. Whether or not the Klan was able to elect any of its members to office in Walsenburg is not definitely known, but it is likely that the mayor was a Klansman. It is also well known that, for two years, the Klan controlled virtually all statewide offices in Colorado. Most of the Klan officeholders were Republican politicians, but a handful of Republican legislators siding with the Democrats kept most Klan-sponsored legislation from being passed. At the end of a turbulent two years, the Republican Governor Clarence Morley and most of the Klan-legislators were defeated for re-election.[11]

The twenties marked a period of growth in Walsenburg. Various water rights were bought and ditch rights secured. Improvements to the paving districts were formed, and the paving of Walsenburg streets went forward at a furious pace.

In 1925 the three-story brick high school building located at 415 Walsen Avenue, designed by the Rapp brothers, was completed. The gymnasium was added a year or two later, built by a contractor named Yanos.

Late in the decade the remains of two Huerfano County soldiers who had died in World War I were returned to the community. The body of John Jenkins was taken to the home of his parents in Pictou, and the body of Mike Duzenack was taken to the home of his brother on West Seventh Street. It seems strange that such a long time passed before these two men were returned home.

In 1927 the members of the Methodist Church turned their attention to the need for a new building. The "little white church" had served the congregation for many years, but the church had outgrown the space. Serious planning and fund-raising began under the leadership of the new pastor, Rev. R. R. Rose.

Once more labor troubles surfaced in the coal camps, this time led by the International Workers of the World, also known as the I. W. W. and nicknamed the "Wobblies." The first hint of a strike was a sort of practice strike called to protest the execution of Sacco and Vanzetti, two anarchists convicted in New Jersey of various crimes. This strike failed to materialize, but the I. W. W. continued its strike talk and in the fall of 1927 called for a general strike.

This strike was not as well supported by the mine workers as the earlier strikes had been. The United Mine Workers had acquired more members, and the company unions instituted by John D. Rockefeller, Jr. had brought about improvements in the lives of miners. The **Independent** reported the following on Sept. 27, 1927:

> *Failure for an I. W. W. strike if called on Oct. 8 is predicted by miners here today following an announcement Saturday and Monday of a 68 cent wage increase for nearly all miners in southern Colorado. Increase boosts minimum daily wage from $5.52 to $6.20, announced Saturday of CF&I for its 19 mines in Huerfano-Las Animas Counties. Nearly all independent mines followed suit. United Mine Workers will kick I. W. W. members out.*[12]

In spite of this large wage increase, the I. W. W. called its strike, but fewer than one-half of the miners in Huerfano County failed to report to work. The strike was declared illegal by the state, but picketing began at several mines.

One interesting aspect of this strike was the use of labor spies by C. F. & I. Information about the use of spies is usually hard to come by, but a researcher using the C. F. & I. Archives in Pueblo, which are slowly being made available to scholars, has shown clear evidence of this practice.

> *The union had 21 demands in total for CF&I and the rest of the Colorado coal industry. The most important of the demands concerned higher wages, but miners also wanted Saturdays and Sundays off, a six-hour workday, a rent freeze on company housing, free first-aid kits, the abolition of physical examinations, "no discrimination on account of age," and that labor organizers "be allowed to come and go to company owned camps." The IWW did not believe that employers would meet all (or perhaps any) of these demands, but it did feel that an extensive list of demands would serve as a good recruiting tool among long-suffering miners.*
>
> *Anticipating trouble, CF&I hired at least three spies in the weeks, months, or years before the strike in order to stay abreast of the Wobblies' activities. The most prolific of these undercover agents were known as "X," "XX," and "X-3". As it stands, the records are silent about these men's true identities. The reports give no indication as to whether the spies were hired from private detective agencies or whether they had worked for the company before. Based on the situation described in their reports, it is clear that each spy was employed before the strike began.[13]*

These spies mailed or called in their reports to the company from time to time. They operated in Trinidad, Walsenburg and Crested Butte. It isn't certain just how effective they were in influencing the strike, but from the tone of their reports, it appears that they may have been long-time employees of the various mines. The spy designated XX reported the following in telling of the intimidation practiced against the strikers:

XX Phones from Walsenburg
9:30 a.m.
Trinidad, Colorado
October 17, 1927

Late Saturday night a delegation of citizens of Walsenburg headed by the Mayor raided the IWW hall, broke the windows and took the furniture, fixtures and literature out in the street and burnt them up. No one was in the hall but Kitto and he escaped thru the backdoor and made his way up to the C & S [Colorado & Southern] depot where he hid in some shrubbery until train time and then went on to Pueblo. The citizen delegations took the guns... in the hall.

Sunday morning the Aguilar and Walsenburg delegates met in front of the hall and went on to Pueblo to attend the conference. Neither Svanum or Franzine or any of the other leaders were there when we got there. I was appointed temporary chairman and the meeting was called for 1:30 p.m. About 12:45 p.m., Svanum, Seidler and Edilla and the balance of the leaders came in and the meeting was called to order. Svanum was chairman.

All the Northern Colorado delegates fought to avoid the strike but Seidler, Edilla, and the delegates from Walsenburg overruled. Onle [sic] one man from Aguilar tried to avoid the strike. This was Razansky. Smith and myself circulated thru the crowd trying to get them to postpone the strike but without any success and when the vote was called it was unanimous for the strike even the Northern Colorado delegates voting for it.[14]

Many of the pickets were women and one particular girl was known as the "Girl in Red." She was "Milka" Amelia Sablich, 19, a Trinidad miner's daughter and she appeared at almost all of the striking camps. Eventually she was injured.

Sheriff Harry Capps appeared at most strike sites with a number of deputies and many arrests were made. The arrestees were taken to the Huerfano County Courthouse and housed in the courtroom as there was not enough room in the county jail.[15] The Colorado National Guard, afraid of a repeat of the previous violence of the 1913-14 strike, sent three planes loaded with bombs and machine guns to patrol over Walsenburg.[16] Strike headquarters at 909 South Main was the scene of one striker's death.[17] The strike dragged on until February 21, 1928, when it finally ended.

Nothing was accomplished for the I. W. W., but the coal operators began to rethink their position on no union recognition and slowly began to negotiate contracts with the more moderate United Mine Workers.

The I. W. W. strike represented the last major coal strike in the southern coal fields. Coal production continued to be strong in spite of the arrival of natural gas in the area.

The Methodists proceeded with building their fine brick church during 1928, and in March of 1929, they dedicated it, not knowing that disaster would soon strike.

Walsenburg looked forward to continued prosperity and growth.

John Albert early pioneer who built an adobe fort on the south end of what is now Main Street. *O. T. Davis photo, courtesy of the Monte Vista Historical Society.*

Rumalda Martinez Atencio 1817-1905, wife of Don Miguel Antonio Atencio, founding couple of the Plaza, along with their friends, the Leon family. The Atencios came from the Rio Grande Valley, NM, to the San Luis Valley to the Cucharas Valley. *Courtesy of the Huerfano County Historical Society, Frances Nelson Vallejo collection (a granddaughter).*

Mexican Residence Adobe houses were the practical living quarters in the Plaza de los Leones days and even today. *1889 photo by O. T. Davis, courtesy of the Monte Vista Historical Society.*

The Sporleder Orchestra in the yard of the adobe Sporleder Hotel in the 1880s. Guests at the hotel included author Helen Hunt Jackson (who described it in detail), Colorado Governor A. Cameron Hunt and General William Palmer.

Photo courtesy of Pueblo Library District, Huerfano County Historical Society project.

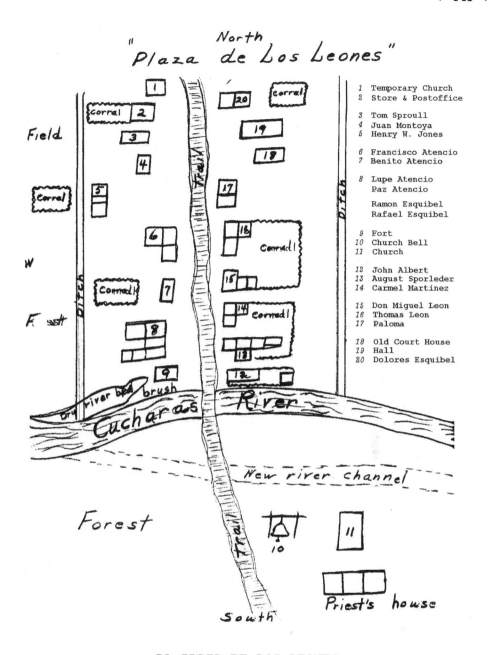

LA PLAZA DE LOS LEONES
...from the collection of Frances Nelson Vallejo.

Map of Plaza de los Leones. The 1875 Plaza later became Walsenburg. This map was drawn by Louis B. Sporleder in 1933 from memory. *Map courtesy of the Territorial Daughters of Southern Colorado.*

Louis B. Sporleder and wife Louise (Unfug) on their 60th wedding anniversary. He was a leading merchant, a historian and a writer. *Courtesy of the Huerfano County Historical Society, Francisco Fort collection.*

Capt. Cornelius D. Hendren, an aristocrat educated at West Point, was in Huerfano County by 1866. *Photo courtesy of Nancy Hutchinson of Pueblo, whose husband is the great-grandson of Hendren.*

Unfug Brothers Trading Post, Seventh and Main Streets in 1872. Wagons brought freight from the nearest railroad, Cucharas Junction, seven miles east of Walsenburg. *Courtesy of St. Mary Parish.*

The Twelve Apostles Twelve early residents of Huerfano County, mostly businessmen and ranchers, taken about 1875. Seated, left to right, A. R. Campbell, Charles Mazzone, Isaac Dailey, Henry Strange, Frank Duhme, John H. Brown, August Sporleder. Standing, left to right: Capt. James Thompson, John Chapell, John Albert, Fred Walsen, Sr., T. L. Creesy. *Photo from the Mazzone family, a copy now in the Huerfano County Historical Society archives.*

↑
Alexander and Lillie Levy.
Alexander, born in Austria in
1849, came to Walsenburg in
1871. A partner in a general
mercantile store with Fred
Walsen, he also entered the
railroad contracting business,
ranching and real estate. This led
to his service as county treasurer.
His wife, Lillie Sporleder Levy,
was a sister of Fred Walsen's wife,
Emilie Sporleder Walsen. *Courtesy
of the Levy family.*

←
Ralph, Archie and Walter Levy,
sons of Alexander and Lillie Levy,
about 1893. The boys were born
and settled in Walsenburg and
engaged in various business
enterprises there. *Courtesy of the
Levy family.*

Chatin Black Smith Shop, built in 1881, located on east side of Main Street between Sixth and Seventh Streets. Chatin also made wagons and cabinets. The Chatin home at the time was at the rear of the lot. *Courtesy of the Pueblo City-County Library District, August and Mima Chatin collection.*

First National Bank building, southwest corner of Fifth and Main, replaced in 1927 by the present building, now the Community Banks of Colorado. *Courtesy of the Pueblo City-County Library District.*

Mazzone Opera House of 1888 was the town's cultural center in the upstairs auditorium, downstairs was the saloon. The Opera House had a two-story outhouse in the back, connected to the upper story by a walkway. After the top floor was removed, the building became the Black and White Grocery on the southwest corner of Main and Sixth Streets. A glimpse of the first school building, an adobe, shows to the right. *Courtesy of the Mazzone family.*

The Palace Livery Stable, next door to John Furphy's Undertaking and Embalming, about 1913. Northwest corner of Main and Fourth Streets, now a part of Dr. David Neece's office. *Courtesy of Dr. David Neece.*

The International House, built in 1898 by Charles and Joseph Brunelli, was later renamed the St. Charles Hotel following the death of Charles. Today, this brick building on the northeast corner of Seventh and Albert, has been reduced to one story. *Courtesy of Norma Lou Brunelli Murr.*

"Bernsteins Undersells" was the motto, and Moritz Bernstein built his department store into one of the largest in Southern Colorado. The store was constantly expanding and moving for nearly 30 years until 1918. Bernstein is the man in the dark suit. *Courtesy of the Rocky Mt. Jewish Historical Society.*

W. R. Faulkner Cheap Cash Store, built in 1882-1884 is now part of the Eagles building, 614 Main Street. Note the business below the store, which was possible when sidewalks were lower. A hotel and later a brothel occupied the upstairs. *Courtesy of the Pueblo City-County Library District, August and Mima Chatin collection.*

Star Grocery, built in 1889 in what was called the Walsen block (cost $8,000), which is on the west side of Main Street between Fifth and Sixth.

Photo courtesy of Gordon Kelley.

Klein Hotel, originally built in 1900 on East Sixth Street. Later it became a 100-room hotel after its sixth addition.
Courtesy of the Huerfano County Historical Society, Huerfano World collection.

Sunday dinner at the Walsen boarding house for coal miners. The waitress is Barbara Froman, later Newman. Her parents ran the boarding house.
Courtesy of the Bessemer Historical Society/Steelworks Museum.

Dick Brothers Wholesale Liquor Dealers delivery wagon in front of the Huerfano County courthouse, 1905.   *Courtesy of the Dick family.*

Old county jail was used in the early 1890s until replaced by the 1896 county jail, now the Walsenburg Mining Museum. The present jail (county and city) was built in 1989.   *Courtesy of the Huerfano County Historical Society.*

Two miners and a day's work. Early miners also had to prop the ceiling and lay track, for which there was no pay. *Courtesy of the Dick family.*

Typical coal mining, back-breaking work in cramped quarters.
Courtesy of the Huerfano County Historical Society, Dr. Harvey Phelps collection.

Baseball was played in every mining camp, and fierce rivalries developed. One player, Ford Frick, became a sports writer, then president of the National Baseball League and finally the National Baseball Commissioner. No information is available about this Walsenburg team.

Courtesy of Denver Public Library, Western History.

Camp House, this one at Walsen Camp, is a typical house found in most mining camps in the area, with a pyramid-hipped roof, and a chimney in the center. The larger, two-story, gambrel roof house in the background was unique to Walsen. *Courtesy Huerfano County Historical Society.*

Mother Jones, a national labor leader, was arrested in Walsenburg for inciting miners to go on strike. She often led marches of women and children in support to encourage the miners.
Courtesy of the Huerfano County Historical Society, History Colorado collection.

Colorado State Troopers at their tent encampment at Fifth and Hendren Streets during the 1913 coal miners strike. *Courtesy of the Huerfano County Historical Society, Walsenburg Mining Museum, Richard and Betty Ridge Collection.*

↑
1913-14 strike in the Walsenburg area forced families to move out of company housing for 15 months to live in tents. People in this photo apparently include one state militia person, officials in suits and miners' families. *Courtesy of Huerfano County Historical Society, Huerfano World collection, taken by A. Donati, donated by Ross A. Hamilton.*

→
Sheriff Jefferson Farr, in office during the violent 1913-14 coal strike, was ousted from his position by the Colorado Supreme Court for election fraud. *Courtesy of the Huerfano County Historical Society, Francisco Fort collection.*

Militia Men in front of the 1908 armory, still standing now but vacant, just north of the railroad depot and across the tracks. The spacious building was used for high school basketball games and even high school classes. *Courtesy of The Huerfano County Historical Society, Walsenburg Mining Museum collection.*

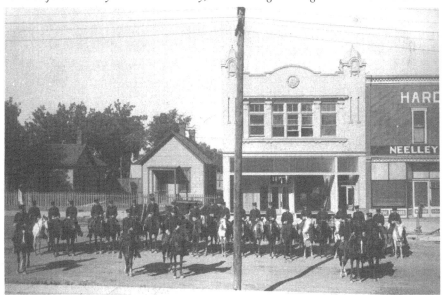

Walsenburg militia face the courthouse. Note the Levy house in the center background, built about 1860 as a two-room adobe. Alexander Levy bought it in 1880. One of the business houses is the Neeley-Caldwell Hardware. Neeley was a gunrunner for the strikers 1913-14 and was later elected sheriff to replace Jeff Farr.
Courtesy of the Pueblo City-County Library District, August and Mima Chatin collection.

Main Street about 1910-1913 between Fifth and Sixth Streets, east side, with Elks convention banners. Business signs: Walsenburg B.P.O.E. No. 1066 Colorado (Elks); the Spanish Peaks Merc. Co.; (street sign in front) Garage Free Rides to All Parts of the City; barbershop with striped pole.

Section of Long Postcard, displayed in its entirety on facing page.
Courtesy of the Huerfano County Historical society.

Polska Hala, or Polish Hall, 909 South Main, was headquarters for the 1927-1928 miners strike of the "Wobblies", Industrial Workers of the World. One striker was killed in the single-story building.

Courtesy of the Wayne State University, Walter P. Reuther Library.

↑ Dr. P. P. Lester, a Walsenburg doctor serving in the state militia during the 1913-14 coal strike. This photo is from a postcard, written on the back of which, is the following information.

Maj. P. P. Lester, Colo. National Guard's Hospital Corps 1913 – 1914. Killed by striking miners while he was wearing the Red Cross badge and ministering to a wounded comrade at Walsenburg, April 29, 1914.

A note with the postcard contains the following information.

Dr. P. P. Lester was a surgeon in the Colorado National Guard. He was killed April 29, 1914 by a gunshot during the Coal Field Wars.

Pro-striker accounts say he was leading a charge of guardsmen. Other accounts claim he was tending the wounded. The incident occurred along the hogback north of Walsenburg.

Courtesy of the Huerfano County Historical Society, Walsenburg Mining Museum collection.

American Legion, Huerfano Post No. 16, stand at attention facing south on Fifth Street, Veteran's Day, 1921. *F. M. Stub photo courtesy of Carol Glorioso and Spanish Peaks Veterans Nursing Home.*

The Walsenburg power plant, built in 1911 to supply electricity to the mines, expanded to serve the towns of La Veta and Walsenburg. Operations ceased in 1978. The plant, just west of Walsenburg city limits, has been placed on Colorado's Most Endangered Places list.
Courtesy of the Huerfano County Historical Society, City of Walsenburg collection.

W. S. CHAPMAN, M. D.

SURGEON FOR ROUSE

Dr. Walter Chapman, a local doctor first employed by the coal companies, delivered hundreds of babies in the area. *Courtesy of the Huerfano County Historical Society and Pueblo Library Collection.*

Judge J. A. J. Valdez served in the state legislature, was Walsenburg's mayor in 1885 and a prominent lawyer. *Photo courtesy of Gordon Kelley.*

Brothers-in-law Fred Walsen and Alexander Levy formed a business partnership in 1876 and ran three stores: Walsenburg, Walsen camp and Huerfano Canon (Farisita). This may be the Walsenburg store in 1880.
Courtesy of Denver Public Library.

Bernstein Store, a leading business in early Walsenburg for nearly 30 years.
Courtesy of the Rocky Mt. Jewish Historical Society.

The former Unfug Hardware building, 424 Main, was called the Neelley
Caldwell in earlier times. Built in 1903 by Blacksmith Paul Frohlich.
Courtesy of the Huerfano County Historical Society.

Colorado & Southern Depot.

The Colorado & Southern depot was east of the present 1927 Union depot building, which combined the C&S and the Rio Grande depots.

Courtesy of Huerfano County Historical Society.

The Fox Theatre, still in operation, was built in 1917 as the Star Theatre. A prized Wurlitzer organ was the centerpiece, and has been restored.

Courtesy of the Huerfano County Historical Society archives, Huerfano World collection.

Walsenburg Creamery, built "on the old power plant" (the Walsenburg Electric Light and Power Co.) was opened as the Brokerage in 1891 by Frank Mauro Sr.
Courtesy of Gordon Kelley.

Old Washington School, built in 1884 at Russell and Fifth Streets, was replaced by the present Washington School building in the same location.
Courtesy of the Pueblo City-County Library District, August and Mima Chatin collection.

St. Mary Catholic Church, dedicated in 1900, with the earlier church to the east (left) above, which opened in 1882. The older church was later demolished to make way for the current Rectory, built in 1921. Later the church steeple's tall spire blew off in an Ash Wednesday windstorm in 1927, and the deteriorating bricks, which had been fired locally, were covered with stucco in 1956, left.
Courtesy of St. Mary Parish.

St. Mary School educated hundreds of students during its 84 years, opening for classes in 1913 and closing the elementary school in 1997. The high school closed in 1971.

Courtesy of Huerfano County Historical Society, Huerfano World/Jay Crook collection.

Whether you call it Huerfano County High School, or Walsenburg High School, or Walsenburg Middle School or Spanish Peaks Library — all have been in this 1921 building at one time or another. The 1923 gym on the right burned in 1974. Note the median in the street. *Courtesy of Spanish Peaks Library.*

Capital (actually Capitol) Hill School, later shortened to just Hill School, on East Indiana Avenue and Polk, was built 1906–1907, and was used mostly as an elementary school, but also at times for the Huerfano County High School. Now a private residence. *Courtesy of the Huerfano County Historical Society.*

The Methodist Episcopal Church South built this church in 1889, at the southeast corner of Walsen and Pennsylvania, and used it until the congregation built the new brick church in 1929. The Walsenburg summer school was held in the building about 1929. *Courtesy of the United Church of Walsenburg.*

When the Walsen and Levy partnership ended, Alexander
Levy continued in business in Walsenburg. The flour sack on
the animal says "Wolf's Premium Flour". The wagon is
labeled "Bernstein". *Courtesy of the Huerfano County Historical
Society, Huerfano World collection.*

The Ku Klux Klan, active in Walsenburg in the
1920s as a protest against rampant crime,
foreigners and Catholics, attracted businessmen
and political figures.

Courtesy of Carolyn Newman.

Original Fred Walsen Check, and cashier's check, from the 1900s and 1890s.
Courtesy The Denver Public Library, Western History Collection.

Methodist Episcopal Church South was dedicated in 1929, just in time for the Great Depression. The debt wasn't paid off for 15 years, in 1944. A 1961 union of the Community Congregational and United Methodist churches led to a new name, the United Church of Walsenburg. *Courtesy of Carolyn Newman.*

Walsen Mine Camp, just west of town with its rows of identical houses, was a typical camp (not a town, camps were meant to be temporary until a mine closed). These houses with pyramid roofs and chimneys up the center were often moved into town upon a mine's closing.

Courtesy of Bessemer Historical Society.

Lamme Brothers, Hospital, Walsenburg, Colo.

Lamme Hospital closed in 1961. Drs. S. J. And J. M. Lamme opened their first Walsenburg hospital in 1919 in a house. Before the hospital opened, serious cases were sent by train to Pueblo. The Lamme building became the Walsenburg Care Center on Seventh Street, now closed.   *Courtesy of Bob and Karen Tripp.*

Ruffini Grocery and Market in 1922, the year Herman Ruffini opened the store at 128 (now 132) West Seventh. He spent some 30 years in the store until he turned it over to his son-in-law, Silvio Michelli.   *Courtesy of Gordon Kelley.*

Sporleder Selling Company deliverymen were ready to go throughout the area, including to their branch store in Alamosa. The Sporleder Selling Company was built in 1908 and incorporated in 1912. *Courtesy of Gordon Kelley.*

U. B. Grocery, next to the Fox Theatre in the 700 block of South Main. Originally the upstairs was the Victoria Hotel, but in this photo it is the Main Hotel. The Major Coal Company offices are on the right. The building was destroyed by arson in 1997. *Courtesy of John Bellotti.*

Krier's Store (Peter Krier) at the northwest corner of Sixth and Main, the early home of Unfug Brothers store, in the center of town, was the perfect place for the town Christmas tree. Usual hours for merchants were 7:30 a.m. to 8 p.m. daily and half day Sundays.   *Courtesy of Gordon Kelley.*

The Krier family at home about 1930. Lucille and Paul Krier, a businessman, and four daughters: Jewel (Geiger), Carol (McInnis), Pauline (Santi) in front and Shirley (Small) on her father's lap. Later Phyllis (Donnelly) was born.
Courtesy of Jewel Krier Geiger.

"**I'll blow you to hell,**" said the state policeman to a newspaper correspondent during the 1927-28 strike by the "Wobblies", the Industrial Workers of the World. Just a few minutes earlier Clemente Chavez had been killed at 909 South Main, the strike headquarters just behind the policeman. *Courtesy of Wayne State University, Walter P. Reuther Library.*

Dave Farr, originally a merchant, he became the state Game and Fish Commissioner, instituting fish hatcheries. Later, he was undersheriff for his brother, Sheriff Jeff Farr. *Photo courtesy Huerfano County Historical Society, Francisco Fort collection.*

Felix B. Mestas Jr., killed in World War II in Italy, was named a war hero. Mt. Mestas near La Veta Pass was renamed in his honor. A memorial with his name, and others who died in the wars, stands on the grounds of the Colorado State Veterans Nursing Home, Walsenburg. *Courtesy of the Colorado State Veterans Nursing Home and Carol Glorioso.*

Clyde Ruiz served in WWII from 1942 to 1946 with the 106th Division, 444th Infantry Regiment. He was taken captive by the Germans and was able to escape along with 6 other soldiers. During this time he was listed as "Missing In Action". Among his awards are the Purple Heart and the Bronze Star. He fought at Normandy, Battle of the Bulge, Ardienne Forrest, Slotburg and Heidishem Germany, and in France. *Courtesy Carol Glorioso.*

Mondo's Poor Boy was the hangout at 225 North Main, an example of a small diner of the 1920s. Armando Cocetti was the long-time owner. When the diner was moved to make way for Loaf 'n Jug, it became a private residence on West Eighth Street.

Courtesy of the Huerfano County Historical Society, Huerfano World collection.

St. Mary's Crusaders Football State Parochial Champions 1941

Backfield (left to right): Anthony Kaporas, FB, 150, Soph.; Ernie Roybal, FB, 145, Jr.; Frankie Stimack, QB, 148, Jr.; Bob Stimack, RB, 142, Sr.; Chuck Cordova, RB, 135, Sr.;

Line (left to right): Fred Toller, LE, 140, Soph.; Ernie Guillen, LT, 140, Soph.; Ray "Butch" Balotti, LG, 141, Sr.; Oris Pacheco, C, 165, Sr.; George Cornali, RG, 137, Sr.; Don Tallman, RT, 147, Jr.; Nabor Martinez, RE, 135, Soph.;

Weight Average: 145 pounds

State Championship Game, Denver, Colorado, December 14, 1941, seven days after the attack on Pearl Harbor. Defeated Regis, 18 – 0, on grass.

Courtesy of St. Mary Church.

A gas station on every corner was typical in mid-20th century. The Arapahoe was on South Main. Al Feiccabrino on the right, and Mr. Johnson the left, operated this Lenzini station. *Courtesy of Joe and Emma Feiccabrino.*

Spanish Peaks Fiesta Royalty in 1954 and their sponsoring organizations included Princess Rosalie Kopine, VFW; Princess Janice Conder, Sportsman Club; Patti Solomon, Lions Club; Queen Rose Marie Ramirez, Los Huerfanos; Princes Carol June Swift, BPOE (Elks); Martha Leyba, Rotary Club; Marilyn Marcon, Civic League; Gerry Vigil, Business Professional Women; Tommi Miller, Chamber of Commerce; Jo Ann Major, Huerfano Cowbelles; Joc McAlpine, (not pictured) Huerfano Basin Livestock Growers.
Courtesy Pueblo Library District.

The 1896 County Jail, 112 West Fifth Street, has been converted into the seasonal Walsenburg (Coal) Mining Museum, including a walk-through mining tunnel. *Courtesy of Carolyn Newman.*

Washington School, built in 1936 at Fifth and Russell, became the Re-1 school administration offices. The upper floor houses the Alton M. Tirey Local History Center, operated by the Huerfano County Historical Society (HCHS).

Photo courtesy Huerfano County Historical Society, Huerfano World/Jay Crook collection.

Billboards greeting travelers to Walsenburg advertised Thach-Weston "sell ranches", Crescent Motel, Burress Memorial (Chapel), Little Pig Inn, Veterans of Foreign Wars, Chamber of Commerce, Klein Hotel, Fawks Drugs, Jimmy Dick Insurance and "See The Land Of The Huajatolla".
Probably dates to about 1950. Courtesy of Huerfano County Historical Society.

Fiesta Park drew huge crowds for rodeos, carnivals and horse racing. Later called the county fairgrounds, now it houses the ball park at the Huerfano County Community Center.   *Courtesy of the Pueblo City-County Library District.*

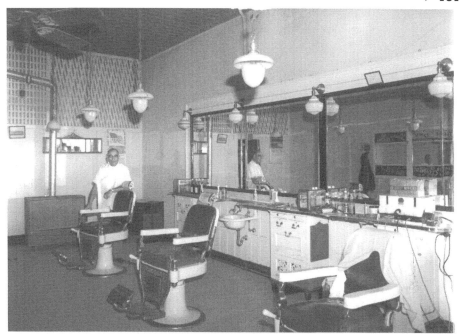

Charlie Fertitta operated his barbershop for 47 years next to Star Drug, 626 South Main.   *Courtesy of Gordon Kelley.*

The First National of Walsenburg board, in the 1970s, consisted of, front, left to right, Alton Tirey, Jim Conder, Ann Kurtz, Gerald Ariano. Back, Floyd Murr and Virgil Ladurini.

Courtesy of the Huerfano County Historical Society, Huerfano World collection.

Third Judicial District Judge Albert Tomsic, a Walsenburg native, served as judge from 1965 to 1986. He was state representative in the Colorado legislature 1952–1962, speaker of the Colorado House of Representatives 1961–1962. *Courtesy of Albert Tomsic.*

Frances Nelson (Vallejo) was county superintendent of schools for 26 years, until 1967 when the office was abolished. *Courtesy of the Huerfano County Historical Society, Huerfano World collection.*

Lathrop State Park, three miles west of Walsenburg, was the first Colorado State Park, dedicated in 1962. State Senator Sam Taylor of Walsenburg was instrumental in the park's creation. *Courtesy of the Huerfano County Historical Society, Huerfano World collection.*

John Mall High School, was partially built in 1974 (the west wing), but the main building on Pine Street was finished in 1976. *Courtesy of John Mall High School.*

John S. Mall, long-time superintendent for whom the school is named, was a teacher, principal, and from 1954 to 1979, superintendent of Re-1 schools. *Photo courtesy of Huerfano County Historical Society archives, Huerfano World collection.*

Peakview School, dedicated September 28, 2004, provides classrooms from Head Start through Eighth Grade.
Courtesy Carolyn Newman.

John Mall High School 1994 Girls Basketball State Championship Team

Mgr. Amanda Busch, Joni Maes, Tracie Trujillo, Bethany Tinsley, Monica Gomez, Ginger Eccher, Teri Jeka, Jessica Mapes, Charlcy Daher, Jennifer Vigil, Gabi Sandoval, Michele Eccher, Michelle Vezzani, Lisa Rice and Mgr. Autumn Tinsley. Front row: Asst. Coach Alan Tinsley, Head Coach Ray Bustos, Asst. Coach Tom Rice.

Courtesy John Mall High School.

Chapter Nine

DUST AND DEPRESSION

On Sunday, March 3, 1929, under the leadership of the Rev. R. R. Rose, the Methodist Church of Walsenburg opened its new three-story brick church. A service was held with special music including a solo, "Open the Gates of the Temple," sung by John G. Lloyd of Cameron, accompanied by his wife, Nell Lloyd. Bishop W. F. McMurry preached the sermon and a subscription of $5,332 was received at the morning service. The church looked forward to a long period of growth and prosperity in its imposing house of worship.

In October of 1929 the stock market in New York crashed, bringing about the financial destruction of many citizens of the United States and plunging the nation into a decade of depression and hardship.

Not everyone realized at once what was coming. Neither of the Walsenburg papers made any reference to the stock market crash on that Black Thursday or for several days thereafter. Life in Walsenburg went on pretty much as before – at least for the time being.

One of the big worries early in 1930 was the fear of an outbreak of smallpox. Dr. S. Julian Lamme asked the schools to exclude all students not vaccinated for smallpox, and the schools complied with his request. In the past, epidemics of smallpox, scarlet fever and other dreaded diseases had been almost a way of life in Walsenburg and the coal camps and were responsible for the appalling death rate of children in the camps. By 1930 with the advent of vaccinations, safer water supplies, and better housing conditions, these epidemics were not the problem they had once been, but it was still deemed prudent to insist on vaccination before children could be admitted back to the schools.[1]

The community was interested in truck farming as an important new economic activity. Plans were developed to make the Huerfano Valley southern Colorado's largest truck gardening area. Many acres of cauliflower, onions and other vegetable crops that were suitable for high altitudes were planted on farms all over the county, and the produce was shipped east by way of the Walsenburg railroads.[2]

Two problems of early Walsenburg resembled the present problems of the area – water and roads. Efforts to secure a larger and safer supply of water were ongoing. Battles ensued over the water in Martin Lake when the owners attempted to sell water to Pueblo County. Members of the Stock Growers Association planned to secure counsel to fight the sale of the water.[3] Eventually this sale was dropped, and the water in Martin Lake remained a part of the water supply of Walsenburg.

Roads were another big concern since in many ways Walsenburg was still isolated. An entrance into Walsenburg on the west side was essential as the only way in at the time was for cars to make their way through Walsen Camp, which began at the west end of Seventh Street. As traffic into the town increased from the west, it became clear that to have cars wandering around Walsen Camp, looking for a way into town, would no longer be acceptable. Businesses along the street were eager to have the new entrance be on Seventh Street, but there were serious problems with this proposal. Flooding occurred from the Cucharas River from time to time. Avoiding railroad crossings was one aim of the highway department, and to do that the road would have to skirt very near to the river. The highway builders wanted to have the road go past the schoolhouse in Walsen Camp, over a hill and enter Walsenburg on Second Street. Today the west end of Second Street ends at Welton Street but continues on as a dirt road into the county.

In time the issue was resolved and the highway came into town on Seventh Street. A number of railroad crossings were necessary, but the commerce on Seventh Street undoubtedly profited by the location of the highway.

Another road much desired by the people of Walsenburg was a road to the east. Plans for this road were often referred to as the Fowler Cut-Off. Efforts to build this road continued for many, many years. Three counties – Huerfano, Pueblo, and Otero – were involved. Over the next few decades various parts of the road were carved out of the prairie. Over the years of its construction, there was always a struggle over whether or not it could be designated a state highway. After a long time the dirt road was finally completed and would eventually become the highway known to all residents as Highway 10, a state highway.

Civic pride has always been a part of the Walsenburg mind and in the early days it applied especially to pride in its many lodges and clubs. In June of 1934 the Elks Club celebrated an important anniversary by taking out a full-page ad in the ***Walsenburg World*** to tell the story of how the Elks Club got its charter.

> *Those Huerfano people who swell up with pride when they can tell the inquiring tourist that Walsenburg has a population of 5,000 have nothing on the "old timer" of nearly 30 years ago. An official report made at that time showed Walsenburg even then had a population of 5,000. "This is brought to my mind," said Adolph Unfug, supervisor of the census in Huerfano County and one of the charter members of the Walsenburg lodge of Elks, "by the efforts Denver is now making to have rural districts added to the city population so that "Greater Denver" can show a population of over 350,000."* [4]

The Elks had to have a population of 5,000 to have a charter and three censuses show that Walsenburg didn't have it. Local Elks were members of Trinidad Lodge 181. In order to qualify for a charter of their own, Edward L. Trounstine, postmaster of Walsenburg, then established a "Greater Walsenburg" population. Rural Huerfano County received mail through star routes radiating from Walsenburg extending to the Apache on the north, south almost to Aguilar, and west as far as Sharpsdale on the

Upper Huerfano, including several coal mine camps. Trounstine estimated the number of people served by the Walsenburg post office certified to a "Greater Walsenburg" population of more than 5,000. The Elks granted the charter on July 15, 1908. "There isn't a thing that you can't put over," said Adolph, "if you put men of vision, push and indomitable will to work for its accomplishment."[5]

The Elks built a fine home of buff brick on the southwest corner of East Sixth and Russell Streets. The three-story building featured rooms for members who needed housing, and a large hall for meetings and social activities. Over the years many community events were held here. Space in the basement of the Elks Hall was rented to the public library until the Elks needed the space for other purposes. In recent years declining population has caused the cessation of the Elks Lodge activities, and the hall was recently sold to a buyer who has turned it into a hunting lodge for guests of a private hunting club in the county.

The papers carried news of some pioneer or other in almost every issue. The *Independent* of April 8, 1930, announced the death of Joseph Brunelli, a pioneer resident who had built the St. Charles Hotel in 1908. The Brunelli clan came from Austria in 1881 and Joseph worked at the Walsen mine. He homesteaded on Bear Creek in 1887 and, with his brother Charles, operated a store and saloon in Rouse in the booming days of the coal camps. After losing the ranch, the family built the St. Charles and for a time the entire family lived in it. The St. Charles was a two-story hotel on the northeast corner of Seventh and Albert Streets, and the hotel was operated for many years.[6] At some point the top floor was removed and the lower floor now houses several small businesses. One of these once held the dental practice of Dr. Fred Menghini. Today that location is a beauty shop.

Another important social observation in the papers was the celebration of the 50th wedding anniversary of Mr. and Mrs. Alexander Levy. The couple had been married at the Sporleder Inn on July 14, 1880. The bride was Lillie Sporleder, daughter of August Sporleder, owner of the inn. Over the years Alexander Levy became one of the most important of Walsenburg's early pioneers. He began his career as a partner of Fred Walsen in the mercantile business. Later Walsen sold his interest in the business and thereafter Levy did business as Levy Mercantile on the corner of Main and Seventh. Levy was also a contractor for grading rights-of-way for railroads and provided most of the ties for them. Much of his wealth came from his railroading activities.[7]

Alexander Levy was a mover in the effort to bring electric lighting to Walsenburg. He called a meeting of the citizens, and the Walsenburg Electric Light Co. was organized and the plant built in 1889 or 1890. It was later sold to the Trinidad Electric Light Co.

Three sons, Archie, Ralph and Walter Levy, and their families, were there to help the Levys celebrate the fiftieth milestone. Another son, Earl, had died in an avalanche as a young man, and two children died in infancy.

As the depression settled in, Walsenburg continued its push into agriculture. Carloads of cauliflower were shipped east, and in September $3,500 worth of sugar beets were shipped from the Joe Corsentino place one and a half miles east of Walsenburg.[8]

Problems arose with algae in the water system, and free water was distributed from the Walsenburg Creamery for several days. The city secured an engineer's report which recommended pre-chlorination of water before it entered the settling reservoirs to eliminate disease germs and prevent growth of algae. More chlorination was recommended after the water left the reservoirs for distribution. Other recommendations included replacement of some of the pipes, larger pipes and more reservoir capacity.[9]

Mayor A. J. Merritt cast the deciding vote in a City Council meeting in early 1931 authorizing the city to spend $141,000 to expand the city water system. Some months later the council reversed itself in favor of more study. The city and its citizens didn't have much money in the days of the depression, so a majority of the council decided that more water would simply have to wait. The water needs would not go away, however, and the city at last was able to purchase the Coler Ditch and other water rights, but it took time and money to bring about the needed improvements.

A new restaurant called the Bluebird Café opened on Sixth Street above Krier's Store.

A sample menu of the new establishment offered the following selections and prices:

> *Roast Beef, Brown Gravy.* . . . . *25 cents*
> *Lamb Stew.* . . . . *25 cents*
> *Calf Liver, Onions or Bacon.* . . . . *25 cents*
> *Breaded Pork Chop.* . . . . *35 cents*
> *Blue Bird Special, Steak French Fried.* . . . . *45 cents*
> *Small Steak.* . . . . *30 cents*

Obviously, it was possible to get a good dinner in Walsenburg without paying a lot of money, but in depression days no one had a lot of money, either.

In 1931 J. L. Brayer, superintendent of Walsen and Pictou mines, announced that C. F. & I. was closing the Walsen Mine, the first major mine ever operated in Huerfano County. An enormous amount of water had to be pumped in order to mine coal. Brayer stated that the company pumped 2,500 gallons of water per minute 24 hours a day. Twelve tons of water were pumped from the mine for every ton of coal taken out. The company believed that the expense could not justify keeping the mine open. The company would continue to mine the still abundant coal seams, but would take the coal out through their other tunnels in the vicinity. Most of the 300 miners would be transferred to other locations, and the 160 or more company houses would be used by the men who worked in other mines.[10]

The Women's Civic League began to interest itself in cleaning up the trash dumps on the outskirts of the city. A welfare worker for the Red Cross reported that the dumps were unsightly and dangerous since children played and dug in them. Infected cuts were frequently treated. The Civic League decided to try to get the city to make April a clean-up month.[11]

The pipe organ purchased for the new Methodist Church arrived and was installed, a cultural event of some importance since music still played a large part in the life of the town. The dedication of the organ was accompanied by a performance of Handel's *Messiah* by the Walsenburg Choral Club and the Monday Music Club of Trinidad. Sopranos of the two clubs were Miss Oliver Cline, Mrs. Fritz Unfug, Miss Elizabeth Cox, Mrs. Marcette O'Byrne, Miss Elizabeth Young, Miss Bettie Law, Miss Cervus Nichols, Miss Lula Kurfman, Miss Charlotte Ermey, Miss Louise Sporleder, Mrs. L. H. Kirkpatrick, Miss Margaret Furphy. Tenors: Dan Ross, Joe Williams, Welling Sumner, James Bainbridge, Fritz Unfug. Contraltos: Miss Esther Waterbury, Mrs. Dan Ross, Mrs. Welling Summer, Miss Elizabeth Lansdow. Bass: David Roberts, Chester Jesse, Louis B. Sporleder, Jr. and William D. Welburn, Jr.[12]

Due to the depression and the severe debt problems faced by the church, this organ was later repossessed. Many years passed before the church again decided to raise funds for a pipe organ. The next time they made sure they had all the money in hand before the organ was ordered. Belle Bonfils of the prominent Denver family was contacted, and she made a donation of $1,000 if the sum was matched by other contributions. The match was made and other contributions came in until at last they had the money and the organ was purchased and installed. It, too, was dedicated with fanfare and a special music program, and today it still provides music for the congregation.

As early as 1931 the depression was beginning to take its toll on Walsenburg. In May of 1931, a group of laborers appeared before the city council to plead for work for the unemployed. Attorney Sam T. Taylor was the spokesman for the unemployed. He represented that there was a great deal more distress among the people of the city than many realized, and that a family had been discovered eating boiled alfalfa and potato peelings from garbage cans.[13]

From this time on through the 1930s, there would be many attempts to find work for the unemployed. Work would be done on community projects, and many found employment on the road improvement projects going on in the city and county.

The deaths of many early pioneers began to be reported.

In May of 1931 Charles Mazzone died at the age of 71. Mazzone had come to Walsenburg in 1874. A few years after his arrival he went to Memphis, Tennessee, and returned with a bride – Miss Caroline Lagomarsino. Thirteen children were born, of whom seven were living at the time of Mazzone's death: C. Victor Mazzone and Herman Mazzone of Walsenburg. The five daughters were Mrs. William Tressell of Galesburg, Illinois; Mrs. Harry A. Grant of Fort Collins, Colorado; Mrs. Frank Yarr and Isabel Mazzone of Walsenburg. Another daughter, Anna Mazzone, was Sister Carmilla of the order of Benedictine Sisters of Atchison, Kansas.

Charles Mazzone had been a prominent businessman and was the owner and builder of the Mazzone Opera House, long a social center in the community.[14]

Other old-timers who passed from the scene included Conrad and Frederick Unfug, two of several brothers who came to Walsenburg in the 1800s. Both were prominent businessmen who were born in Germany. All of the brothers engaged in various forms of business as the town of Walsenburg grew and prospered.[15]

A community garden which would cost about $1,500 was planned for the relief of the unemployed. The site chosen was ten or twelve acres on the Sefton place near the St. Mary Cemetery just south of the Walsenburg city limits. A plan for a pump irrigation system was discussed. Workers would be paid minimum wage, and the vegetables grown would be distributed among workers or sold in local markets. A contract for cauliflower was already in hand, and other crops were being discussed.[16]

The garden grew to fifteen acres when crops such as lettuce, carrots, onions and peas were planted. The pumping experiment, if successful, was thought to be a great advantage to many land owners along the Cucharas River. Many small farms lay along the river from the outskirts of Walsenburg to nine miles to where the

Cucharas River crossed the east-bound road. These farms were largely owned by Mexican-American farmers and supplied mostly the needs of the families who owned them.

In March of 1932 the **Walsenburg World** reported another big change in the town.

Old Landmark Falls Before Man's Hands

One of the oldest buildings [southwest corner of Main and Seventh] in Walsenburg is being torn down to make room for a new business. The building was built about 1880 by Fred Walsen and Alex Levy. At the time it was built it was the southern most building in the little settlement. Main Street ended abruptly just a short way from there by the rugged fence of a pole corral. There was no building West of it with the exception of a large hay barn which was built at the same time as the building. The part of the block including the Lamme Hospital was nothing but a large corral. To show that little was thought of a city at the time of the building of the store, when the city was laid out with streets and alleys, the back of this building extended about three feet into the surveyed alley and this condition has existed to the present day.

The building was first occupied by the Levy Mercantile Co., then by the Star Theatre. After the theatre was moved to its new building which the Valencia theatre now occupies, the building became the property of the Lenzini Motor Co. and was changed into a tire shop. It was first occupied by Mose Daher, later by Dan Bergano, and then the Lenzini Motor took the business under their own management putting Joe Yourick in charge.

On the site of the old landmark the Lenzini Motor Co., plans to erect a modern filling station built of brick and stuccoed. Mr. Joe Yourick will have charge of the new business place.[17]

In later times the building was used as the office and showroom of Zorc's building supplies company. At the present time it is owned by the Black Diamond Corporation and has been turned into an office and art gallery.

Entertainment was always important to the community and music was at the center of it. Music Week was celebrated each year with concerts, operettas and other musical activities.

Dancing was another popular activity and, in the spring of 1932, Ray Laster, an employee of the post office, leased the Aguilar pavilion for the summer months. He had been in charge of the dances held at the Maccabee Hall in Walsenburg and had staged several dances in Aguilar.[18]

The Walsenburg community garden prospered as may be seen in this newspaper item:

Walsen Community Garden Attracts Attention of Colorado

From W. M. Case, extension horticulturalist at the Colorado Agricultural College came this assessment concerning the nineteen counties with special garden programs. "One of the most outstanding subsistence gardens in the state and the earliest planted is the garden at Walsenburg, which is sponsored by Huerfano County, City of Walsenburg and the Huerfano County Chamber of Commerce.

"B. W. Allred, county agent, planned and has charge of the garden, which was planted to show that coal miners can add to their incomes by growing garden crops during periods of slack employment at the mines.

The garden produce, which consists principally of cabbage, cauliflower, peas, onions, and celery, will be sold to reimburse the county and chamber of commerce for funds advanced for the garden. Part of the produce will be canned or dried and given to Red Cross for the needy. Laborers supplied by the Red Cross are paid in food or clothing only vouchers for the work done being cashed at the city stores in exchange for goods. Funds that would ordinarily have gone directly to charity are used to hire labor."[19]

Throughout the year work and talk continued on roads, water, and other needs, but attention also turned to the national election of 1932.

The election of Franklin D. Roosevelt was reported in an inch and a half headline before the state and local offices were decided.

By the next paper the reports were in and the Democrats had won in the state. Alva Adams became the governor, and the party controlled the legislature for the first time since 1917. In Huerfano County three offices held by Democrats went to Republicans and four held by Republicans went to Democrats.[20]

In spite of the change in the nation, the problems of the depression deepened, and there were daily increases in people applying for financial help, including the old age pensions provided by the state. One of these applicants attracted the notice of the newspaper due to her pioneer lineage.

Pension Asked by First Native

A small, bent little lady, dressed all in black, with a black shawl over her head was ushered by friends into the office of County Judge W. W. Hammond this afternoon, and from all appearances she appeared to be the same as scores of others who have visited this office to apply for old age pensions.

However, upon questioning this old, neat little woman one would find that she wears the mark of distinction for she is Doloritas Albert, the first person to be born in Walsenburg. Doloritas is the daughter of "Uncle John" Albert, one of the first settlers in this region in the days of the early west and prominent in early day history of Huerfano County.

She was born May 11, 1868 to become Walsenburg's first native. She has lived in this county all of her life and now makes her home on East Sixth St.[21]

As the year went on and the programs of the New Deal began to be put in place, both community activities and relief activities continued in Walsenburg.

The Community Leisure Time Association opened its first reading room for the general public, using donated books and magazines. The organization also made plans to build a municipal park on the east side of Main Street between Fourth Street and Colorado. Later this was the location of Ludvik's and the fire station. The land was donated by the Martin family and the Elks Lodge and would be called Martin Park. The park would include a bandstand, and a Civic Band was organized even before the park was built.[22]

For some time the two newspapers had been published separately every other day, but in May of 1933 it was announced that henceforth the paper would be published as a daily and would be called the *World-Independent*.[23] With this merger the decades of furiously partisan reporting from the two papers would be exchanged for a single paper with no particular political bias.

Sports were always of great interest in Walsenburg, and the population was undoubtedly thrilled with the following headline on May 30, 1933.

OVERHEAD WINS INDIANAPOLIS RACE

Fred Frame Is Injured in Crash
After He Has Driven 200 Miles.

Babe Stapp Leads Pack at 250 Mile Post but
Gives Way on Last Half of Race.

Mark Bilman Wrecks at Same
Spot Few Seconds After Frame.

Indianapolis, Ind., May 30 - (AP) Will Overhead won the Indianapolis Memorial Day race today. At the two hundred fifty mile post Babe Stapp was leading the string of roaring cars but gave way to Overhead on the last half of the 500 mile grind.

Fred Frame, one of the leading contenders for first place cracked up after driving two hundred miles and injuries force him out of the race. Mark Hilman wrecked at the same spot a few seconds later and was taken to the hospital.[24]

No doubt this was thrilling news for the sports fans of Walsenburg, but they had never heard of Will Overhead since no race car driver of that name ever existed. The local paper had a new reporter on night duty, and he teletyped to a Denver paper asking the result of the race. The Denver reporter replied in journalist jargon that "will overhead Indy race." The phrase meant that he'd send a wire as soon as he had the outcome, but the Walsenburg man interpreted it differently.

Thus began one of Walsenburg's chief claims to fame. A check of the next few papers for a correction revealed no such correction. Maybe the word got around town by word-of-mouth.

The story of Will Overhead continues to surface from time to time. One story says that it was written up in one or more journalism texts. The story was even stolen in 1947 when humorist H. Allen Smith attributed the tale to an Indiana location. The Walsenburg editor, in spite of an understandable desire to forget the whole thing, wrote a column denouncing the writer's theft of Will Overhead. In later years Walsenburg honored Will for a couple of years by calling the summer festival "Will Overhead Days."

Soon Walsenburg had something more important than a car race to worry about. The Rev. J. B. Liciotti, pastor of St. Mary Church, announced that the Catholic grade school and high school would be unable to open that year because of financial difficulties. This threw the public schools into a panic while trying to figure out how to absorb an additional 640 students.[25]

In the fall, however, after St. Mary's had been visited by a number of Catholic dignitaries, it was announced that the school was too important to close and money would be found to keep it open. The high school remained opened until 1971, and the elementary school hung on until 1997, to serve the Catholic youth of the community.

Other activities continued during the summer. Martin Park was dedicated and band concerts were given each week. Archie Levy turned his swimming pool on West Seventh Street over to the city and the C. L. T. A. (Commission on Leisure Time Association) undertook to operate it for the benefit of the young people of the town at no charge.

The community was saddened in August 1933 when word was received of the death of E. L. Neelley in a car accident in Arizona. Neelley was the candidate for sheriff whose suit in 1915 had resulted in the ouster of Jeff Farr. After serving two terms as sheriff, Neelley had moved to California. His funeral was held at the Community Church and he was buried in the Masonic Cemetery.

Relief funds were cut off to Huerfano County in October. The state had instituted something called the UR tax, which involved automobile tags, with the proceeds going to finance relief aid. Huerfano County apparently had not cooperated with this effort, and its failure left many families in desperate straits. The tax was soon declared unconstitutional, and the need for providing relief fell on the counties.

Also in October the paper reported an anniversary celebration:

> *Mr. and Mrs. Telesfior Garcia, old-time residents of this city, celebrated their golden wedding anniversary today, Oct. 20, with a renewal of their vows at the six-thirty mass at St. Mary's Church, Rev. J. B. Liciotti performing the ceremony. Twenty-five friends were present to witness the ceremony and later joined the couple at a breakfast held in honor of the occasion at their home at East 7th St. Mrs. Garcia was presented with many attractive and appropriate gifts.*
>
> *Mrs. Garcia has lived in this city since 1874. Prior to her marriage to Mr. Garcia in 1883, she was the widow of Jose Dolores Esquivel who was sheriff of Huerfano County in the 1880s. Mr. Esquivel was killed on duty Jan. 15, 1881. He was shot in the back by an unknown assassin while he was taking prisoners to jail.*
>
> *Mr. Garcia, before he came to Walsenburg, where he met and married his present wife, made his home in Talpa, Colorado. In his younger days he was an instructor in the public schools.*[26]

More road activity was soon reported with the announcements of blueprints for the road north to Pueblo.

> *The highway leaves Walsenburg by way of Walsen Ave. but at the end of the pavement goes straight on across the hogback north of the city and runs in that direction for about two miles when it takes off at an angle and runs due northwest of the present highway and without a curve or crook for about eleven miles or somewhere in the vicinity of the Schlink store north of the Huerfano River.*[27]

This exit from Walsenburg is very much as it is today with the exception of the connection in town from Main Street to Walsen Avenue. This problem would cause headaches later on, but for the time being it was easier for people to arrive in Walsenburg from the west and leave it to go north to Pueblo than it had ever been before.

The lengthy life and career of Alexander Levy ended in Walsenburg on October 27, 1933. After an illness this noted pioneer died at his home on Main Street.

From the earliest days of La Plaza de los Leones, Levy had been a central figure in the history of the town and county with his many business ventures. He and his wife were active in every civic and social area possible. The town mourned the loss of this vital man.

The newspaper reported his funeral:

> *Funeral services will be held tomorrow afternoon at the home on Main St. for Alexander Levy, pioneer settler of this city, who died early yesterday morning. Rabbi Zigmond of Temple Emanuel in Pueblo will officiate at the ceremonies, and the Masonic Lodge will hold services at the grave. The B'nai B'rith, a Jewish organization, will attend the funeral services. Interment will be in the Masonic cemetery under the direction of the Unfug Peet Mortuary.*[28]

According to his granddaughter, Levy did not actively practice his Jewish faith during his long lifetime in Walsenburg, but neither did he disavow it as is evidenced by the presence of the rabbi to conduct the funeral.

In later years the descendants of Alexander and Lillie Levy sold the house and property to the city of Walsenburg. The house was demolished and the land added to what is known as Heritage Park, located between the train depot and law offices next door on the east side of Main Street. A plaque is dedicated to the lives of this pioneer couple and their descendants.

It is difficult for today's residents and for travelers passing through the city to imagine a time when Main Street did not curve past the United Church to join Walsen Avenue. It is even harder to envision Walsen Avenue as a divided street with a median filled with grass, trees and shrubs. The median became the center of a long controversy with the highway department; the dispute went on for some years before it was finally resolved by removing the median.

Throughout the depression years, in spite of all of the economic problems that enveloped the area, work continued on civic projects including work on the fair grounds in the southern end of the city. This project was undertaken by the American Legion. Their plans called for extensive renovation of the area, and they hoped to have it all done in time for a grand 1933 Fourth of July celebration. The **Walsenburg World** reported on the plans.

> *Surveyors and workers started the buzzing away at the local fair grounds today. After a few more weeks of construction Walsenburg will claim one of the best amusement parks in the southern part of the state. Commander Charles Tallman, head of the American Legion post in this city, stated that work will begin at once to tear down the old stables and shacks at the back of the grandstand, and the workers will start immediately on a regulation one-half mile race track which will be forty feet wide and sixty feet on the curves.*
>
> *The ball playing fields will be set in the middle of the race track, the grandstand is to be moved to the west side of the fence. Another softball playing field will be constructed. It is said that it will take at least two to three weeks before the construction which is undertaken by the American Legion will be finished and ready for the public. Plans are also going ahead for a big Fourth of July celebration in Walsenburg with horse races and a rodeo being one of the high lights of the day.[29]*

Turkeys were another economic asset to the community with thousands being raised, slaughtered and shipped to market each year. Apparently Walsenburg was a major supplier of Thanksgiving turkeys. It also seems likely that the turkeys bought by the Methodist men to supply the weekly turkey dinners were bought, live, from some of the turkey growers in the area. A turkey processing plant was located in Loma Park.

Much of the agricultural activity slowed or stopped entirely during the depression. Dust storms and drought reduced the successful growing of marketable crops, and many farmers lost their holdings. The great shipments of cauliflower ceased, and agriculture has never regained the place it once held in the economic picture of Huerfano County.

In spite of this, efforts continued to be made in the area of agriculture. The community garden was a great success, and the mine camps sponsored garden contests among their workers. There was even an effort by some mine camps to provide workers with small farms to boost their income in the times when the mines were not working, but not much came of this.

In late November of 1933, Postmaster Eugene Vories announced that President Roosevelt had approved the construction of a new post office in Walsenburg to be built at a proposed cost of $68,200. The site had not yet been chosen, but efforts to choose one began at once.

Several hundred county men got jobs when more projects were approved by New Deal agencies. These projects included the Bear Creek, Ideal and Santa Clara road projects, the City of Walsenburg flood control project, the La Veta and adjacent small road project, the City of La Veta's flood ditches and improvement of the city dam project, the Gardner road west, including Pass Creek, the Upper Huerfano and Mosca pass road project and a project allowing an administration office force.

Still later more projects were approved for the graveling of Highway 69 from Walsenburg to the Custer County line, Cucharas and Rattlesnake Butte roads, improvements and construction work on Turkey Ridge, Lascar and Mustang roads, and the improvement of Turkey Creek and Williams Creek roads.

All of these projects, which were spread throughout the county, were about roads which are still in use today by residents and visitors alike. Throughout the dark days of the depression, improvements continued to be made in the rural west through the means of the many efforts of the federal government to provide employment for needy citizens.

In other areas of need, citizens were called on for help. Amanda Simpson, the county superintendent of schools, requested the donation of old school books for the many tiny county schools which had no money for the purchase of books. The Community Women Workers announced that work would begin on toys for poor children and asked anyone who had old or broken toys to donate them. The women would then refurbish them to provide Christmas joy for children who would otherwise not have any toys.

More paving projects were announced, and the Colorado Civil Works board announced three new projects for Huerfano County. These included general repair on the Wheatridge and Apache roads, additional flood protection for Walsenburg and laying a pipeline from Walsenburg to Toltec. The project also included building a grandstand at the Huerfano County athletic ground, but only if the school board approved and agreed to furnish the materials in the amount of $2,000.[30]

The site for the post office was finally selected on the northeast corner of the intersection of Russell and East Sixth Streets. The property, including a large brick building which was known as the Vaughn boarding house, cost $9,500.[31]

By May the new stadium at the high school was almost finished, and the school board announced that negotiations had been completed for the installation of a standard football lighting system. Citizens were urged to visit the stadium to see what it was like.[32]

Over the years Walsenburg and Huerfano County have mercifully been spared most of the weather scourge known as tornados, but in June of 1934 the first such tornado was reported. The property described in the following news story was located east and north of Highway 10 about twenty miles or more from Walsenburg, now the Turkey Ridge Association.

A tornado, first on record in the history of Huerfano County,
swept several buildings and a shed from their sites at the ranch of

George Niebuhr, postmaster, yesterday afternoon, and piled them as a twisted and broken mass of wreckage about 300 feet north of their foundations. Eight men were in one of the sheds but no injuries were reported.

The tornado in wrecking the building left its freak markings on the damaged property. All of the men were working in a large shed which was about 160 feet long and 25 feet wide. The shearers were working in the west end of the building, but about 500 head of sheep were in the east end. The wind lifted about eight feet of the east end of the shed into the air and carried it about a block away, twisting the corrugated iron of the building into a mass which appeared as thought it had been crushed in the hand of a giant like a piece of tinfoil. However, the 500 sheep which were under this section of the building were not touched, not one even being moved or injured by the gale. The pens were in good shape, $1500 worth of wool remained on the ground as it had been piled inside the shed, hay was still in its stack in its proper place, nor could anything which was kept in the shed be found out of place.[33]

The year 1937 brought the first coal mine story in a long while and it was a delightful one.

Popeye is Sissy Compared with Molly the Mule

A.A. Wheelock, stable boss at Cameron Mine, has mules that are taught to be tough. A cave-in at the mine this week fell directly on Molly, a hard-working old girl, and buried her beneath 30 ft. of dirt and rock. Workmen were busy from 8 a.m. to 4 p.m. before Molly was located under the debris. Upon being uncovered she merely kicked up her heels and returned to the stable without a scratch.[34]

The islands of greenery on Walsen Avenue were finally declared a menace. The state had threatened to re-route Highway 85 if they were not removed. Businessmen declared their dislike of the islands, and so the fate of these green areas was determined. The ever-active Civic League, however, promised to remove the shrubs from the area and see to it that they were re-planted in other areas. Walsenburg has long been known for its devotion to trees and greenery around the city.

The new post office had been finished for two or three years, but late in 1937 it received an important embellishment. The paper reported it proudly:

> *A beautiful mural painting of the Spanish Peaks was erected in the Walsenburg Post Office Tuesday and has been acclaimed by critics as the most beautiful interpretation of the Twin Peaks ever made. The painting is by Ernest L. Blumenschein, president of the Taos Artists' Association. He made the mural especially for the Walsenburg post office at the request of the U. S. Treasury Dept.*
>
> *The mural depicts the Peaks in Indian days as Blumenschein imagined it appeared in 1850. The mural is nine feet long and four feet wide and the artist worked on coloring effects for more than a year. The first sketch was made last year when the Peaks were capped with snow.*[35]

The sketch mentioned in this story now hangs in Blumenschein's home in Taos, which is operated as a museum. Many works of art were created during the depression in the government's program to help support artists. Not only paintings, but also literature was created with these programs, especially books of interviews and stories about early residents. Many researchers have been greatly aided in their work by these writings.

The Blumenschein mural, protected by a clear covering, is still in the post office lobby above the door to the postmaster's office. In the early '70s it was appraised at $40,000.

Christmas time always brings interesting stories to newspapers and the early days were no exception. The following story harkens back to Walsenburg's earliest days.

Judge Luz Gonzales Celebrates 70th Christmas in Walsenburg

Judge Gonzales told how Christmas brought no toys, no elaborate gifts and certainly no brilliant decorations in 1876.

Christmas was observed by feasts that often took weeks to prepare. Wild meat was served and plenty of beans and wheat. Most commodities were obtained by trading. Baking soda was a luxury and women dug the crust of earth from around a soda spring to use in baking. Wheat was ground by hand. Coffee was made with one-fourth coffee beans and three-fourths dried peas. Many candles were made. Clothing was spun from wool raised on the ranch.

The Judge explains that paper sold for 25 cents a sheet and he remembers writing his letter to Santa on a dried pelt. "And then people complain of hard times today," the Judge chuckles.[36]

Not all December news was as pleasant as the recollections of Judge Gonzales. A 1937 newspaper told of the December 24 death of an important member of the community:

Mrs. Maria Prisciliana Nelson died at her home on W. 7th early Sunday morning. Mrs. Nelson, whose husband, John Nelson, preceded her in death three years ago, was the grand-daughter of Don Francisco Antonio Atencio, who homesteaded the land which is bordered by the present site of the post office and St. Mary's School and extends a quarter of a mile to the west, including most of Main St. and the downtown business section. The land was proved in 1874.

The Atencio family came here in 1868 from Conejos County. Mrs. Nelson's parents were Miguel and Rumalda Atencio.

Frances Nelson, assistant to the county superintendent of school's office, a niece of Mrs. Nelson was adopted by Mr. and Mrs. Nelson when she was a little girl. She is the only survivor.[37]

The date of the arrival of the Atencio family may be in error. Many of the Atencios came at the same time as the Leon family in 1859. The Leon family established the village known as La Plaza de los Leones while the Atencio family settled further west near the end of the present day Seventh Street in a village known as Tequisquite.

Among the efforts of the various agencies to help people mired in the depression was the Farm Security Administration. In

Huerfano County this agency worked to improve living conditions for farm families.

Marked improvements in living conditions have been made by the twenty-two families which have been helped by the Farm Security Administration in Huerfano County, says Anna L. Catchpole, county home supervisor.

Twelve yards have been improved by cleaning, planting flower gardens, or fencing. Four homes have had screens repaired or replaced. One home has a repaired roof. Eleven have repaired or replaced curtains, rugs, and bedding. Two homes have new walls and one has a repaired windmill. New cupboards have been placed in two. Ten families have improved their poultry flock. Twelve are keeping complete farm and home account books. Families have canned 3,844 quarts of food, stored 2,966 pounds of vegetables and 3,300 pounds of fruit and 1,020 pounds of dried vegetables.[38]

Work continued on roads and other county projects. More work was approved for the fairgrounds including the completion of the grandstand and exhibit buildings. Also a caretaker's house was to be built and landscaping done. All of this was a project of the W. P. A., Works Progress Administration.

Another improvement was reported at this time when $50,000 was appropriated to build a railroad overpass on Highway 160, just west of Walsenburg. Bids were opened and contracts let, but the project soon ran into a major difficulty. The overpass was being built over the old tunnels of the Walsen Mine, and cave-ins soon began, leaving a hole beside the highway and endangering the whole project. An ingenious solution was decided upon. In its June 19, 1938, edition the *Denver Post* reported on the matter.

MINERS WILL PLUG OLD WORKINGS
TO AID BUILDING OF ROAD

Daredevil coal miners have been drafted into service to build the "foundation" for the approach to the new $81,000 overpass crossing the D. & R. G. W. tracks on Highway 160 west of Walsenburg. The roadbed is being constructed directly over the *workings of old Walsen mine, offering some of the strangest problems the Colorado state highway department has faced.*

A portion of the old mine "honeycomb" has already caved, leaving a gaping hole directly in the path of the new highway. The crater-like opening has revealed a ragged entrance to the yawning shaft of the old mine – it is thru this entrance that skilled coal miners will crawl down into the belly of the mine to build bulk-heads at the various openings of the workings, preparatory to blasting the shaft full of sand.

The plan for filling the mine was conjured by J. P. Baca, resident engineer of the state highway department. He will personally direct the undertaking.

Bulkheads made of timber, chicken wire and burlap will close off 300 feet of the mine shaft that lies beneath the roadway. A hydraulic mine fill using water and sand, will then be made. Water will be pumped thru a four-inch pipe under 150-pound pressure, then thru a pile of sand into the mine. The water will run thru the bulkheads, but the sand will pile up, filling the shaft solidly beneath the road. It is expected that the fill will require two weeks.[39]

The Walsen Mine had closed in 1931 due to the increasing seepage of water which made mining the coal too expensive. For this road project six former miners were employed to go back into the abandoned mine tunnels. The task carried considerable risk just as mining coal had been risky, but the old-timers succeeded in building the needed bulkheads. A month later the Walsenburg paper recorded:

Walsen Mine fill reported as successful. Work is moving in high gear on the fill, as a constant stream of water washes tons of sand down into the abandoned workings of Walsen Mine. An average of 700 truckloads of sand is used daily and it is estimated that 6,000 cubic yards of sand will be used. Water is pumped from the Cuchara River and trucks haul sand from the river bed. J. B. Baca, engineer, reports that the mine is filling rapidly. Baca and a crew crawled into the flooded mine for an inspection.

Bulkheads built to catch the sand are holding well. The bulkheads were built so that water would pass thru and the sand will pile up. The water travels on down into lower reaches of the mine and empties into underground streams.[40]

This dangerous undertaking proved to be highly successful. The overpass was built, and thousands of cars pass over it each month of the year. A deep gully runs along side the highway at the approach to the overpass which undoubtedly represents part of the caved-in tunnels. At its peak the Walsen Mine had 157 miles of underground tunnels. Several other mines were located in the same area along Highway 160, so as modern day residents and tourists drive this stretch of road, they are passing over the deep tunnels in which early miners toiled.

One could never be sure just when Walsenburg's early history would come to light in the more modern days of the 1930s. An item in the **Walsenburg World** recounted the following:

Remodeling of Mazzone Hall Recalls Colorful Memories

Memories of such famous characters as H. A. W. Tabor, P. T. Barnum and Bob Ford were recalled in Walsenburg today as workmen ripped heavy coats of paper off the walls of Mazzone Hall at the [southwest] corner of Sixth and Main. The building which was erected in 1888 at a cost of $10,000 was once the meeting place for the West's most colorful characters. When first opened the building housed an extravagant saloon on the ground floor, and Walsenburg's first opera house with a seating capacity of 200 on the second floor.

Tabor, Barnum and Ford were only a few of the famous men to stop and refresh themselves at this famous bar. The building was built by Charles Mazzone, who came to Walsenburg in 1874 and lived here until 1931. Mazzone's son, Victor, recalls dances in the hall at which admission of $5 was charged. He says Bob Ford, killer of Jesse James, was a frequent customer of the amusement center.

The building served as Walsenburg Opera House from the time it was built until twelve years ago. It is now being remodeled to make a modern grocery for a Safeway store.[41]

The long decade of the 1930s drew slowly to a close. Road projects continued. The green islands on Walsen Avenue were torn out. Coal continued to be mined, but natural gas was beginning to make strong inroads. Plans were made to remodel the county jail due to three prisoners who tunneled their way out but who later turned themselves in. The plans included concrete flooring, new plumbing and remodeling of some of the cells. There were also plans for a catwalk to connect the jail and the district courtroom, but this was never built.

Walsenburg continued its optimism, however, and in 1939 big plans were made for a celebration to advertise southern Colorado coal in hopes of revitalizing the mining industry, the first Black Diamond Jubilee.

This would be an enormous event for the city and county. There would be a rodeo, ball games, and horse races. Residents would dress as miners or cowboys, men would grow beards, and women would wear bright-colored cotton clothing. The town was decorated from one end to the other. C. F. & I. sent a miniature of the steel mill with working parts. A special train would come from Pueblo to carry people from that city. The governor of the state, Ralph Carr, was coming to officiate. At the opening ceremonies a mile-long parade with cowboys, bands, floats, and decorated cars would follow the opening speeches.[42]

Rain forced a one-day delay in the start of the Black Diamond Jubilee, but in spite of that, the event ran for the full three days. The people of the town were thrilled with the success of the exposition and made plans to make it an annual event.

Shortly after the big celebration, a mysterious robbery took place in June 1939 at the county courthouse. Burglars ransacked and set fire to valuable records in the vault of the County Treasurer, F. H. Danford. From $800 to $1,000 was taken, but there was no apparent reason for the arson. They entered through a window on the south side of the courthouse and entered the vault through a steel door in Danford's office. A heavy bar was used to break open a wooden door connecting two rooms of the vault. Officers believe a fire was started in both the cash room and record room after filing cabinets had been ripped open and records were scattered. A briefcase belonging to F. E. Shepherd, who was auditing books of the county offices, was emptied into the fire. Valuable reports of a financial nature were destroyed.[43]

Over the next few weeks this story continued through the papers. Extra workers were hired at the courthouse to try to reconstruct the burned records. Eventually the auditor, F. E. Shepherd, was arrested in Prowers County and held on a charge of swindling. It was believed that he may have caused the burning of his briefcase.

A complete audit of the county's books was conducted following the burglary, and many delays in business were caused by the difficulties.

Some months previously the Lenzini Garage had burned to the ground but was soon replaced. In December a grand new garage opened with prize drawings and free grease jobs offered to invite the public to see the new facility. A. S. Lenzini drew all the plans for the new building. Lenzini, in his career, had advanced from grocery clerk to the managership of a big motor company. He was married to Nichie Santi of Pictou, and the couple had three children, Michael, Elsie Marie and Sandy, Jr.

On this note of a big business opening, a long, difficult decade of dust storms and depressions drew to a close, and the city looked forward eagerly to the 1940s.

Chapter Ten

WAR COMES TO WALSENBURG

Although the Great Depression was still dragging on, January 1, 1940, a new decade, seemed to bring renewed optimism to Walsenburg that its future would be bright.

The Junior Chamber of Commerce settled on May 30, 31 and June 1 as the best days to stage the annual Black Diamond Jubilee. The city council wrestled over the problem of land for a new water filtration plant and how to finance the project. The high school planned a Shakespearean festival directed by William O. Eastman. Students of the Honor Society would present *The Taming of the Shrew*, and faculty members would present excerpts from *A Midsummer Night's Dream*. A below-zero cold wave gripped the city, but, other than that, things looked better.[1]

Much of the first year was concerned with the new filtration plant. A $15,000 bond issue was floated and the city condemned the land necessary to build it. There was difficulty in agreeing on a price with the owners, Milton Utt of La Veta and James A. Utt of Avondale, but eventually, through the condemnation process, the 0.84 of an acre of land was obtained, and the city was able to take immediate possession.[2]

The courthouse, built in 1904, was beginning to show its age and the county commissioners decided that some of the fancy trim had to be removed. Workers began removing cornice stones from different locations at the top of the courthouse. There was a fear that these huge round stones might fall and result in serous injury.[3]

In May a sensational murder occurred in the city. Dr. J. F. Baca, a member of the prominent Baca family of Trinidad, who had practiced in Walsenburg for sixteen years, was shot three times by a young husband named Andrew Spendow, Jr. in the kitchen of the home of the young man and his wife. Dr. Baca did not die at once and was taken to the Lamme Brothers Hospital where futile efforts were made to save his life. Before his death Dr. Baca was able to dictate and sign the following statement:

> *I, Dr. J. F. Baca, believing myself about to die do hereby make the following statement in the presence of Jack Lacy, Dr. S. J. Lamme, Irene Stringari, and George Miller.*
>
> *I was in the home of Andrew Spendow, Jr., when after treating his wife I went to the kitchen to wash my hands. As I was washing my hands Young Spendow stepped in the door and fired three shots. I don't know why he did it. We were the best of friends.*[4]

Spendow was captured and charged with murder. During the trial much conflicting information came to light.

The Spendows had consulted Dr. Baca because Mrs. Spendow was pregnant and feared a miscarriage. On the day of the shooting, Spendow had summoned Baca to see his wife. Dr. Baca found that she was having a miscarriage. He sent the husband for gauze while he went for proper instruments. He returned and cared for her and later loaned his car to Spendow. Shortly after Spendow's return, he talked to his wife and then went into the yard. He returned, grabbed a gun and shot Baca.

Before Baca's death, Dr. Lamme testified that he asked him if he had performed an illegal operation, an abortion. Baca denied it. Spendow claimed that his wife told him that Baca had operated to take the baby from her. He claimed he saw evidence and became ill.

The Spendows had been to see Baca the previous day. She claimed to have been doing laundry and lifting tubs of water and complained of pain.

Mrs. Spendow had been hospitalized following the shooting. She had suffered from "milk leg", a condition of swelling sometimes associated with pregnancy. She testified that she had gone to Baca and asked him to take her baby from her. She said that he had given her medicine to prevent her having the baby and that she had taken it a number of times. She repeatedly said that she and Dr. Baca knew of the abortion attempt. Under cross-examination by Spendow's attorney, she admitted that the story of lifting tubs of water was a lie.

On July 3, Spendow, who was only seventeen years of age, was convicted of voluntary manslaughter and sentenced to 7 years, 11 months, and 28 days. In passing sentence, Judge East stated that the evidence in the case indicated that the crime was committed in the heat of anger, and that it was the result of failure on the part of the defendant to govern his "ungovernable and unreasonable" temper.[5.]

So many years after the crime it is impossible to determine the complete truth in such a sensational crime. The Spendows were very young and her true feelings about having a child cannot be known. Dr. Baca had been a respected member of the medical profession for many years. He seemed truly stunned at the actions of the young man who shot him. Like so many other stories from the past, the whole truth is lost in time.

When war news began to fill the papers in 1940, the nation decided to begin registering aliens within its borders. As a coal-mining area, Walsenburg and Huerfano County had plenty of non-citizens, but the new law had unintended consequences. The following story about such a matter appeared in the local paper.

Citizens when single, aliens when married; husbands became naturalized – oh, what's the use? When is a citizen not a citizen? This question got a good working over this morning at the post office, where Postmaster George Niebuhr is conducting the alien registration that got underway Tuesday.

It's all very complicated, but nevertheless a fact, that three ladies appeared for registration as aliens who were born and raised in this country. And what is more they are aliens in the eyes of Uncle Sam.

It happens this way. The three ladies were born in the U. S. which made them citizens. But – when they grew up and were married, all married men who were not naturalized citizens. Thus they lost their citizenship. Since that time, all the men have become citizens by naturalization, but their wives because they married aliens became citizens of another country.

Are you following?

Now, they are forced to register as aliens in spite of the fact that none of them has set foot outside the borders of the U. S.

P. S. They're all planning to enter naturalization classes at once to regain their status as citizens of the U. S.[6]

Although there was as yet no sign that the United States would enter the war which was raging in Europe, a national draft was set up. In Huerfano County, Otto G. Klein, Dr. G. S. Mallett and Thomas S. Young were named to the draft board, and the board and its staff immediately set up quarters to begin registering young men.

In late October five local men were called in the draft lottery. Franklin Roosevelt was re-elected in a landslide and Huerfano County remained largely in the Democratic column with only three Republicans gaining office. Frances Nelson was elected to become county school superintendent, a post she would hold until 1959, when the school districts were consolidated and the county system ceased to exist.

Not only were young men beginning to be drafted into service, but others were volunteering for the armed services. In late January twelve local men – John A. Bucci, Max Talmich, George S. Spock, George W. Judiscak, Leo Gallegos, Silvirio Escobedo, John F. Ladurini, Eloy H. Cordova, Thomas E. O'Rourke, William J. Olguin and Louis Lee Archuleta – left Walsenburg for service.[7]

The community was saddened by the death of Sen. Charles Hayden, a man widely known in local and state politics. Sen. Hayden, 69, was found dead of carbon monoxide poisoning near the old Ideal mine.[8]

With the war in Europe coming closer, the nation turned its attention to patriotism. Walsenburg responded by sponsoring a week of Americanism activities beginning with a mass meeting and a parade. The meeting after the parade offered the following program:

Selection by band
Singing of "America" led by H. F. Scott
Invocation, Father Raymond Newell
Introduction of Chairman Fisk
Welcome Address, Mayor Andy C. Schafer, Jr.
Presentation of Resolutions, I. E. Schachet
Address, "The Part We Play in Americanism", Star Caywood
Singing of "God Bless America" by audience
Selection by band.[9]

The year continued with many activities. The final installations were made on the city's water mains in preparation for getting the filter plant on line. The new city hall in the 100 block on the north side of East Sixth Street was opened for inspection with the formal opening taking place a day or two later. The building had been purchased and remodeled for $7,900 and marked the first time that all offices and shops of the town were under the same roof.

The city and county were already underway with projects designed to help people affected by the war. In March the Huerfano County Red Cross chapter prepared the first quota of clothing for aid of suffering war refugees. The collection included clothing, layettes and blankets, and represented thousands of hours of work by the women of Walsenburg and the county. Everything had been sorted and packed into several huge boxes. It may have been the first effort on the part of area women, but it would certainly not be the last.

Even in the face of increasing war news and continued hardship from the depression, Walsenburg could find pride in new buildings. The new Fox Theatre, for example, was welcomed enthusiastically.

Emphasizing streamlined simplicity that is the keynote of present day architecture, Walsenburg's new Fox show house is indeed a typical example of "The Theatre of tomorrow" – theme of

*its architect. Plans for the building were made by Walter Simon,
leading theatre designer.*

*The towering concentric circles that compose the top of the
building are a spectacular feature. These have been stuccoed a
glittering white and contrast effectively with the speckled blue
terra vitra that has been used for the lower walls. A harmonizing
yellow mortar has been combined with the terra vitra and succeeds
in giving a colorful effect without being too bizarre.*[10]

Archie Levy offered the pool on the Levy property on West
Eighth Street to any civic or city organization who would sponsor
it in order for young people to have a place to swim. Only a small
amount of work would be needed to make it useful. A WPA project
was authorized for improvements to the Civic League Park on
First and Pinon. The bandstand and seats would be removed, and
a wading pool and tennis courts would be installed. Walsenburg
intended to continue its improvements if at all possible.

In 1941 the library board started planning for a Silver Tea, a
fund-raising event coupled with a social occasion. The board had
an unusually difficult time selecting a date since some other
activity always seemed to interfere with their plans. At last a date
was chosen and plans were laid for this activity.

The selected date was December 7, 1941.

The attack on Pearl Harbor that day, of course, changed many
plans including those for the Silver Tea. The tea was postponed
for a week and, when it was held, raised a little over $5.00 for the
library. The library board and its supporting organizations then
began to look for ways to aid the war effort.

War news quickly began to dominate the newspaper. Detailed
instructions of a program to prevent sabotage for the protection
of industries in Huerfano County were received by Sheriff Claud
Swift from the Colorado Council of Defense.

An incident soon occurred which many believed to have been
sabotage. A switch had been partially opened on the D&RG branch
line near the Turner Mine. The act was discovered by Frank Vigil,
foreman of a maintenance crew, shortly before the regular trip

over the line. Vigil reported that he rounded a curve on the line just before approaching the switch and, noticing evidence of tampering, managed to stop the small maintenance car. An investigation ensued but the matter was never solved.[11]

Many activities now began to support the war effort. High school students formed groups to buy defense stamps. Farmers and ranchers pledged to increase production of agricultural products. Citizens were asked to guard against war discussions, the war department announced that no more weather reports would be published, and residents were asked not to cut through railroad yards. The local county court was swamped with requests for birth records as many people sought birth certificates to prove their citizenship. A rationing board was soon set up to be ready as rationing of various commodities was announced.

The war hit home in Walsenburg with the following story:

> *The first evacuees from Honolulu to Walsenburg since the beginning of the war were Mrs. R. L. Noonan and 5-year-old daughter, Sheila, who arrived Saturday night following a hurried trip from the Hawaiian Island. Dr. Noonan is the son of Dr. and Mrs. G. M. Noonan of Walsenburg. Noonan is on duty with the Navy and was at Pearl Harbor but was not injured.*
>
> *Mrs. Noonan reports she was given a 24-hr. notice that she must leave the islands on Christmas day. She and her daughter boarded a transport on Dec. 26 and arrived in San Francisco on Dec. 31. Three transports were in the group making the voyage, which were convoyed by Navy vessels. Approximately 2,000 persons were carried to the mainland, including a boatload of Navy families and wounded, one Army transport and one civilian ship. Except for the anxiety and hurry to get aboard, no incident occurred during the trip, Mrs. Noonan said.*
>
> *Dr. Noonan was on duty at Pearl Harbor on Dec. 7, when the Jap attack occurred, but was uninjured. Mrs. Noonan says she saw him for the last time the day before the attack, and has had several short letters from him since.*
>
> *The Noonans sailed for Honolulu early this year, after the doctor had received a commission in the Navy medical corps. Mrs.*

Noonan will spend several days here before going to the home of her parents in Wellington, Kansas.[12]

The first casualty of the war was reported to Walsenburg soon after. Bibian B. Gonzales, son of Mr. and Mrs. Albert Gonzales, was killed in action near the Hawaiian Islands in the Japanese attack. Gonzales was a graduate of St. Mary School, class of 1940. He entered the U. S. Navy in November of that year as a Seaman, first class.[13]

This was the first loss, but it would not be the last to be reported in the Walsenburg paper in the next four years. Determined to do their part for the war, a number of efforts were launched in the town of Walsenburg. The public library board and its supporters started a Victory Book drive. Donations of books were solicited and workers to repair, pack and send them were recruited. Businesses donated supplies, and, on at least one occasion, a trucking company shipped the books free of charge. Hundreds of books were sent to bases and hospitals over the course of the war.

Bond drives were a big part of the war effort, and Walsenburg routinely surpassed the set goals with several hundred thousand dollars in war bonds purchased over the next few years.

It was quickly perceived that there would be labor shortages on the home front, especially in the agricultural areas. Both Huerfano County High School and St. Mary High School responded to this need by pledging to supply needed farm labor.

Scrap drives became a big item in the war campaign. Drives were organized to collect every sort of material that could be used. Striving to find all the metal possible, area ranchers even began digging up old appliances, vehicles and the like which had been dumped into arroyos for erosion control.

Waste cooking fats were another badly needed commodity. The loss of the Philippines, the Dutch East Indies and Malaya had cut off at least half of the nation's normal imports of fats and oils. Fats were used not only for food, but to make the tough paints and varnishes needed for planes and tanks and guns and ships.[14] At one point the city shipped 250 pounds of brass keys to aid the military.

All of these drives proved to be highly successful as the citizens turned out to do everything they possibly could to advance the nation's war efforts.

For the first time in thirty-one years, the annual St. Mary Church fair was cancelled, with the war cited as the reason.

At the same time that the town was working for the current war, the town's past occasionally intruded itself into the papers.

Old Gun Found Here Recalls Pioneer Days of County

Speaking of armaments (and who isn't these days), a relic of a bygone year has come to light in Walsenburg recently that is a real collector's item, according to experts.

The relic – the barrel and part of the stock of an old cap-and-ball rifle such as was used by pioneers in this section – was dug up recently by Joe Mestas of Loma Park, who was excavating for the basement of a new house. Altho the barrel has accumulated considerable rust during its stay in the ground, it is still in a remarkable state of preservation.

The gun is a .45-calibre or larger and was equipped with a maple stock. It bears the name of S. Hawken, former early-day St. Louis gunsmith, whose work was highly prized among pioneers and Indian-fighters of around 1850.

L. B. Sporleder, Sr. of Walsenburg, one of the county's pioneers, identified the weapon, and related that a number of the guns were in general use in the western area as late as 1860. Hawken, according to his recollection, came to Pueblo in the 1860's and continued to manufacture precision arms.

The entire gun is hand-made, and the barrel forged in octagonal shape. Precision rifling is to be observed in the barrel.

Altho it is not known who owned the gun, it no doubt was a factor in early life in this section, since a number of exciting battles and skirmishes were fought at the time this type of armament was in general use. Adding a grewsome (sic) note, two notches have been carefully filed in the barrel near the ramrod guide.

Mr. Sporleder says the cap-and-ball type of gun was an innovation in this section during the early days, and was used to replace flintlocks and smooth-bore "squirrel rifles" brought by Southerners earlier.[15]

As always the city was concerned with water, and now the first mention of an attempt to buy the Martin Lake system, also known as the Coler Ditch Company, surfaced. The council began to look at a plan to buy the system which for years had been used for irrigation in Pueblo County. Almost as quickly as the offer was made to sell the system to Walsenburg, the offer was withdrawn. This issue would be visited again and again until a final solution was reached some years later.[16]

In the meantime land around Martin Lake was used as a city park with playgrounds and other facilities. It was called Huajatolla Park, and its opening in July of 1942 was celebrated with games, cow-milking contest, music, swimming exhibition and a band concert.[17]

The war continued to dominate the news even with all of the civic activities going on. In September Mrs. And Mrs. Mike Buku of Cameron received word of the death of their son, 2nd Lt. Mike J. Buku, in action in the Aleutian Islands.

The first trial blackout in the city was deemed a success. Lights were extinguished at nine p.m. at the sound of the siren. The scrap drive continued throughout the county with members of the Walsenburg Lions Club staging a "commando raid" at Cucharas Camps, where they collected 1500 pounds of scrap metal in the form of bedsteads, old stoves and other items. It was announced that drivers who violated the 35-mile speed limit would face denial of gas rationing books.

The county-wide scrap drive kicked off on October 14 with the fire siren signaling the start. Workers would have a free breakfast before fanning out across the city and county to find scrap metal.

In March of 1943 the Walsenburg USO had a successful opening day, according to Mrs. M. E. Cowing, chairman of the ladies who were maintaining the center. Ten servicemen registered during the time the building was open. Some stopped in on their way through Walsenburg, and local men who were home on furlough also used the center.

Periodically the paper printed letters from servicemen such as the following:

> *From Cpl. Gerald Mauro, stationed somewhere in North Africa.*
>
> *Dear Editor: Haven't got much to do for a while tonite, so I thought I would drop you a few lines. I guess you are wondering how come I'm way over here in Africa. Well, I'll tell you. I got sorta bored and disgusted over in the States, so I decided to drop everything and take a little cruise. I wasn't particular as to where I was going. In fact, I didn't even know where my destination would be when I got on ship. You know how it is – just wanta go somewhere and don't care where. Well eventually I ended up in Africa, and believe it or not, it's a pretty darn nice country. I have grown so fond of travel that I just decided I would go on horsing around – at least, probably for 6 months after this old war is over.*
>
> *Seriously though I just wanted to write to tell you how grateful I am for the issues of the World-Independent that I have received. I enjoy them a lot, and I'm always looking forward to them. Hoping everything in Walsenburg is "tomatoes", I remain,*
> *Gratefully, Cpl. Gerald Mauro*[18]

Just a short time after celebrating the 60th wedding anniversary of Louis B. Sporleder, Sr. and his wife, Louisa, the community was mourning the death of Mr. Sporleder in 1943, that grand old pioneer who had influenced the life of the community in so many ways. C. O. Unfug, a member of another pioneer family, wrote this tribute.

> *The most dominating trait of his character was his love of Freedom, an unbounded, unrestricted freedom of thought and action. His ideal was the "free man" who thinks for himself and trods not in the old traveled ruts of others.*

He was eternally searching for the truth in all things. A solemn and religious regard to spiritual and eternal things was as indispensable to his thinking as life itself.

His love for knowledge drew him into a world that few in this life ever know. His library was filled with the works of the great thinkers. His knowledge was profound. The realm of his thinking spread in many directions – to philosophy, nature, the arts.

His hobby was writing. Putting his thoughts into writing was one of his recreations. He often said that he could not refrain from recording his thoughts with the hope that someone might get some benefit, some degree of inspiration from them sometime. He wrote much and some of his historical sketches are now preserved in the archives at the University of Colorado. The State Historical Society has gained much from his historical knowledge of Southern Colorado. His advanced years seemed to have little effect on his great mental capacity for remembering detail. His mind continued to be a veritable fountain of ideas up to the last. He was just putting the finishing touches in some of his writings for want of physical strength before he was compelled to retire.

Mr. Sporleder kept up a lively correspondence with many writers and scholars throughout the world. Many of these contacts were Europeans until the war prevented the exchange of such letters. All regarded him with esteem, and some made visits to Walsenburg to become personally acquainted.

His love for the Spanish Peaks was unbounded. They were as much a part of his life as food and shelter. One of his great ambitions was to awaken southern Colorado to the possibilities of the Spanish Peaks as a recreational area. He knew every trail, every spring, their plant life, their history, traditions and legends as no man did or perhaps ever will. A cordial invitation was always ready to enjoy the environments of "his" mountain.

In all his greatness he was simple. He lived simply. He often said: "A view of the world based alone upon mere observation of physical existences and experience will always be prone to failure for it will never explain the best and noblest thing a man possesses – his soul." [19]

So as Walsenburg mourned its dead in the global war, it also mourned the passing of another of its pioneers.

The city's war efforts went on without pause. In April of 1943 another large group of young men left for their army exam. A new scrap drive was planned which would include tin cans. Thousands of dollars in war bonds were bought. The Office of Price Administration required all restaurants to file a true copy of each menu, bill of fare or price list. This was to establish ceiling prices in eating places. Two jeeps were bought for the army by city school students. They had put $1,860.35 in the general "jeep" fund, according to S. M. Andrews, city superintendent.

Some of the high school students went to summer school so that they might graduate in three years and be able to help the war effort sooner.

Dr. G. R. Mallett, mayor of Walsenburg, ordered a halt to all forms of gambling in town including the operation of slot machines. Something like 160 slot machines were removed from places of business and all such places were warned to stop all forms of gambling.

> *"It is my purpose in this matter to keep the new ruling in effect for the balance of my term in office," Dr. Mallett said today. "With present conditions with relation to juvenile delinquency at a peak and with criticism directed toward the community from nearby Army posts, no other action could be taken than to order all forms of gambling out."* [20]

The army gave thanks for the two jeeps bought by the fund-raising of city students and sent Pfc. Elmer Stillwell, of the 254th infantry company stationed at Camp Carson, to give jeep rides to students. Some 300 to 400 boys and girls and their teachers were given a thrill by being driven around town in a jeep, a new type of vehicle at the time.[21] The deaths of Macaques (Max) Vigil and Pedro Maes in North Africa were reported. Mrs. Lillian Roybal was doing her share in the war effort by working in an aircraft factory in California, while her husband, Rudy Roybal, served in the Marine Corps.

There were still lingering effects of the depression and one of these showed itself in nutrition problems for school children. The efforts of a defense group resulted in the Penny Milk program through which 916,023 half-pint bottles of milk were served to area children in the preceding school season.

> *An outstanding contribution to the recreation facilities of Huerfano County was made Sunday by Milton Utt of La Veta, prominent rancher, when he deeded a 40-acre tract of beach and recreational land adjoining Martin Lake to the HCAND (Huerfano County Association for National Defense) for future development at Huajatolla Park. Although the park has been under development during the past two years, thru an agreement with Utt, the action in deeding the land to the Association was his contribution to the continuing program in the county.*[22]

Huajatolla Park had a grand opening July 4 with races and contests for all ages, a miniature train for youngsters and a short patriotic program at seven o'clock. Several thousand people attended the opening, thus proving that the residents of the town and county were not so focused on the war that they could not take time out for recreation.

Two new reservoirs, the Cucharas and Bradford, were sold to the Huerfano Valley Ditch and Reservoir Company. This addition to the water rights of the county was of enormous importance. Both were east of the city and the purchase added more than 62,000 acre feet of water to the city's supply.

Crops in the area were saved when a weeks' long drought ended with nearly two inches of rain in August, but even the end of the drought pales beside the huge headline on the paper of Sept. 9, 1943.

Italy Quits!

Doubtless this first sign that the war would someday end brought new hope and renewed effort in Walsenburg as well as across the nation that the tide had definitely turned and that the United States and its allies would ultimately be victorious.

Many activities were carried on to raise money for the war effort, but one event deserves mention.

Huge Turnip Brings $2,000 At Auction

A record-breaking turnip, 23 inches in circumference, today brought a total of $2,000 in war bonds at an auction held at the regular Rotary luncheon this noon. Successful bidder was John Kirkpatrick of the Walsenburg Mercantile company.

The turnip, one of the largest ever seen in this locality, was raised in a Victory garden at Cucharas Camps, by L. H. Kirkpatrick, and was placed on the block at the club meeting to help the current Third War Loan campaign.

The bidding started at $100, but reached the $2,000 figure in very short order. Some are suggesting that there was some collusion in the Kirkpatrick clan, but the truth is that probably there is a bit of friendly rivalry between the brothers.[23]

While the Italians may have quit the war, the German army had not, and the battles in Italy went on. Two Huerfano County men were reported to be in the thick of the fighting in the battle for Salerno on the Italian mainland. Tech. Sgt. Raymond M. Harrison, son of Mr. and Mrs. Jack Harrison of Walsenburg, and Sgt. John Ladurini of Toltec, son of Mrs. Ida Ladurini, were both involved in the battle in which the German army was ultimately forced back.

The exploit inspired two Walsenburg residents, A. S. Lenzini and Frank S. Mauro, to pledge themselves to buy a $25 bond for every enemy soldier killed in that action.

Crime did not leave Walsenburg alone during the war. In October law enforcement officers found themselves investigating the fatal stabbing of William Ugolini at the hands of Esequiel Baca in front of a West Seventh Street tavern. Following an inquest, Baca was ordered held for trial in the killing.

War news of all sorts filled the newspapers. 2nd Lt. Malcolm J. MacDonald, son of Mr. and Mrs. Malcolm J. MacDonald, Sr., was officially listed as a prisoner of war in Germany. Mildred Garbiso was listed as the area's first member of the Women's Army Air Corps. She left for training in Denver. Five members of the Marck family were in service. Four sons and one daughter of Mr. and Mrs. Pio Marck of Walsenburg were making their contribution to the war effort. The five were Adolph, Albert, Ruth, Ernest and Louis.

More local citizens entered service. Aviation Cadet Richard J. Ridge, son of Mr. and Mrs. Charles V. Ridge, completed basic flying training at the Pecos Army Air Field and went on into advanced training. Miss Theresa Dissler was accepted for service in the WAVES, the Navy women's auxiliary.

Esequiel Baca was tried and convicted of the slaying of William Ugolini. The jury deliberated for only one hour, and Baca's attorney announced that they would file for a new trial.

A moment of triumph was celebrated by the Methodist Church with a service to mark the paying off of all church debt. The Rev. Wilbur E. Hammaker of Denver, bishop of the church, preached the dedicatory service. The pastor, Rev. C. H. Hatfield, and the church members had been engaged for many years in paying off the debt incurred with the building of the red brick church just as the Great Depression struck.

St. Mary Church members mourned the death of their priest, the Very Rev. R. L. Newell, who died in a car accident. The Rev. Howard L. Delaney was named to succeed him.

By this time the activity in coal mines had slowed down from its heyday in the early part of the century, but work still continued, sometimes with unusual results as in the following story

Discovery of a loaded pit car in an abandoned section of the old Walsen mine, which has been loaded and sitting there for the past 55 years, was discovered Saturday by workmen in the Cameron mine when they cut thru into the old workings, it was announced today by Charles McBrayer, superintendent of Cameron.

The car was found by Gaetano Savio, mine foreman, and George Race, fireboss, after workmen had cut into the old room. According to the best available information, the car was loaded and left there in 1889, when the Walsen mine was operating.

The cut-thru was made from the Cameron side. At present, the car cannot be removed until more excavation is done, but it is planned that the car will be removed intact and placed on display.[24]

An annual event from the high school had been the El Fandango performance by members of the Spanish Club. The students in the group performed dances of Mexico and New Mexico and also offered songs and skits. In 1944 the sponsorship of the club was assumed by Miss Martha King, a member of the distinguished King family of Gardner. She remained as the sponsor long after she became the bride of George Spock, and the activity flourished under her guidance.

In 1944 the scene of the entertainment took place in the fictional Mendoza family's patio, where members of the family were entertaining a goodwill ambassador from the United States. The dances included *Chiapenecas*, *La Varsovianna*, *La Cuna*, *El Jarabe*, and popular Spanish songs such as *"Farolito"*, *"Adelita"*, and *"Besame Mucho"*.[25]

For many years the Spanish Club entertainment was an extremely popular event in Southern Colorado. The inter-city bus from Pueblo would stop at Huerfano County High School to drop off passengers who had come to see El Fandango. Audiences of 1,000 were not uncommon.

Unfortunately, over the next few decades, El Fandango declined due to fewer students who wanted to commit themselves to learning to dance, but in recent years the program has been enjoying a revival under the leadership of Gretchen Sporleder Orr and Mary Jo Micek Tesitor.

Soon the attention of the citizens of Walsenburg and the rest of the nation turned to D-Day, the invasion of Normandy by Allied Forces, and the beginning of the end of the European war. The invasion was announced in the *World Independent* with a banner headline and several stories including maps and pictures detailing the plans of the campaign.

While the attention of the town was focused on the war, the workers at Cameron Mine were working on their antique coal car.

Old Pit Car Taken from Mine Tuesday

A memento of the past – a loaded pit car abandoned in one of the fartherest extensions of the old Walsen mine 55 years ago – was brought to the surface by workmen at the Cameron mine yesterday.

Workmen, led by Supt. J. L. McBrayer and Mine Foreman Gaetano Savio, placed the car on new tracks and brought it out at 4 o'clock yesterday afternoon. A party of others made the trip into the mine – including Dep. State Coal Mine Inspector Myron D. Williams, E. G. Turner, Robert Hepplewhite, Richard B. Morris and James Madison of the World-Independent, Ray Lees and Ralph Taylor of the Pueblo Star-Journal and Chieftain staff, Bob McAlister, CF&I mine inspector and various members of the mine staff.

It is not definitely known why the car was left in that section or who was working in the place at that time. Entry to the area was made from the south, although the Walsen workings drove in from the northeast.

No difficulty was encountered in removing the car and its load of coal. Although the metal wheels and reinforcements were rusted somewhat and the coal discolored by water action, it was in sound condition and now rests on the Cameron tipple. No check was found on the car.[26]

During its most productive years, the Walsen mine had 157 miles of underground tunnels, according to a map which hangs in the Walsenburg Mining Museum. Such a large number of tunnels may make it easier to understand how a fully loaded coal car could simply be overlooked. The tipple was the elevated structure at the opening of the mine where coal cars were tipped or dumped before returning to the mine. The check which would normally be found on a loaded car referred to the round, numbered disc which identified the miner who had loaded the car and to whose account the weight of the coal should be entered.

A recent article in **True Sport Magazine** about Ford Frick, the president of the National Baseball League, prompted school superintendent S. M. Andrews to discuss Frick's stay in Walsenburg with the **World Independent**. Frick, who returned to Walsenburg for visits from time to time, was the son-in-law of Mr. and Mrs. F. E. Cowing. His wife was the former Eleanor Cowing.

Andrews reported that he had become acquainted with the Frick family of Brimfield, Indiana, when he was principal of the town school. He boarded at the Jacob Frick home when young Ford was in the third grade. After Andrews became superintendent of the high school in Walsenburg, Frick wanted a job. Andrews hired him for the commercial department.

Frick instructed the first course in journalistic writing ever to be taught here. C. O. Unfug, then publisher of the **World Independent**, was one of his students. Later Frick moved to Colorado Springs where he taught in the public schools and at Colorado College. He next joined the staff of a Colorado Springs paper where he covered sports and general assignments.

Andrews remembers that Frick gained national acclaim during this period for an eye-witness account of the Pueblo flood of 1921. The entire city was inundated and completely cut off from the outside world, but Frick joined with a barnstorming flyer of the Springs and the two flew over the flood. This is believed to have been the first eye-witness account of this type written after visiting the scene by air and Frick's story was carried in virtually every paper in the nation. Shortly thereafter Arthur Brisbane, then editor of the New York American, realizing Frick's talent, offered him a position on that paper, and later he joined the sports staff of the New York Evening Journal.[27]

More war casualties among Walsenburg and Huerfano County men were reported. Pfc. Tom M. Dunich died of wounds received on Saipan Island. William Zanon was killed in a plane crash, and Ralph Valdez was wounded in Marine action.

A Walsenburg connection to the plight of Jews in Germany was revealed in the following story about the 1944 high school summer graduation.

Salutatorian of HCHS Class is a Refugee from Germany

A young refugee from German brutality in East Prussia will be salutatorian of the graduating class of the summer session at Huerfano County High School at commencement ceremonies to be held tomorrow evening in the auditorium of the school.

The salutatorian is Miss Lee Bain, 17, foster-daughter of Mr. and Mrs. Joe Bain who came to this country in 1936 as a refugee. Her removal from Prussia came thru the efforts of a Jewish relief society. In that year, she was 9 years old; she knew not a word of English and had never been far from her home.

She was sent to a home in Denver along with many others, and thru the good efforts of the relief organizations, all the youngsters were cared for until foster-homes could be found. Mrs. and Mrs. Bain took the child on the basis of her picture, and brought her into their home here. She entered Washington school and rapidly learned the language and the customs of the Americans. She has been active in school affairs and extra-curricular activities and is an accomplished public speaker.

Now Miss Bain, formerly Anniza Kreshevsky, is graduating with her class with her American classmates. She will enter Baylor University in the fall. Thru the intervening years, no word has been received from her parents or other members of her family.[28]

Two items reveal the war news from Europe. Helen Unfug, well-known local singer, was said to be with a USO show in France. Paris had been freed from Nazi control, and General Omar Bradley had ordered armored equipment into the city. Things were looking up in the war effort.

Back in Walsenburg, members of the St. Mary parish undertook two major projects. They opened a campaign to clear the parish of all debt, a matter of $50,000, before the jubilee observance. Secondly, the women of the parish joined a nationwide effort to gather collections of old but usable clothing to be shipped to the European liberated nations.

A great day occurred for education in Walsenburg in early October of 1944. The final bonds for the red brick Huerfano County High School were paid. The entire bond of $90,000 was cleared when the members of the HCHS committee voted to pay the final $6,000 to bond-holders. The original issue of the $90,000 in bonds was made October 1, 1919, following a special election in June of that year.[30]

A newly printed book made headlines at this time. As a feature of the Jubilee Anniversary of St. Mary Parish, the Rev. Howard Delaney had written a book entitled *All Our Yesterdays*. This small book contained much information not only about the Catholic parish but also about the general history of the town and county. Copies were distributed to members at the climax of the celebration.[31]

Although Walsenburg was not many years from the 90th birthday of its founding, there were still members of the community who had been part of the turbulent years of the area. The death of one such person was reported in November.

Famed Law Enforcement Officer Dies
Silverio (Shorty) Martinez dies of Heart Attack

Huerfano county residents were today mourning the passing of Silverio (Shorty) Martinez, pioneer enforcement officer in this area, and one of the most colorful figures in recent police annals, who died suddenly of a heart attack at noon Saturday.

The famed officer, noted for his 6 foot 6 inch height and for his reputation of utter fearlessness had been closely identified with local law enforcement for the past 40 years serving many years as deputy and under sheriff under both Harry J. Capps and Jeff Farr and many terms as a member of the Walsenburg department.

He went thru some of the most trying times in the history of the county, including the days of the strikes and during the time when desperados preyed on citizens in this locality. It is said that he had *a reputation of always "getting his man." One of his outstanding achievements was the solving of the $5,000 Oakview mail robbery of 1922, bringing the thieves to justice nearly two years after the robbery was committed.*

Martinez entered the law-enforcement profession in 1900 and held various positions in the city and county until a few months ago when he retired from the city force.

He was born July 30, 1873 in Walsenburg and was a continuous resident of this city.[29]

Had there still been two newspapers in Walsenburg at the time of Martinez's death, the stories about him might have been quite different. As one of Jeff Farr's crew, Martinez was feared by many, especially among the mining families. He was noted not only for his actual height but also for his penchant for wearing high-heeled cowboy boots and unusually tall hats to increase his fearsome size even more.

The deaths of more young men were reported from time to time including S-Sgt. George Bechaver, Steve J. Glinsky, former city treasurer, and Pvt. John Archuleta. The family of Levio Amidei finally received word that he had been a prisoner of the Japanese since the battle of Corregidor.

The town and county continued to experience labor shortages due to the war and the schools continued to help out as much as possible.

Local School Children Go to Work to Help Turkey Harvest

As a result of a special appeal to students thru the school yesterday, the picking sheds in Loma Park are filled with workers today – most of them boys and girls up to 15 years of age. These, along with a few adults, are picking the thousands of turkeys ready for markets, and it is anticipated that the entire crop will be on its way this week.

Prior to the school appeal, fear was expressed that not enough workers could be found for the huge task, but officials of the city schools, St. Mary school and HCHS cooperated in releasing the youngsters.

More than 100 are on duty today, and the feathers are really flying, according to Felo Martinez, manager of the local War Manpower commission. It is estimated that some 10,000 birds will be included in the shipments.[30]

Clearly Walsenburg never shirked its wartime duty to help out. Bond drives continued to bring in money, young men continued to fight, and school children were willing to pick turkeys. What more could be asked of a small town?

While most of the men who served during the war did their duty without any outstanding heroics, one Huerfano County man was identified as a bona fide war hero. The paper reported the following exploit:

Huerfano County Man is Identified as War Hero

A Huerfano county man, Pfc. Felix Mestas, Jr. who was killed in action on Sept. 29, has been identified as one of the outstanding heroes so far in the Italian battle, according to information released yesterday.

Pfc. Mestas is the son of Mr. and Mrs. Felix, B. Mestas, Sr. of La Veta. Although his death was reported several weeks ago, details were not released until after Combat Correspondent Gerald Root of Lansing, Mich., dug up the information from friends of the man.

Mestas was a Browning automatic rifleman in the 350th regiment, now known as the "Battle Mountain" regiment, and it was in the Battle of Battle Mountain that Pfc. Mestas distinguished himself by killing 24 Nazis with the rifle and accounting for two more with hand grenades, according to reports.

Members of the battalion took up positions on the mountain two days before the attack, and stood off a number of counterattacks on Sept. 29. Finally the Nazis attacked in force, and the men realized they would have to retreat since ammunition was running low.

Peck said Mestas insisted he leave first, and on looking back, saw the former Huerfano county man standing in full range of the enemy, shooting his heavy rifle from the hip and later ac-

counted for two more with hand grenades. Peck and two other riflemen were the only survivors of the squad.[31]

Private First-Class Mestas was later honored by having a mountain peak, formerly called Baldy Peak, just off Highway 160 on La Veta Pass, named for him.

In April the first act was played in what was to become Walsenburg's most celebrated political dispute since the days of Sheriff Jeff Farr. In the race for mayor of the city, Joe Mosco, Jr. defeated James B. Dick, Jr. by one vote, according to unofficial returns. The official vote was conducted on Friday, and the canvassing board found errors, but no fraud, in the vote. The official count was therefore deferred until the election laws could be checked. On April 9 the vote was declared to be a tie with each candidate having 636 votes.

> *Wide public interest is being manifested in the method by which the city election will be decided between the mayoralty candidates, according to information gathered by the World-Independent today. One faction which appears to have considerable support suggests that the matter be decided by the toss of a coin. This group suggests a public meeting be called to which admission is charged to watch the coin-toss. Proceeds would be placed in a fund to buy a sidewalk cleaner or street-sweeper or some other municipal benefit. Others suggest that both serve alternately, one in the morning and one in the afternoon; others are urging the candidates to split the term. One suggests no contest be declared leaving the present mayor Herman F. Mazzone in the chair.*[32]

On April 19 the matter of who would be the mayor was resumed with the following report from the local paper:

> *Fast plays give city four mayors in half an hour. In a breath-taking quadruple play believed to be unmatched in Walsenburg municipal circles, the community had four mayors in the space of less than thirty minutes last night as members of the retiring council and those elected to the new council met to accomplish the*

change in administration. The play, engineered with dispatch and precision, saw the mayoralty chair pass from Mazzone to Dick to Benine to Mosco almost so fast that the many spectators had difficulty in following the procedure.

The meeting started with members of the old council occupying the chairs for the purpose of completing final business before retiring. At the close of the business session, Dr. C. A. Brunelli introduced a resolution calling for the breaking of the tie by means of a lot; the measure was seconded by James Phipps and was passed 5 to 1. Drawing was arranged by placing the names of the two candidates in capsules which were placed in a hat. Justice of the Peace Fred I. Barron drew the winning capsule which contained the name of James B. Dick, Jr. Dick then was elected by the retiring council. Mazzone swore everybody in.

Immediately after Dick took the chair and said he felt the election had been conducted in the American way and pledged himself to non-political administration. After a lot of other commotion, new resolutions were introduced with the upshot being that Mosco became mayor.[33]

So, for the time being, Joe Mosco, Jr. became mayor of Walsenburg. The paper is unclear about the brief time when a Mr. Benine was mayor, but perhaps that is understandable in such a confused situation. The matter seemed settled at the time, but it was by no means over as subsequent actions proved.

For the moment Walsenburg was able to turn its attention from local politics to the impending end of the long, costly World War II.

Clothing was collected – 8,286 pounds of it – to be shipped overseas for those who had lost everything in the war.

The war in Europe ended in May, and the mayor proclaimed V-E day in Walsenburg. Mr. and Mrs. Leonzo J. Martinez welcomed a new daughter and named her Victoria Elaine in honor of V-E Day.

The release of German POW Malcolm MacDonald was announced, and each paper carried the names of other area men who were released after the end of fighting in Europe.

Suits were filed in the still-simmering matter of who the mayor might be, and the legal matters were to be decided by Judge David M. Ralston in county district court. Several days after the court hearing, the judge decided the suit in favor of Joe Mosco, Jr.

In August the atomic bombs were dropped on the Japanese cities of Hiroshima and Nagasaki, and all the world knew that the war would soon be over.

The end was announced in Walsenburg with a five-inch headline —

JAPS FOLD!

Changes came swiftly in the lives of people. Wartime controls were cut, and many rationed items would soon be on the free list. But a new group of draftees reported to Denver for physicals. Not everything would change overnight.

The ongoing mayoral dispute would now be heard by the Colorado Supreme Court due to an appeal by James Dick, Jr.

A local man, Levio Amidei, arrived home after three years spent as a prisoner of the Japanese. He had been captured at the fall of the island of Corregidor. As a prisoner, Amidei had been sent to Japan from the Philippines, and he told of the conditions in the camps. His family received three postcards and three letters from him during the years of his captivity, but he received more than 45 letters from his family. He told of his joy when American forces liberated the camps.

With the end of the war, the city was able once again to turn most of its attention to civic matters. The mill levy was raised to provide funds needed for maintenance, to employ an extra policeman, and to establish a pound for stray animals. Several new doctors set up practice in Walsenburg. Businesses began to expand with Pritchard Lumber Co. adding a new warehouse, Santi Motor Company had a new site on North Main Street, the O'Byrne Hardware Co. planned extensive remodeling and Fashion Mart installed several new display cabinets. Pictou Mine was set to open within sixty days while Cameron Mine would soon shut down. Walsenburg was returning to normal.

The Colorado Supreme Court handed down its decision in the matter of the mayor of Walsenburg. Colorado's Supremes decided that James B. Dick, Jr. was the mayor and Joe Mosco, Jr. was forced to step down.

Efforts to secure a hospital for the city began, and land was leased for an airport. The county was expected to receive $200,000 for Highway 69 from Walsenburg to Gardner and beyond. Ralph Levy, son of Alexander and Lillie Levy, was named police chief for the city.

The Coler Ditch Reservoir Co. proposed to sell Martin and Horseshoe Lakes to Walsenburg. No decision was reached at first, but the water would be used for recreational purposes, for domestic water use and to supply industries which might locate in the county. About 4,600 acre feet of water would be added to the city's water supply.

In 1948 plans were made to honor Dr. Walter S. Chapman for his 50 years of service to the area. A testimonial dinner would be held at the Community House. Dr. Chapman came to Huerfano County in 1900. He married Stella Alethea Keys, who was a teacher at Rouse. Two children, Walter and Francis, were born to the couple. Dr. Chapman served in the 7th Cavalry in the Spanish-American War. He served as coroner during the coal strike and continued his practice.

At the time of the dinner honoring him, Dr. Chapman was seventy-six. He lived well into his 90s and continued his practice throughout this time. Many residents of Walsenburg remember being treated by him, and there are many anecdotes which testify to his competence as a physician.

The Coler Ditch system dropped its original asking price of $65,000 for Martin and Horseshoe Lakes to $50,000 and on October 7, 1948, the city of Walsenburg agreed to buy them. These purchases greatly expanded the water supplies of the city and continue to do so to this day. In more recent years the two lakes and the surrounding territory have been turned into

Lathrop State Park, but the city leases the two lakes to the state for the recreational uses of the park and continues to use the water for domestic purposes.

An early day pioneer, F. E. Cowing, gave an interview to the paper in 1948 and related many interesting bits of Walsenburg history. Mr. Cowing had lived in the county for 69 years.

He was born in Buffalo, New York, in March, 1856, and came to Walsenburg in 1870 with two schoolmates. He had a large flock of sheep in the Spanish Peaks area and in 1882 became the deputy county clerk. He and a partner, L. C. DeCamp, opened a general store in Gardner. He married Susan Evans in Cincinnati, Ohio, in 1883, and the couple built a home with the first bay window in Gardner.

In 1889, they moved to Walsenburg and opened a general store on the site of the present Unfug-Peet Mortuary, until the business block built by Fred Walsen was completed. In September, Cowing moved his general store to the present site of the Star Grocery and remained in business until he retired in 1919.

Not more than two dozen American families lived here at that time. The block had the Cowing store and two residences – Fred Walsen and Charles Unfug. Where Krier's store now stands was a long adobe building which housed the court house.

Despite the sparsely populated community, dancing was the favorite recreation. These dances were held in the old Mazzone hall. Upon entering the hall, the ladies would sit on one side and the men on the other. Upon being asked to dance, the ladies carefully would lay aside their mantillas or shawls which would be replaced by the gentleman upon finishing the dance. Shawls were worn instead of hats and the stores carried a large supply of shawls along with their staple groceries.

Wagons were the principal means of transportation and it was nearly a daily occurrence to see a runaway team going thru the town. Great caravans of horses met at the old Unfug Bros. Store to make their trips to the nearby coal mines which had begun operation.

One of the unforgettable incidents was the time upon visiting with Mr. T. L. Creasy at a dance hall and gambling house owned by Bob Ford, Mr. Cowing was mistaken for Frank James, brother of Jesse James who was killed two years before by Ford. He was identified before any gun play took place. The well-know "Soapy" Smith was a character often seen on the streets.

One of the Cowing daughters, Eleanor, married Ford Frick.[34]

The **World Independent** also reported on the building of the jail which now houses the Walsenburg Mining Museum. Until the new construction, the jail had been a small, one-room building built in 1878. Since it was considered unfit for further use, the grand jury meeting in 1896 agreed that a new one should be built.

Within two months the county commissioners were discussing the matter seriously. Bids were called for since it was desired to get the new jail built before winter set in.

The contract for the stone and woodwork building was granted on June 17, 1896, to George Keyes of Pueblo for $5,210, and the work of the cells and steel construction was contracted to the Diebold Safe and Lock Co. of Canton, Ohio, for $4,685. This made the total proposed cost for the jail only $9,895.

Work began almost immediately when twenty men began to lay the stone foundation. By September the steel for the inside arrived, and the stone masons finished their work on October 2.[35]

The description of the interior of the jail is quite similar to its current configuration. The building served as the Huerfano County Jail until 1989 when it, too, was deemed unfit to hold prisoners, and the county came up with the financing to construct the modern jail across the street from the venerable old structure. In 1994 the county commissioners permitted the Huerfano County Historical Society to use the lower part of the jail for the Walsenburg Mining Museum, a use that continues to the present time.

The closing year of the tumultuous decade of the 1940s saw various changes in the configuration of Walsenburg and county activities. The public library moved to the top floor of the old

C.O.D. grocery since the Elks wanted their space back. The purchase of Martin and Horseshoe Lakes was finally completed, and the city council approved an ordinance authorizing the issuance of $100,000 worth of bonds to buy them and improve them. Talk began about consolidation of the many small schools into as few districts as possible.

The Spanish Club was invited to present El Fandango in the Denver Auditorium in July. Miss Martha King was the director of the popular dance program.

Work was at last underway in building an airport building. After many years of planning an airport here, there, and everywhere in the county, a site four miles north of the city and one mile east of the highway had been selected.

In November the county school reorganization plan was finally approved. There would be three school districts – Walsenburg, Gardner and La Veta. Nothing has changed in this plan except that Gardner became part of the Huerfano Re-1 School District in 1959, while La Veta is Huerfano Re-2.

With these events the decade that had begun in depression, and continued through a world war, which saw the deaths of many city and county young men, drew to a close. Future years would see Walsenburg as a less eventful but still vibrant small town between the mountains on the west and the sprawling plains on the east. Like other small towns, Walsenburg would continue to thrive.

Chapter Eleven

TOWARD THE END OF THE CENTURY

Following the turbulence of the war years, Walsenburg, like all other small towns in the nation, settled into a quieter existence. The usual problems occupied city government – obtaining more water rights and improving the delivery system to the town. The area of the town grew with the annexation of Loma Park, an area on the west side of town, which had once had railroad lines, a turkey processing plant and homes. About one hundred residents were added to the town with this annexation.

War loomed again with the coming of the Korean crisis, but while this war would affect the area and put many young men into harm's way again, it did not have the total impact of the worldwide war. The first member of the organized reserves to be called from Walsenburg to serve in the new conflict was Gerald Ariano. Soon after that five county men were called in the draft: Dino D. Avellani, Edward Huerta, Robert Charles Colnar, August Mike Amedei and Peter John Condor. In Korea the Marines stormed ashore on two coasts.[1]

In 1952 Miss Ernestine Guerrero had been appointed postmaster of Walsenburg to replace George Niebuhr, who had retired. Now, however, the matter of the postmaster examination came into play and two veterans, James J. Tesitor and Ernest P. Bellotti, came in ahead of Miss Guerrero on the test. Tesitor had ten veterans preference points and Bellotti had five, which would have placed both of them ahead of her, but, in addition, they had scored higher on the test than she had. Protests were lodged on her behalf, but the test scores won out with the post office department, and James J. Tesitor became the postmaster. He would continue in this position for twenty-eight years.[2]

Captain Raymond Waski, a St. Mary graduate, came home for a four-day furlough. He had entered the Air Force in 1942, was discharged in 1946 and recalled in 1948. He spent the next three years in the Far East. "People here just don't know what it's like there," said the veteran of 135 missions against the Communists. "I think there is a natural tendency to take that war lightly and it shouldn't be treated that way." Of the nineteen original pilots in his flying squadron when the outbreak first occurred, Waski said he was the only one alive now.[3]

For many years the education of children in Walsenburg and Huerfano County had been widely spread with children of Gardner and the outlying coal camps having their own schools. In town the elementary schools and Huerfano County High school had separate administrations and school boards.

The state now mandated the reorganization of the county schools and a committee was chosen to deal with the matter. The committee members were James Phipps, Frank Vanotti, Fred Paddock, Harry Capps, E. B. Tatman, Harry Willis and George Robert Pepper. Alternates were Arthur Benine, Frank Brunelli, Ralph Read, Mrs. Cora Hribar, Earlin Busch, Phil Miles and Joe Waggoner.

In addition to the work of this committee, the decision was made in Walsenburg to close the venerable Seventh Street School. The red brick building was built about 1907 for about $7,000. It had been used for nearly half a century for first and second grade children. As many as 3,000 children may have studied there.[4]

Coal mining continued to exist and also to decline in the county. In early 1955 Huerfano mines employed eighty-six men and saw 7,769 tons of coal brought to the surface. Accidents continued to kill miners, but not on the scale they had previously seen.[5]

The summer of 1955 saw great excitement in the city and county with the promise of a huge $11 million industry planned. A firm called Cotarco leased 600 acres of city-owned land near La Veta in a 99-year lease to be used for its own and other industrial plants. Cotarco's plans were for a coal carbonization process, and a fertilizer plant was planned to use the gas which the carbonization process would produce.[6]

A small acreage owned by a La Veta man was included in the area desired by the company. This parcel was obtained by the city by trading a larger acreage to the land-owner in exchange for his bit of land.[7]

> *Carbonization is the driving out of volatile matter by the application of heat. The volatile matter in coal begins to come off at around 400 degrees C. and continues to be removed up to 1,000 degrees C. at which temperature all but 1 to 2 percent of the volatile matter has been removed.*
>
> *The devolatilized residue is called coke, if it is of a firm consistency and almost completely devolatilized.*
>
> *However, when the carbonization is stopped at 500 to 700 degrees C., the residue containing some 10 to 25 percent of volatile matter is likely to be friable and rather soft. This residue is called char.*[8]

The company planned to stock 500,000 tons of coal, which was said to be enough for 100 days of operation. Figures representing millions of dollars were mentioned that would be spent for construction, sales and advertising, labor, maintenance and utilities. It seemed that this would be the biggest thing ever to happen to Huerfano County. Newspaper articles referred to the county as the next big industrial area for the state.

Big plans were made for the ground-breaking for the firm. The governor was expected to attend. The paper issued a large edition filled with articles about Cotarco's coal carbonization process and with many ads from businesses and organizations welcoming the new industry.

Dignitaries, escorted by the state highway patrol, began arriving in Walsenburg at 12:30 p.m. on June 18. A luncheon catered by Shosky's Café was held at the Elks Hall, and speeches by John Dinise, president of the Huerfano County Chamber of Commerce, Mayor George M. Turner of Walsenburg and Mayor Paul Gilbert of La Veta were heard.

A motorcade formed at 2:30 p.m. for the trip to the 600-acre tract near La Veta which had been leased to the company. The national anthem opened the ceremony, followed by the invocation by the Very Rev. Howard L. Delaney. Addresses of welcome were made by locals, and these were followed by Gov. Edwin C. Johnson, and John Gordon, vice president and director of Cotarco, used their shovels to break ground for the new industry. Several other speeches followed the groundbreaking, and then the group returned to Walsenburg where they were entertained with cocktails at the Dallafior Bar and, later, with a smorgasbord dinner at the Community Center.[9]

A few months passed and anticipation built again for Cotarco, and its plans with the purposed issuance of "anticipation bonds" to finance the construction of the plants. John Gordon, managing director of Cotarco and vice president of Umbaugh Chemicals, Inc., stated that if these initial warrants were bid in and purchased, then plans and specifications for the initial construction would immediately be advertised by the city in agreement with the two firms. Construction would actually begin very soon.[10]

There may have already been some concern about the viability of this project when the council ratified ordinances permitting the city to issue up to $21.6 million in anticipation warrants for the construction and equipping of plants for the two companies under the terms of Senate Bill 313. The council also approved 99-year leases to the companies of the plants to be constructed with funds derived by the sale of the warrants. Both of these measures passed by a vote of only five to three.[11]

The excitement generated by this industrial promise continued. Ray Umbaugh promised that their plans would likely be increased due to a greater market than they had anticipated. Hiring would begin soon with as many as 500 men to be hired for the construction process and about 217 permanent employees when the plant was ready. Umbaugh told the council that a soil-testing laboratory would be set up immediately. When asked what "immediately" meant, he replied "in about a month."

A railway spur, miles of roadway, two artesian wells, storage tanks, a cooling tower, trucks and automobiles were among the miscellaneous items for which Walsenburg was asking bids. Specifications called for the Cotarco coal carbonization plant to produce low temperature char, fuel gas and other products.[12]

The first real sign of trouble appeared with a question about whether the city warrants were constitutional. Sen. Sam Taylor, who represented the two companies and who had been involved with the planning from the beginning, assured the town that the warrants were constitutional. The senate bill on which they were based had been sponsored by Gov. Edwin C. Johnson and overwhelmingly supported by the legislature. It was intended to allow poor sections of the state the opportunity to attract industry to move in and take advantage of the tax-exemption benefits which the law allowed.

In February the city council chose to amend the warrant ordinances to change the manner or order of retirement of the warrants. This postponed the bidding of them until February 21.[13]

Umbaugh now filed a test suit charging that attacks had made bidders withdraw. The suit named the City of Walsenburg and Attorney General Duke Dunbar as co-defendants. It asked for a "judgment or decree" not only on the constitutionality of Sen. Bill 313 but on the validity of the leases entered into by Umbaugh and the City of Walsenburg.[14]

While all the legal action was going on, John Gordon told the Chamber of Commerce that Umbaugh-Cotarco was "here to stay." The lawsuit would probably postpone the bidding indefinitely, and many questions were now being asked about the whole project.

In May the city was given the right to lease the Umbaugh and Cotarco tracts for crops. The lawsuit was to test the constitutionality of Sen. Bill 313 and the legality of the leases with the city which were based on the bill.[15]

This was apparently the beginning of the end for this much-anticipated industrial project. The land-owner who had traded his land to the city for a larger acreage nearby was eventually able to

246 ◆ Walsenburg – <small>CROSSROADS TOWN</small>

profit from his trade in selling off parts of it, but this person appears to be the only one who benefitted from this grandiose plan. At the time of the plans, only three coal mines were still operating in the county, and they would have been unable to provide the vast amounts of coal needed for the operation. No plants were ever built, and the highly anticipated jobs never materialized.

Ordinary life must go on even in view of the excitement of a new industry, and the community was always interested in school news. In the midst of all of the excitement about the Cotarco project, school superintendent Merle V. Chase resigned to take a position in Longmont. The board immediately began looking for a replacement. They quickly settled on John Mall, who was then principal of Washington School, thus beginning Mall's twenty-five years in that position.[16]

In September of 1955 the city believed it had reached an amicable settlement with the Utt brothers of La Veta over rights involving Martin and Horseshoe lakes, parts of which were owned by the two brothers. With the agreement, the city gained full ownership to the water of the two lakes, the Coler Seepage Reservoir, the water in the Coler Ditch, plus the land involved around them.[17]

Unfortunately this proved to be not quite as definitive as the city had hoped. In later times further litigation was necessary with the Utts before the ownership of this vital water was finally settled.

Floyd Jeter reached an agreement on the leasing of a radio tower and planned to build a small building to house his radio station. Jeter and his station continued to serve the community for years.[18]

One of the oldest commercial firms in Walsenburg, the Sporleder Selling Company, which had been operating under that name since 1908, was broken into three parts in June. The feed department was sold to C. S. Sporleder, Jr. who would continue at the same location under the name of "Sig Sporleder Feeds." The grocery department became the property of A. R. Pazar, John F. Pazar and A. R. Benine, who operated it as The Wholesale Food

Company. The Sporleder Selling Co. continued with investments and securities under the management of C. S. Sporleder, Sr.[19]

Another major change in the appearance of the downtown area began when James Benine, owner of the Black and White grocery, then located in the old O'Byrne hardware building at the southwest corner of Main and Seventh, purchased the Mazzone building. This structure at the corner of Main and Sixth Streets had once been the famed Mazzone Saloon and Opera House. Benine's plans for the building included removing the upper floor, where the auditorium was located, and remodeling the lower floor to house the Black and White Grocery.[20]

For some time discussions about the reorganization of the various school districts throughout the county had been going on, and a plan was finally agreed upon. The plan called for the consolidation of the twenty-six school districts into two. The La Veta district would be called Huerfano Re-2 and Walsenburg and the rest of the county would be Huerfano Re-1. The Re stood for Reorganized.

Huerfano County High School would no longer operate as a separate district but would be combined with the elementary schools, to become a first-class district with a single board of education of seven members.[21]

An unheard of event occurred in the city election of 1959. The mayor's post was won by Mrs. Ethel Stacy, and two other women won the positions of city clerk and treasurer. In addition three women were elected to the city council. This was startling to the men of the city who were accustomed to running everything.[22]

Lamme Hospital, which had long been the only local hospital available to residents, announced its plans to close, and the community began looking for some way to build a community hospital. Petitions were circulated for the formation of a hospital district, and then presented to the county clerk with a total of 2,584 names. Land was offered for the proposed hospital. A 35-bed nursing home would open in the former hospital. Some federal funds were received from the Hill-Burton Act, and a bond issue of $250,000 was passed. The hospital would be located in the northeast section of town.[23]

For some time Harold Lathrop, director of the state park and recreation board, had been seeking sites around the state which would be suitable for state parks. Now Lathrop told the Walsenburg Chamber of Commerce that he was favorably impressed with the potential of Martin Lake as a site for a park development.[24]

The idea of a state park came a few steps closer when certain state agencies signed options for acquiring land from the Utt brothers of La Veta. The proposal included the enlargement of Horseshoe Lake to approximately 180 acres. Camp sites, picnic grounds and roads were also to be built by the state.

All of these plans were carried out and, in June of 1962, hundreds of people came to Martin Lake for the Lathrop Memorial Park dedication. Between the time of the first proposal and the completion of the park, Harold Lathrop had died and the state chose to name the park in his honor. At the celebration the Lieutenant Governor Robert Lee Knous spoke, and Mrs. Lathrop was an honored guest. Lathrop had founded the state park system in Minnesota and was given the job of establishing a similar system in Colorado. He is believed to be the only man to have launched two state park systems. Lathrop Memorial Park was the first state park in Colorado. [25]

During the spring and summer of 1962 further funding for the hospital was secured, and construction was begun on the facility located in the northeast section of town on Indiana Avenue.

In late 1963 a special edition of the **Huerfano World** was planned to welcome the newly completed hospital. A crowd of several hundred people was present for the dedication. On the same day the hospital got its first patient. Bill Billingsley was brought in for treatment at the new facility after being bucked from a horse. [26]

The Morning Glory Mine was sold by George Turner, Nick Balich, George Dunich, Andy Conder and Abel Gomez, Jr. to Jack Fink, Tony Just and Abel Gomez, Jr. This was one of the last working mines in the area.[27]

Although coal mining was no longer a factor in the county economy, the memories of the coal camps lingered on. The famed 1921 Pictou baseball club decided to have a reunion. Eight of the original fourteen players met at Shosky's on Saturday evening and continued the next day with an afternoon tour of the old baseball fields at Cameron, Walsen and Pictou. They then attended a baseball game at the Old Pictou ball field and watched kids of the Old Timers League play. A banquet at Shosky's followed the ball game. The players in attendance were Mike Bechaver, first base; Alex Muir, third base; Morgan Roberts, left field; Lucian Farmer, pitcher; "Pee-Wee" Judiscak, shortstop and captain; "Babe" Shosky, second base; and John Bechaver, catcher and outfielder.[28]

The war in Vietnam had been raging for several years, but 1966 brought the first mention of the death of a Walsenburg man. Matthew Krist, a hospital man, was listed as killed in a South Vietnam battle.[29]

School news now began to dominate the newspapers and would continue to do so for a long time. Most of the focus was on the need for a new high school. One of the chief problems with the Walsenburg High School building was the lack of adequate science labs. The age of the building and the other buildings as well came into play. S. M. Nation, then the publisher of the *Huerfano World*, wrote a long article on the history of the schools and urged voters to consider building one or more new buildings.

A bond issue was proposed for $134,000, which would include an addition to Gardner School. The bond issue was overwhelmingly defeated in an election where 74% of the qualified voters turned out. Virgil Ladurini, school board president, said, "The board has not given up. We're still searching for a way to solve the problems of obsolete buildings and crowded conditions. We need the opinions and suggestions of the people to help us. If need be, we will have another bond election in early spring."[30]

The death of a prominent citizen and community leader was noted in July of 1968 with the drowning death of Star Caywood at Martin Lake. He, his wife Virla, and Art Benine had been fishing on the lake when a sudden strong wind overturned their boat.

James King, Jr. of Walsenburg saw the boat capsize and swam out to Caywood's wife. King's father helped Benine, who was clinging to the boat. Caywood's body was recovered a day later in about six and a half feet of water.[31]

Shortly after the death of S. M. Nations, publisher of the *Huerfano World*, a new publisher arrived to take over the management of the paper. Jay Crook, 33, a native of Garden City, Kansas, came to Walsenburg from Holbrook, Arizona, where he had been the editor of the *Holbrook Tribune News* for three years. Crook and his wife, the former Sandra Crist, had a baby daughter, Cari.[32]

The Walsenburg Pavilion on West Eighth Street, built by Archie Levy, Sr. in 1925, had long been a city institution of great importance. It was the site of many dances accompanied by big-name bands from around the country, including Paul Whiteman and Conrad Nagel. Built of pine slabs, the building had a fir promenade which was salvaged from the old Washington School when it was razed. The flooring was of solid maple. The Pavilion was sold in the late 40s to the Slovenian Lodge and was used for dances, conventions, and other activities including wedding dances and receptions.[33] One current resident recalls with pleasure the dances that were held there. She told of how elderly couples took to the dance floor along with elementary age youngsters – all experiencing great joy in dancing the polkas and other folk dances which were the heritage of the ethnic groups in Walsenburg's society. Dances declined in favor of other forms of entertainment, and the last use of the pavilion was as a roller skating rink. On August 26, 1969, this venerable structure burned to the ground.[34]

School news once again took center stage when Walsenburg High School hosted a North Central evaluation team. North Central was an organization of educators whose purpose was to evaluate the programs of high schools and accredit or not accredit them according to their findings. The high school had enjoyed accreditation for many years. This time, however, the reports were not favorable in many areas. The need for a new school was cited, and the possibility of losing accreditation was raised. The school had no indebtedness, and the support per pupil was $100 lower than the state average.[35]

In related news a few days later the possibility of closing St. Mary High School was raised, and John Mall resigned as superintendent of Re-1 schools, citing health reasons. He asked for another assignment in the district.

Once more the question of the building needs of the school district came to the forefront when the school board asked a cross-section of community leaders including businessmen, ranchers, farmers, civic leaders and school supporters for recommendations. Citizens were invited to tour the high school building on Walsen Avenue, and one rancher's wife reported being shocked after seeing the building with its outdated facilities. Joe Crump, representing the ranching community, complained that ranchers would bear most of the burden of the cost of a new school. As owners of large amounts of land, ranchers often had higher property taxes than those who owned only a home. Some asked what mill levy would be needed as compared to several years ago.

The outcome of all of this was the decision of the Re-1 school board to hold a special bond election for a new $1,400,000, sixty-thousand square foot, high school building to be built where John Mall High School now stands.

Following this decision the community and the school district went into full campaign mode to support or oppose the bond issue.

A full page ad with pictures of teachers telling what a "yes" vote would mean to their educational programs appeared in the *Huerfano World*. The ad featured Frank Montera, music; Joe Dosen, social studies; William Crump, math; Consuelo DeVan, physical education; Jim Robertson, counselor; Alice Davis, history; Michael Lynch, English; Robert Hemphill, industrial art; and Evelyn Heikes, librarian.

Joe Crump stated that stockmen would not support the bond issue in spite of the fact that Huerfano County had one of the lowest mill levies in the state. Dr. Arthur B. Vialpando M.D. was quoted as saying that he would leave if the school bond failed.

Teachers announced that they would not seek a salary increase to show support for the bond issue. Shortly before the election, a full-page ad appeared with 100 names of people who planned to vote yes on the matter.

On December 17, 1970, the school bond vote once again failed by a 2-1 vote. Superintendent Jearl Nunnelee said that the board might be coming back with another issue soon.[36]

A further blow to the school district occurred early in 1971 when St. Mary Parish announced the closing of St. Mary High School at the end of the year after fifty years of operation. The top three grades would be affected, and some thirty-four students of St. Mary's had already transferred to the public school. This increase strained the already over-stretched school. An official said, "We finally got them textbooks, but we still don't have enough desks." Superintendent Nunnelee said, "We face serious problems in accommodating the additional St. Mary students next year and something will have to be done to provide another building."[37]

Split sessions for pupils were considered, as well as attempting to find additional classroom space. St. Mary's opted to close out the ninth grade, which added even more students and consequently more space needs to the public schools.

Again the board chose to attempt to pass a bond issue, this time for only $600,000. This, too, was rejected. The board had only three years in which to make major fire and safety repairs to the high school building. This was deemed impossible without a bond issue. Eventually space was leased at St. Mary's for one kindergarten and two fourth grade classes. This lease was good for only one year.[38]

In the midst of all the bad school news, a good item finally appeared. Edgar DeVan was selected teacher of the year in a landslide vote of the school community. One of thirteen children, Mr. DeVan, whose father had worked in the coal mines, taught history, ecology, senior social problems, minorities and biology, in addition to being the head football coach.[39]

Two months later the announcement came that Mr. DeVan was one of four finalists for the honor of state teacher of the year. In his philosophy of education, he said, "Man, if he has everything but lacks pride, has nothing."

He continued by saying that students must learn to respect a person for what he is, not for what he can or cannot do. He tried to follow the three Fs in dealing with students: treat students fairly, be friendly to all students, and be firm.[40]

While Edgar DeVan was not selected as the state teacher of the year, he continued to earn the respect and devotion of students and community for his 37 year long career in the Walsenburg schools.

The school board attempted another approach to obtaining the bare minimum for the needs of the school. Plans were drawn up for a nine-classroom building which would house the junior high grades and provide laboratories for science classes. Funding would come through a lease-purchase agreement. In March a contract for a lease-purchase building for $148,000 was let. The board also raised the mill levy to 10.5 mills to help furnish the new building.[41]

This prompted a move by a taxpayers group to recall the school board. The members of the school board were Darwin Smallwood, Virgil Ladurini, Anthony Pando, Don Wagner, Earl Tatman, Tom Zellar and Andy Ritz. The taxpayers group pushing for the recall included Fred Eccher, Christie Mosco, Joe Crump, Van Lawson, Don Andreatta, Bob Andreatta and Mike Lenzini.[42]

The board refused the demand to lower the mill levy. Board President Anthony Pando stated, "Walsenburg High School can be closed down in 1975 by the state industrial commission for safety reasons if district Re-1 does not do substantial remodeling. We will also probably lose our North Central accreditation because the high school building is such a poor facility." The taxpayers group countered with a claim that the board had deliberately let building maintenance go in order to force a bond issue.[43]

At a group meeting the taxpayers group offered no solution to the very real problems of the schools. Asked how they proposed to deal with the matter, they gave no answer.

The recall petitions were filed, and, on May 25, 1972, the voters recalled the entire school board. Comments from outgoing board members were that any new board members would not find solving the problems an easy matter.[44]

In June a heavy turnout of voters elected a new board: Ben Vigil, Jr., Earlin Busch, Sergio Abila, Christie Mosco, Norma Lou Murr, Donald Noga and Thomas Conder.[45]

The first attempt to fire Superintendent Nunnelee came in June when the board suspended him from all duties and exempted him from pay. Two representatives of the State Department of Education, however, informed the school board that they could be sued individually or collectively if they ruled his contract invalid. The board backed off and ratified Nunnelee's contract in July.[46]

By late fall the new school board began to change when, in short order, Tom Conder and Sergio Abila resigned. They were replaced in January by August Andreatta and John E. Rodriguez.[47]

For a time in 1973 the community was able to put aside all of the school turmoil and turn its attention to celebrating the 100th anniversary of Walsenburg.

Local mailers with postage meters began using special stamp cancellations with the words "Cultural Crossroads" across a background drawing of the Spanish Peaks. The drawing was by Jeannette Thach, a local realtor and a member of the noted Faris family. From March through July, the Walsenburg Post Office would use a special stamp cancellation of three lines on letters mailed at the post office. The lines included "Centennial 1873-1973", "Land of Huajatolla" and "Cultural Crossroads."

Telos Rodriguez, chairman, reported that letters from across the U. S. were accumulating awaiting the March 1 date for first-day cancellation of Walsenburg's special centennial post mark.[48]

The principal centennial celebration came on July 27, 28 and 29 with activities on Main Street including food and craft booths. A pancake breakfast on the courthouse lawn was followed by the Centennial parade at 10 a.m. A *charreada*, which was a Mexican-style rodeo, was presented at 2 p.m. by the Pueblo Charro Club, and this was followed by a Walsenburg Spectacular, sponsored by Arts 'n Things Council. [49]

While the centennial celebration was taking place, the school board continued to wrestle with its problems. In March the board fired Superintendent Nunnelee with no reason given and the rest of his contract was bought out. The recall was considered the most likely reason. Norma Lou Murr and John Rodriguez voted against the resolution of dismissal. John Mall was appointed as temporary superintendent.

With the addition of another new board member, Marge Figal, the board appeared ready to look again at a new building. In June the board gave approval to a lease-purchase arrangement with Ecco-leasing of Denver. This would be a 12,500 sq. foot Butler building to be ready for the 1974-75 term. There would be eight classrooms for sixth, seventh and eighth grades and three high school science labs. [50]

Don Noga resigned from the school board, Lowell Elisha of Dove Creek, Colorado, was hired as superintendent, and Ed Cruz was appointed to the school board – all in July. [51]

The board again chose to place the matter of the new school before the voters and, in November of 1973, the electorate approved $300,000 to build what is now the West Building at John Mall High School. [52]

For a time it seemed that things might become a bit quieter in Walsenburg. San Isabel Electric expressed an interest in buying the power plant. Early in the new year the city council eased the way for a new Safeway store at Seventh and Albert Streets. Safeway had purchased most of the properties on the block. Fifteen people applied for the Walsenburg High School principalship. El Fandango, which had not been held for a year or two, was back under the direction of Chuck Vialpando and H. W. Morales. The old jail, which had been garnering much criticism, would not be closed. Instead the wiring and ventilation systems were updated along with the plumbing. Senator Sam Taylor announced his retirement after serving in the state senate for forty years. All was calm and well in Walsenburg. [53]

The calm did not last. Early on the morning of July 11, 1974, Melvin Higgins passed by the high school building and saw smoke. He tried to knock on doors in the area and at last Mrs. Maurice Page, hearing the commotion, got up, saw the fire and called it in.

The volunteer fire department responded quickly as usual, but it was too late to save the building. By morning a large crowd had gathered to watch as the firemen went about the dangerous work of mopping up.

> *It wasn't just the smoke – Wiping the tears from their eyes many onlookers found they were not alone in their grief as they watched the flames devour the stages, the gym, etc. Said one: "It wasn't just a building burning, you see, it was a hall of memories. It was pomp and circumstance, proud graduates and beaming parents and dedicated teachers, caps and gowns marching down the aisle through many a commencement. It was the teams and the thrill of the crowds roaring their approval at the ball games. It was prom night and one's best date.* [54]

The raging fire gutted the gymnasium, cafeteria, industrial arts shop and art room and the boys' shower. The academic section was water soaked and smoke damaged, and two classrooms nearest the gym were partly burned.

> *"It was definitely arson," stated Fire Chief Andy Ritz, "The call came at 4:10 a.m. and as I rounded the corner it was already a blazing inferno. I figure the fire was set perhaps around midnight and smouldered for hours. Supt. Lowell Elisha, returning from a brief vacation, was by the building around 3 a.m. and saw nothing wrong."*

To assist with the investigation into the disastrous fire, the local police called in the Colorado Bureau of Investigation. Teen suspects were soon being questioned. It was determined that the front door of the building had been forced open and a hacksaw and a blade were found inside. Efforts had also been made to break into the school vault, and the library on the third floor had apparently been entered. Entry to the gym had been made through the southwest window. Paint remover had been used to start the fire.[55]

The school board went into special session and established committees to look into how to prepare for the opening of school less than two months away. By July 18 they had awarded a contract to clean-up the building. The work went rapidly, and by the end of summer, with the aid of teachers and student workers, the undamaged parts of the building were ready for school to start.

By September the middle school students were ready to move into the new building as were the science students of the high school.

After a great deal more discussion, the Re-1 School Board finally set into motion a new bond election to provide funds to build a complete new high school and a gymnasium for the old building, which would now become the middle school. The amount of the bond was for $1,250,000 which ultimately proved to be somewhat inadequate.[56]

Voters approved the new high school by a vote of 2–1 which must have been gratifying after the defeat of previous bond issues by the same margin. Demolition of the remaining wreckage would come first. When the new construction was complete, Hill School would be closed. Students there would go to Washington School, and the middle school students would be housed in the remaining portion of the old high school.[57]

No one was ever charged with the arson of the gymnasium.

During the spring and summer, revised building plans for the high school were presented. A social occasion honoring retiring Sen. Sam Taylor was held. Six positions on the school board were open for election due to the number of appointees' terms running out. The new Safeway store opened. The City accepted the water treatment plant subject to final approval of Economic Development Agency officials.

In mid-May the following school board members were sworn in: Shirley Martinez, Fred George, Norma Lou Murr, John

Rodriguez and Earlin Busch. Only Murr and Busch remained of those who had won election following the recall two years earlier.

While construction of the new building was progressing, the school board made a historic decision. By a unanimous vote they chose to name the new school in honor of the man who spent his career devoted to the children of Walsenburg as principal, superintendent and assistant superintendent. The school would be called John Mall High School.

The board was quoted: "Board members agreed it was fitting recognition of John S. Mall, who, over the years, has been seen at diverse pursuits throughout the district from helping move a pile of bricks that covered a hidden water line to making a tough administrative decision that would affect the whole district and community; from crawling under school buildings to trace a maze of heating and plumbing lines to wading through a maze of federal red tape and regulations when Title I first came to Re-1; from passing lollipops to all the elementary kids at Halloween to placing his tall but spare frame between the hot tempers and impatient fists of overly emotional football teams."[58]

On a cold, windy day in December of 1975, the cornerstone of John Mall High School was laid. Students had prepared the contents: a scroll signed by all students, a copy of the school newspaper and other memorabilia. The ceremony was conducted by the local Masonic Lodge with Earlin Busch, Re-1 Board president, leading.

Changes had come to the school district while all this was going on. Samuel S. Conaway had been hired as high school principal. Lowell Elisha had requested a leave of absence for health reasons and had been replaced by Dr. Robert Hall.

By July of 1976 John Mall High School was completed and accepted by the Board. "A heck of a building for the money," was the enthusiastic reaction of Re-1 Board of Education members, school administrators, architect and construction foreman, who toured the nearly completed John Mall High School throughout the day and evening Tuesday. The keys were presented to Earlin Busch."[59]

There followed a flurry of moving activity. Teachers and staff had prepared for this by doing all the packing of materials, textbooks, library books and audio-visual machines before the end of school in the old building. Trucks went back and forth daily hauling loads of boxes and depositing them in the designated rooms. With just a week until the opening of the school, faculty members worked furiously to get their departments ready. A number of willing students were hired by the district to help. Against all odds the school opened on time with everything in reasonable order.

An open house and dedication ceremony were held for John Mall High School on September 12, 1976.

"It's the fulfillment of my dreams for a good education for all the children of this district," declared John S. Mall at Monday night ceremonies dedicating the new high school which bears his name. An estimated 350 townspeople took part in honoring the man who came to Walsenburg in 1952 as principal of the elementary school and continued to serve the educational needs of the community for a quarter century. Expressing his pride in dedicating the new high school to "a man who has filled every need," Earlin L. Busch, president of the school board, told listeners he felt, "the time to honor a person is when he's living, not after he's dead." He recalled that Mall filled whatever need arose, from repairing a furnace to reorganizing a batch of small school districts into one, from doing a bit of janitorial work to settling a squabble on the football field."

Other guests, Dr. Calvin M. Frazier, Commissioner of Education, Dr. Robert Hall, master of ceremonies, and Virgil L. Ladurini, past president of the school board, also paid tribute. Other dignitaries included: Frances Nelson, Sam Conaway, principal, Larry Crosson and William Duran, Pam Crump, Student Council president, the Rev. Caro Russell, and Father John Sullivan. Visitors were invited to tour the building and parents could follow a mini-schedule of a high school student's day.[60]

Everybody moved into the new building and settled down to go to work. Unfortunately, problems with the building surfaced almost immediately. The heating company refused to guarantee its equipment due to the high electric voltage fluctuation. The roof leaked, too.

During that first fall, which proved to be a rainy one, teachers often had to duck under a waterfall which came through a joint in the ceiling between the cafeteria and the academic wing. The gymnasium, whose roof sported exposed insulation batts with no ceiling tiles, built up water in the insulation necessitating some means of letting the water down so that a basketball game did not have a floor filled with water. Bill Crump, assistant principal, was sometimes seen firing BBs into the insulation batts to allow drainage of the water. The heating system worked in reverse, causing extremely high temperatures in the winter, especially in interior rooms, for example, the library. Over time and with the expenditure of more money, most of these problems were solved.

While the school board struggled with the new school, the city addressed other problems. Plans were made to create a new city hall complex in the old Safeway building at the corner of Sixth and Albert Streets, but costs slowed the project for some time. San Isabel Electric Co-op continued its interest in purchasing the city power plant which was located west of the city and had once been part of the Walsen Camp complex. Eventually this was placed before the voters and approved.

In March of 1977, the community was saddened by the death of Sen. Sam Taylor. A memorial to Taylor called him "A man of character, integrity and ability." Flags flew at half-mast over the state capital. Born Jan. 4, 1903, in the Las Animas mining community of Hastings, Sen. Taylor worked in the mines during his younger years, before attending the University of Colorado and later its law school. He married Nina Luckenbaugh, and they had one son, Sam. Jr. The senator served in many capacities in the state legislature. His funeral was celebrated by Monsignor Howard L. Delaney with the Rev. Father Maurice Gallagher.[61]

Under the sponsorship of Earl Boyer and Richard Maes, the Spanish Club of John Mall High School was doing excellent work. El Fandango dancers were performing at various events during the spring, and the club itself participated in the Pueblo Foreign Language Fair at the University of Southern Colorado. The students brought home five first places, two seconds and a third. Those participating included Darrell Archuleta, Brenda Ruiz, Sandy Salazar, Jaydah Bellah, Leroy Salazar, Doretta Garcia, Deann Martinez, Laverne Maes, Billy Armijo, Ray Hernandez, Donald DeVan, Bernadette Gonzales, Cathy DeHerrera, Cindy Knowlton and Gary Johnson.[62]

Fall of 1978 saw the arrival of the first exchange student in Walsenburg in many years. Kari Lofthus came from Oslo, Norway, to live with Sig and Ruth Sporleder and Gretchen, Karl and Eric. Host families at the time were hard to find and the question of a home for a Norwegian student came up in a conversation with the Sporleders at the Gardner Chuckwagon Dinner. Daughter Gretchen pushed the idea of having the Norwegian girl, and the result was her arrival in Walsenburg in September. "I was really, really lucky," Kari said of her host family. "She's a terrific girl," Ruth Sporleder said. "We're enjoying her a lot."[63]

Kari Lofthus participated in as many school activities as she possibly could, including journalism, photography and El Fandango. She also made friendships which have endured to this day.

La Plaza de los Leones continued to be the town's major festival. Officials called the 1979 event "One of the best" and reported that 50 dozen burritos, 30 dozen tostadas, 30 cases of pop and 150 pounds of menudo were served. There were thirty entries in the parade, and Walsenburg Middle School took first place in marching bands, while Antonito High School placed second. Eighty runners aged 11 to 52 took part in the second annual distance run at Lathrop State Park.[64]

James J. Tesitor, one of the last politically appointed postmasters by President Harry S Truman, announced his retirement after 28 years of service. He accepted the appointment from Truman just a few weeks after graduating from Pomona College in California in 1952.[65]

In a later interview Tesitor told of his early life. He was the eighth of nine children born to Nick and Josephine Tesitor. James was born a mile east of Walsenburg on what is now the Corsentino ranch. The family moved to town when he was six months old. He made the trip in a little wagon pulled by his older brother, Carl. He was a basketball player in high school, and, with the encouragement of his coach, Gaston Santi, he applied to Grinnell College. He worked his way through his second year but dropped out when he came home and found that things were difficult for his family. In 1942 the draft caught him, and he and others from Walsenburg went to the medics at Camp Berkley, Texas. He entered officers' candidate school in the Medical Service Corps and graduated as a lieutenant. He was discharged as a captain and remained active in the military reserve and later the Colorado National Guard. For a time, he worked at the Rouse coal mine with his brother, Anthony. Together with his brother Sam (Sen. Sam Taylor) he went into business when they purchased the Tressler Insurance and Real Estate Co. and later the Dick Abstract Co. The economy of Huerfano County was declining at the time, and he decided to go back to college, this time at Pomona College in California. After graduation with a degree in economics he took the postmaster's exam, received the appointment and came home for good. He and his wife, Rubie, were very active in church, school and municipal affairs in the community.[66]

After a few years of relative calm, school problems again took center stage in the community. Superintendent Robert Hall had resigned after a stormy relationship with both the school board and many of the teachers. He was replaced by Walter L. Way of Aspen, Colorado.

Within a short time Way began to discuss financial difficulties he found in the district and requested that the board hire Michael Bouzos as business manager. Since several teaching positions had been eliminated, the Walsenburg Classroom Teachers Association had understood that no new administrative positions would be created. Way responded that Bouzos was actually a replacement for Carlos Maldonado, the former director of federal programs for the district.

Way continued to insist that there were major financial shortfalls in the district, and, to solve the problem, he proposed eliminating faculty positions and changing several others, effective October 1. Those affected would be music, home economics, two spelling teachers, making one English teacher half-time, several classified positions and the reassignment of a librarian.

Not too surprisingly, the teachers' association reacted badly to the idea of discharging teachers under contract soon after school had begun. With the aid of Wayne Hopewell, Uniserv director for the Association, the battle was joined. Teachers announced that they would work with the district to help cut $16,000 from the budget but claimed that more time was needed on other proposals. After a meeting with Hopewell, which lasted until 2 a.m., WCTA adopted the following resolutions in a unanimous vote: 1. To support utilization of the full resources of the United Teaching Profession for any members who are RIFed (Reduction in Force) and 2. Should the board RIF any member at the time, the WCTA shall meet immediately to consider appropriate organizational response.

A community-wide meeting was held at Washington School to inform the public of the financial problems. Superintendent Way was still holding out for firing people, but the board began to feel the opposition of the community as well as of the teachers to this drastic approach. The board members directed administrators to come up with a package of reductions that would have the least effect on all personnel. In board meetings and in the community, various ways of saving money were discussed, including the first suggestion of a four-day school week.

The issue was finally resolved when Golden Cycle, a housing development west of town which had owned many, many acres, sold all its property and paid its back taxes of $110,000. An additional $27,000 for special education was also received. The crisis was averted.[67]

Another prospective economic boost to the area was discussed frequently during this period of time. This was the proposed CO_2 pipeline to be built by ARCO (Atlantic Richfield Co.) near Sheep Mountain in the Gardner area. Much hope was held out for this enterprise. It was eventually built, and for the next two decades supplied much of the tax revenue for both county and the school district.

In 1981 the John Mall High School Panthers won the district basketball tournament and were on their way to the state tournament in Denver. They were pictured on horseback on the front page of the **Huerfano World**. The team made it all the way to second place in the tournament, but greater consequences resulted from the tournament than merely bringing home the second-place trophy.

Some citizens who attended the tournament felt that the town did not get enough recognition because "nobody knows where John Mall High School is."

As a result, the Huerfano Re-1 Board of Education moved to phase "Walsenburg" back into the name of the high school while retaining the dedication of the entire complex to John Mall and calling the gym John Mall Gym. [68]

Some citizens were pleased by this decision, but others were not. Members of the faculty and staff were especially distressed since they felt that the name added distinction to the school, and that it was wrong to honor a living person and then take that honor away. Many continued to think of the school as John Mall High School and resisted making changes. The custodial staff, for example, just never found time to take the words "John Mall High School" off the front of the building.

After a couple of years of rather poor press, Superintendent Walter Way finally received recognition for his skills as a wood carver. He carved an image of an Indian from a long trunk and presented the 25-foot statue to the city. The city accepted the gift and placed it on a pedestal in the Triangle, a piece of land in front of the Methodist Church which had been created years before in the change which joined Main Street and Walsen Avenue. At the time, Way reported that he was looking for a log from which to carve a miner. This search was successful, and the Indian statue was later replaced by a statue of a coal miner on his way to work.[69] Later it was placed at the Mining Museum.

In the spring of 1983, it was noted that the 50th anniversary of the Will Overhead blooper was approaching. For years Alan J. Gould, general sports editor for the Associated Press, decorated his office with a framed copy of the May 30, 1933, *World Independent* front page. Jay Crook, current editor of the *Huerfano World*, had calls from sports publications around the country, the Associated Press, and a couple of big city newspapers. Journalistic jargon caused the error which had an non-existent race car driver named Will Overhead winning the Indianapolis Five Hundred.[70]

In honor of the occasion the Chamber of Commerce decided to change Whoopee Day to Will Overhead Day in the upcoming year.

Once again the city elected a woman mayor when Betty Dick Ridge carried three of four wards over Leo Maes. Music director Ione Glumac and high school and junior high school bands marched in the Cheyenne Frontier Days parade in Wyoming. Pete Gomez III, son of the high school wrestling coach, won the 105-pound state wrestling championship.

By May of 1984, all plans were in place for the first Will Overhead Day. A royal blue shirt with a specially designed Will Overhead emblem in black was the clothing for members of the Huerfano County Chamber of Commerce.

The festival was a huge success with a sidewalk breakfast, an Overhead $500 golf tournament, a four-person mini-marathon, and a parade down Main Street. George Zanon, retired printer and former co-owner of the *World Independent*, was the grand marshal for the parade. A free day at Lathrop Park offered food concession booths, arts and crafts and the like. Five thousand or more people attended, twenty-five county organizations were involved, and there were sixty-five entries in the parade. Art Gaytan and Dick Dissler won the $500 team golf tournament.[71]

Joan Eagle in partnership with her husband, Ben, opened a new business in Walsenburg called Chipita Accessories. Ms. Eagle had long enjoyed a hobby of beading earrings and accessories, and she now enlarged her hobby into a business. Operating from a small building on East Seventh Street, she employed a number of local people who beaded the earrings and other items from her designs. In addition to the high-priced earrings, belts and hatbands were popular. Chipita products were soon owned across the country by many celebrities including Willie Nelson, Burt Reynolds, Hank Williams, Jr., Cher, Emmy Lou Harris, Barbra Streisand, Patti Reagan and a Miss America. With this kind of publicity, the business flourished.[72]

A few years later Chipita Accessories found itself in a struggle for survival due to an obscure provision of the Department of Labor which prohibited at-home labor such as was done by workers in the county, mostly women, beading the earrings from Joan Eagle's designs. This dispute went on for a long time with the Eagles fighting for the rights of their workers and their company. The money earned by these workers was extremely important as many of them came from low income households. Eventually these rules were changed since the work they did could not be called dangerous, and the workers were able to go on making the popular jewelry.

A new battle now began to brew in school matters. Art teacher Alexis Betts was already a member of the school board, and Larry Crosson, high school counselor, wished to run. The school board had passed a policy which stated that a school employee could not be paid while serving on the Board of Education. A law suit had been threatened by the Walsenburg Classroom Teachers Association.

Teacher attorney Larry Hobbs of Denver stated, "...both are tenured employees and that the new policy violates their rights to be free of adverse employment practices due to participation in community affairs and that they are being pressured to withdraw from nomination and election." The case would be heard by Judge Harry Sayre of Trinidad. District Judge Albert Tomsic had disqualified himself since his wife was a teacher in the school district. The board policy had been adopted on a 4–3 vote after several weeks of study.[73]

Actually at this time, no lawsuit had been filed. A preliminary injunction had been asked to prevent the board from enforcing the policy until a lawsuit was filed, if that became necessary.

In the meantime six people were seeking election to the four vacancies on the board – Larry Crosson and Marge Figal, District B; Alexis Betts and Margaret Galvan, District F; Shirley Hribar, District C; and Art Vigil, District D. The election came several days before the scheduled hearing before Judge Sayre.

When the votes were counted, it was clear that Betts and Crosson had won the two contested Re-1 seats by decisive margins.

At the hearing Judge Sayre requested both counsel to prepare statements supporting their positions. He would sign one or the other by June 1 of that year.[74]

When Judge Sayre at last issued his ruling on the policy, the teacher-board members won. Judge Sayre ruled that the district could not withhold payment of salary from the two in accordance with an Re-1 conflict of interest board policy since they were tenured teachers with salary rights protected by Colorado Teacher Tenure laws. His ruling would apply to other tenured employees but not to non-tenured teachers or other employees. The request for an injunction was withdrawn.[75]

Only one other teacher has taken advantage of this ruling. Elaine Lenzini, mother of Alexis Betts, later ran for the school board and won. She served for several years before and after her retirement from teaching.

A new manufacturer arrived in Walsenburg and began training workers. Mountain View Manufacturing, maker of firefighter's safety clothing and rain wear, had selected Walsenburg as a site and had begun operation at 408 Russell Avenue. G. B. "Jerry" Fitzgerald was the owner, and Ernie Reynolds of Walsenburg had been hired as general manager.[76]

This business proved highly successful and continues in operation to this day.

Once more an action of the school board made news. The matter came up shortly after the board had adopted its budget on a 4–3 vote.

> *The Board again considered the question raised last meeting about the high school name, citing confusion to visitors when the entity is called Walsenburg High School while the cornerstone, building sign and other symbols say John Mall High School. A motion was made to return the name to John Mall High School as originally designated when it was built in 1975 to eliminate the discrepancies. Aye votes were recorded by Crosson, Betts, Hribar, and Rodriguez with Naranjo, Schmidt and Vigil opposed.*[77]

The views of people varied on this matter, but it appears that most members of the educational community were happy to have the name back, and the honor bestowed on John Mall restored. John Mall still lived in the community and had never stopped offering his services to the school district all during the controversy. For example, he appeared at the office of Principal Bill Crump one morning carrying two or three small wood and glass cases. He had noticed some unused space above the crowded trophy case and had decided to fill that space by making the additional space for more trophies.

The early months of 1986 brought a number of changes to the community. District Judge Albert Tomsic retired after twenty-one years on the bench. A graduate of Huerfano County High School, he served overseas with the Far East Air Forces during World War II. He received his law degree from the University of Colorado and was admitted to the Colorado Bar in 1951. He practiced law in Walsenburg and served five terms in the state legislature. Claude Appel was named to succeed Judge Tomsic as District Judge.[78]

The Walsenburg Downtown Development Committee bought the house across from the courthouse, the home of the late Ralph Levy, Sr., who had been a Chief of Police. The site was to become a park, and the committee agreed to place a plaque to commemorate the pioneer family of Alexander and Lillie Levy, who had originally owned the house. The Levy family had asked that the park be named Levy Park, but the city council voted 5–4 to name it Heritage Park.[79]

For some time planning and work on a proposed Mining Museum had been ongoing. The site would be the lower floor of the county-owned building on the south east corner of Main and Fifth. This was one of the earliest buildings in Walsenburg and had once housed the offices of physicians and attorneys as well as housing businesses on the lower floor. Work was already proceeding on refurbishing the building when the Museum received a $15,000 grant from the Boettcher Foundation and a $1,000 donation from the Walsenburg Civic League. Walsenburg miner John Biondi was acting as site manager. Plans included an opening date of mid-June for the museum.[80]

In March of 1987, Bill and Joan Crump retired from the school district. A terrible post-prom accident killed the daughter of a local doctor, Jennifer Lisonbee, and injured Mitch Abila, Glen Glorioso and Frank Pineda. Mitch Abila died of his injuries a few weeks later. The accident had been caused by fatigue, not alcohol or drugs. Superintendent Walt Way resigned to take a position in Elizabeth, Colorado. Walsenburg voters finally said yes to San Isabel and the local electric utility would be sold.[81]

On July 4, 1987, the long-awaited Walsenburg Mining Museum opened its doors in the back part of the old Kearns and Cole building on the southeast corner at Main and East Fifth. The building had been built in 1883 and used by the Dick Brothers. As a museum, it featured newly remodeled rooms with traveling exhibits, photo exhibits and memorabilia. The museum owed much of its existence to the hard work of Christine Schmidt, Dianne Hanisch and John Biondi along with the efforts of many others. [82]

Conditions in the 1896 county jail continued to be a problem as had been the case for a number of years. Now the inmates were threatening a lawsuit over conditions, and the sheriff was also making demands. Finding the funding for a new jail seemed now to be mandatory. The Planning and Zoning Board recommended to city council that a special use permit be granted to Huerfano County for the construction of a $2.3 million law enforcement complex, south of the courthouse. Within a month or two the clearing of the site of the old Pritchard Lumber Co. was underway to make room for the jail.[83] The new jail opened in 1989.

At the same time that the struggle for a new jail was going on, problems with the hospital kept surfacing. The land on which the hospital had been built kept sinking and causing great difficulty with electrical and other systems. A solution had to be found.

The possibility of a Vets Home grant was raised, with the home to be built in conjunction with a new hospital. A Colorado Energy Impact grant of $500,000 was promised with more money coming from other sources. An effort began to ask voters to pass a bond issue for $5.2 million to build the hospital. A site west of Walsenburg across from the entrance to Lathrop Park was chosen. The election was held on May 2 and passed overwhelmingly. Seventy per cent of eligible voters turned out with a vote of 1849 to 378 or 6–1.[84]

Two deaths of note occurred during this time. Dr. James M. Lamme, Jr. passed away. He was born November 26, 1919, the first baby born in the new Lamme Hospital, the building which is now the Walsenburg Care Center. He received his M. D. degree from the Long Island College of Medicine in Brooklyn, New York, and later served two and one half years in the Navy. He returned to Walsenburg and joined his father in practice. During his years of practice, Dr. Lamme delivered more than 3,000 babies, whose pictures he kept in a scrapbook.[85]

A few months later John Mall died. Born in Leadville, April 24, 1910, Mr. Mall lost his parents and grandmother in the flu epidemic of 1918. Mall and one of his brothers were placed in St. Vincent's Orphanage in Denver. He attended Regis High School and Regis College. He came to Walsenburg in 1952 as assistant principal of the high school under S. M. Andrews. He was the principal after Andrews' death until he was named superintendent. In a *Pueblo Chieftain* interview, his youngest son, Louis, was quoted.

Some men measure their success by their wealth, but my father was not a rich man. He was never paid very much for what he did. He got wealth from the love that the community and the family had for him, and his love to the family and the kids.[86]

The Malls had seven children and later became the legal guardians of five nieces and nephews who had lost their parents, relatives of Mrs. Mall, in a car accident. They raised them as their own. It was also noted that Mr. Mall's devotion to the school, which bore his name, never ceased. The night before his death, he had been directing traffic at John Mall High School for the graduation crowd.

Joan Crump won election as mayor and was sworn in on January 11, 1990. She was the sister of Betty Ridge, who had been mayor 1983 to 1987, thus giving two women of the Dick family the top job in Walsenburg politics.[87]

The first Gulf War in 1991 did not consume the news as earlier conflicts had, but Huerfano County men answered the call as always, and the names of those serving were carried in the paper. They were Donald R. Andreoli, Tony R. Encinias, Wayne Espinoza, Lee Gallegos, Pete Gomez III, Mitchell R. Gordon, Joseph E. Hibpshman, Michael Scott Kay, Victor E. Lopez, Christopher L. Manzanares, Charles Martinez, Jr., Thomas R. Martinez, John M. Ortega, Kenneth R. Thompson and Jimmy VanLue. Others would come later.[88]

Groundbreaking for the new hospital and veterans home was held after several delays.

Both the hospital and the wing intended for the veterans' home were built. The hospital was dedicated and opened, but the veterans' center went through a long period of time when it could not achieve recognitions from the Veterans Administration. Some of this difficulty arose from having too many residents in the home who were not veterans or family members, and some for deficiencies cited by the VA. Eventually all of these problems were overcome, and the needed certification was received.

Mayor Joan Crump died in August of the following year of complications of bronchitis. A special election was held to fill the mayoral vacancy caused by the death. Jay Crook, editor of the *Huerfano World*, was elected by 55% of the votes cast.[89]

Over the years Walsenburg had its share of violent crime, although the numbers were small compared to larger towns. One such crime shocked the town when the body of a young man, Charles "Chuck" Grandbush, was found in his home. His skull had been crushed by numerous blows from an object, such as a hammer, as Grandbush slept in his bed. In less than a month charges were filed against his girl friend, Lyana Salazar. She soon pled guilty by reason of insanity and was sent to Pueblo for a mental examination. Following the examination, she was returned to jail in Walsenburg until her trial. Statements made to police were admitted against the objections of her attorneys, who claimed she was not properly advised of her rights. She either withdrew her plea of not guilty by reason of insanity or had been found sane.

Her trial was then moved to Pueblo, probably due to the publicity in Walsenburg. In June of 1993 she was found not guilty by a six-man, six-woman jury after four hours of deliberation. The possibility of a bungled investigation existed. Salazar may also have been using large amounts of drugs, according to the forensic doctor at the Colorado State Hospital who examined her. The crime is still officially unsolved.[90]

The Fox Theatre on Main Street had been largely closed for a number of years. In the early 90s the building was acquired by the Huerfano Youth and Arts Foundation. George Birrer, youth center president, said, "This is a giant step forward in our effort to provide the young people of this area with a place to congregate and an outlet for their energy."[91]

Incorporated by the Optimist Club, the group immediately began to seek grants to renovate the theater. Plans included making it available for theatrical and musical groups from the outside. Movies would be shown on weekends. Shakespeare's *A Midsummer Night's Dream* and Agatha Christie's *The Mousetrap* were presented by the group, and the success of these offerings helped to secure more grants to continue the renovation of the theater.

St. Mary Credit Union, which had begun as a union for parish members only, celebrated fifty years in business. In the early 50s the directors chose to expand and open its doors to all community members. By the 50th year of operation, the credit union had four and one-half million in assets and 1680 members.

The First National Bank celebrated ninety years of business. The bank had been chartered in 1903 by Fred O. Roof, J. B. Dick, William Dick, George Dick and J. B. Farr. It was descended from four earlier banking establishments in the same location. The 1903 building had been razed in 1927, and a new $75,000 brick building was built. The officers at the time of the celebration were Gerald Ariano, chairman of the board and director, Virgil Ladurini, Floyd Murr, Fred Menghini and Alton Tirey, directors.[92]

At a later date the bank was sold and is now part of the Community Banks of Southern Colorado, but it continues doing business at the old location on the corner of Main and Fifth Street.

As if to show that it was still a river to be reckoned with, the Cucharas River chose the summer of 1993 to once again flood south Walsenburg after torrential rains at Navajo Ranch. The south Main Street bridge, Bear Creek bridge and Ysidro bridge were all closed, and nearby residents were advised to evacuate. Max Sanchez attempted to go under the railroad at Eighth and Leon, and found his pickup swept away by the flood waters. Sanchez and his passenger escaped the truck, which ended up south of Fiesta Park on the east side of town. It was the worst flood since 1977.[93]

The Walsenburg Mining Museum was preparing in 1995 for an important move. The 1896 jail had been made available by the county commissioners. Plans were made and efforts were put forth to secure more photographs and more artifacts. A $24,000 grant from the State Historical Society was obtained, and in-kind contributions were offered. It would take some time and more money, but eventually the museum opened in its new location.

Members of the committee at the time were Christine Schmidt, JoVonne Fitzgerald, Gerald Lamb, Viola Archuleta, Betty Ridge, Norma Lou Murr, Florence Rogers, Carolyn and Alfred Newman, Jr., John G. Bechaver, Walter and Molly Bailey, Ben Eagle, Nick Faris, Dianne Hanisch, Joyce Kramer, Vivian Price, Nancy Christofferson and Pat Lepka.

After many years of trying to secure a prison of some sort for the county, contracts were finally signed for the construction of a private prison operated by the Corrections Corporation of America. This company, which managed several private prisons in Colorado, had a contract with the State Department of Corrections to house minimum security prisoners. The construction and operation of the prison provided many jobs for the community, and the prisoners were active in service projects.

Prisoners were soon arriving at the newly completed prison. Of five separate buildings, three are housing units, with three pods. Each contains 42 to 46 cells, and has a recreational area, and two or more handicapped cells. Medical facilities, exercise equipment and classrooms for inmates were included. The prison was located just east of I-25 near Walsenburg Sand and Gravel Company. It was one of the largest employers in the area.[94]

One new business arrived in Walsenburg, and an existing one opened a large new location. Bill and Virla Downey opened the Main Street Office Supply, and both newcomers soon became active in community affairs. He became a member of the school board.[95]

Zorc Building Supply began the construction of a large new building, constructed by the Duran Construction Company, on Seventh Street. The new building staged a grand opening in June of 1998.[96]

The Huerfano County Public Library, under the leadership of Sylvia Rael, the first fully-qualified librarian the institution ever had, completed a massive remodeling paid for by a large grant.

A few years later, threatened with drastic budget cuts from the county, the library and the Friends of the Library mounted a successful campaign to establish an independent library district with its own mill levy. The vote to make the county library an independent library district passed by a 2–1 vote and became the Spanish Peaks Library. Donna Allenbaugh, library director, and the Friends of the Library had worked long hours to make this dream a reality. The library continued to expand services and collections. Use of the library increased dramatically until space became critical, and the board of directors and, later librarians, began to look at ways and means of expanding the facilities.[97]

As the end of the century approached, the citizens of Walsenburg were experiencing the same trepidation about the coming of the new millennium, largely due to the fears that all computers would crash and cause chaos in a world dependent upon them. For the most part, however, the people of the town looked at this change as they had all of the other drastic changes the community had experienced in its long history, as just one more problem to be endured and somehow solved. Walsenburg would continue on its quiet, though sometimes turbulent, way.

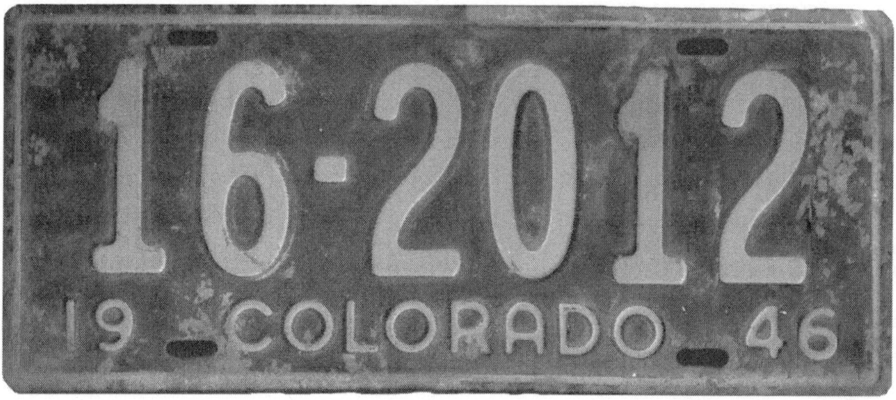
16-2012
19 COLORADO 46

Chapter Twelve

INTO THE TWENTY-FIRST CENTURY

On the morning of January 1, 2000, the people of Walsenburg awoke to find that their lights turned on, their refrigerators were still operating, their computers went online on command, and Safeway was still able to provide for their grocery needs. The dreaded new millennium had arrived with none of the feared interruptions in services. Life would go on in the little town as always.

Walsenburg is never far from its past. In a local newspaper column, Nancy Christofferson reported that in the 1910s Walsenburg had two newspapers, two schools, at least fifteen saloons, nine hotels, twenty-four wholesale and retail groceries, meat and merchandise businesses, ten physicians, and two dentists, two undertakers, three drugstores, three furniture and hardware businesses, six churches, a dairy, two banks, several feed and livery stables, blacksmiths, three confectionary/bakery shops, two lumber yards, numerous restaurants and cafes and all kinds of services.[1]

A few years earlier, Christofferson had also published a book on the coal mining history of the county. Entitled *Coal Was King*, the book presented information on each of the dozens of coal mines in the area.[2]

In January Effie Faris George celebrated her 107th birthday. Born in New Orleans, Louisiana, in 1893, she married Kalil George in 1910 and moved to Walsenburg. She was one of a few thousand people in the country to be born in one century, live an entire century, and continue into a third century. Mrs. George died the following year at the age of 108.[3]

St. Mary Church celebrated its 100th birthday with an ice cream social for parishioners. Monsignor Howard L. Delaney and

Bishop Arthur N. Tafoya assisted Pastor Richard Wehrmeyer in various church services during the centennial celebration.[4]

A new statue of a miner was placed in the Main Street Triangle. Carved by Community Corrections of America inmate J. Robert Winters in the prison workshop, the statue is of cottonwood. Renovation of the courthouse began with the replacing of the roof and work on the parapets, cornices and gutters. Maurice Brau was sworn in as mayor, replacing Fred Rodriguez; Paula Sterk Conder, who had served twenty-one years as city clerk, left office due to term limits.[5]

A new spirit seemed to have arisen in Walsenburg with a desire to change things.

In 1996 Marti Henderson bought the building at 118 East Sixth Street. This structure had been the Oxford Hotel and later, in 1939, had become the Kirkpatrick Hotel. At one time, part of the lower floor had housed the post office, and another part had been used as the bus station. Henderson completely renovated the structure, adding bathrooms to the upstairs rooms and decorating with Victorian furnishings. A banquet room and restaurant were installed in the lower floor. The new business was named La Plaza and opened for business on Memorial Day 1997.

The restaurant failed to attract enough attention, and that portion became a breakfast room for hotel guests and for catered luncheons and banquets.

Realizing that La Plaza was not generating enough business, Henderson decided to do what she could to help revitalize the downtown area. She bought three properties on Main Street, located on the west side between Sixth and Seventh Streets. Her properties also included the vacant lot where the historic Mazzone Opera House once stood. Three shops were located in these buildings, which had been refurbished to reflect the style of the era when they were built, and the corner lot has been turned into a small park.

Cowboy Connections, featuring western wear, was managed by Henderson with the help of Deb Williams and Marianne Smithey.

The Antique Mall was actually several small mini-stores with local people offering various wares, mostly antiques.

The Southwest Store offered anything to do with the southwest including home décor, jewelry and pottery.

Henderson's idea in the beginning was to offer tourists more reasons for coming to Walsenburg and staying longer than servicing the car would take.[6]

Other new projects greatly improved the appearance of Main Street. Rich McEntee, owner of the Black Diamond Housing Park, a few miles west of Walsenburg, opened an office and art gallery on the southwest corner of Main and Seventh Street, where the Walsen and Levy store once stood, and re-opened the service station on the northwest corner of these streets. The noted O'Byrne Hardware Store occupied that site in earlier years. Both of these buildings were decorated to correspond with the Black Diamond Housing. Star Drug had a face lift, and a day spa under the management of Patty Corsentino Kelley opened a few doors north of the drugstore. A coffee shop opened just north of the Silver Scissors Beauty Parlor at 510 Main. Other buildings have been sold to buyers with plans for innovative retail opportunities.

The new spirit in Walsenburg was not limited to businesses. The city long struggled with keeping the swimming pool open for the youth of the community. It had been a losing battle due to poor construction years ago. In 2003 the city council was told that the old pool was beyond repair. The council consulted a pool designer and learned that a new pool would cost about a million dollars and would be a simple pool. The council decided to work toward the creation of a water park in the same City Park location on Seventh Street. The water park would have two pools and a lazy river. The main pool, designed for family use, would be from zero feet to three and a half feet in depth. A very large pool with water buckets and water cannons for children and teenagers was included in the second pool. Two projected water slides – a small one and a large one, three stories tall and 160 feet long, would be added last. The lazy river plans included hundreds of feet of flowing water tied into the swimming pool at the end. Councilman

Maurice Brau believed that the water park would be a huge boost economically to the community since tourists would want to stop and stay for several hours. For some time members of the city council were reluctant to begin until the money was completely in hand, but due to the risk of losing some grant money that had been obtained, council voted to begin the project.[7]

Education is never far from the minds of the people of Walsenburg whether the subject is how well the schools are doing, what more is needed or how much will it cost. For several years there had been concerns about education in the lower grades. Many residents did not like having the fifth grade students in the same building with the junior high students. At that time fifth through eighth grades were located in the Walsenburg Middle School, the red brick building on Walsen Avenue. When the building was first built, it had been the Huerfano County High School and was later renamed Walsenburg High School. After the construction of John Mall High School in the mid-1970s, the red brick building had become Walsenburg Middle School.

School district administrators were not in disagreement with the parents of fifth graders, but there simply was not room for them in Washington School, which now housed kindergarten through fourth grade.

So the idea of an early childhood learning center was born. The first mention of such a center came in late spring of the 1996-97 school year. The school superintendent at that time was Glenn Davis, and the members of the school board were Mickey D'Ambrosia, Al Manzanares, Tom Vail, Marge Figal, Elaine Lenzini, Anita Cordova and Jaye Sudar-Thomas. Suggestions were made to lease a building, separate off a portion of Washington School, or to place a modular classroom on part of the Washington playground. None of these ideas found much support, and the discussion of the matter was dropped for a few years.

In the fall of 1998, the school board directed Davis to investigate the possibility of building such a school for pre-school and kindergarten through first grade. New board members in 1998 were Jim Eccher, Sue Powell and Dave Mockmore.

Early in 1999, the Early Childhood Learning Center study committee was formed. Its members were Julia Marchant, principal of Gardner School, Susan Murdock, Ellie Linke, Marie Nigrini, Edi Sheldon, Theresa Martinez, Tom Powell, Elaine Lenzini and Dave Mockmore. The focus of the early meetings was on how to fund such a building. The idea of including the Head Start early childhood program now entered the picture. Two new board members, Jill Davis Homerding and Ernie Reynolds, had also joined the discussion.

Within two years the committee was exploring the idea of building as much as possible to start and planning for an eventual kindergarten through eighth grade facility. The architectural firm of Lantz-Boggio was chosen to prepare a facilities assessment and to deliver a master plan. This plan was delivered and reviewed by the committee and the school board in the spring of 2002. Superintendent Davis said, "At this juncture in the process Lantz-Boggio, represented by John Quest, and Houston Construction, represented by Ken West and Paul DePatie, stepped up big with no guarantee that they would profit and helped us greatly with projecting costs." [8]

In June of 2002 the school board at last decided to propose a bond issue to the voters for $5,755,000 with about half a million going to the Gardner School addition. This addition would consist of a science classroom and a pre-school classroom.

Until now the science classes at Gardner had been held in a rickety, single-wide trailer and the pre-school was housed half a mile away in an aging Forest Service building.

Many people came together to work hard on the Vote Yes on the 3A campaign. I told Don Diones (a representative of the George K. Baum Investment Bankers, Inc.) that it might take three tries to pass a bond issue, but the "Committee for Education" only planned for one. Lynette Kleinschmidt and Jill Davis Homerding were co-chairpersons, Marge Figal, treasurer, and Sue Powell, secretary. Their members were Julia Marchant, Jaye Sudar-Thomas, Pamela Levie, Mary Anderson, Carolyn New-

man, Ernie Reynolds, Valerie Halvorson, Sandra Wagner, Judy McCutcheon, John Figal, Dianne Hanisch, Patricia Martinez, Cathy Harmes, Jolette Martinez, Yvonne Griego, Sharon Ulrich, Francie Davis, Theresa Martinez, Antoinette Vigil, Gaye Davis, and Mickey D'Ambrosia. The committee worked tirelessly on fundraisers, presentations to groups, letters to the editor, house to house, and phone campaigning.[9]

The bond issue passed by a margin of fifty-eight votes.

Funding was later increased through the talents of the school district's grant writer, Gaye Davis. Her efforts brought in a total of $1,232,600, which local taxpayers did not have to fund. These grants allowed the district to add classrooms to house second and third grades as well as the original classes. Another grant provided a new roof, heating and air conditioning, upgraded wiring and other improvements to the west building of John Mall High School, which now housed the junior high classes.

Ground breaking was held on July 15, 2003, with a gold-shovel ceremony.

One aim of the school board was to have the building as solidly built as possible, unlike John Mall High School, which had been built as cheaply as possible. The foundation for the building that would become Peakview School included removing forty inches of soil, which contracts and expands, and replacing it with soil which does not. A total of 140 pilings, averaging twenty-five feet long going down to bedrock, were put in place. These were approximately thirty inches in diameter with an inner circle of two-inch rebar put in place before concrete was poured. It was believed that this foundation was solid enough to prevent problems in the future.

Following the dedication of the building on September 28, 2004, the school opened under the leadership of Principal Patricia L. Martinez.

A descendant of pioneer John Albert, Patricia Martinez was born and raised in Walsenburg. She left at the age of eighteen and went to college at the University of Colorado at Boulder, where she graduated. She spent five years in Boulder and then went to Seville, Spain, where she earned credits toward a degree in Spanish. Returning to the United States, she taught at Trinidad State Junior College in a special services program.

She next decided to return home to Walsenburg and taught for eleven years in the Gardner School and ten years at Washington School. Deciding to become an administrator, she took the necessary courses for certification as a principal and spent a year in Mexico near Talapa as the principal in a small, primitive village.

Returning once again to her home town, she became the principal of Washington School and then moved into the leadership position of the bright, new Peakview School.[10]

Martinez is extremely enthusiastic about everything surrounding Peakview School. She has high praise for her dedicated staff of teachers and their commitment to children and parents. The relationship between the faculty and the staff of the Head Start program continues to grow and improve.

The gymnasium is used and loved by all students. Head Start children use it as well as the public school students. All junior high games are played in this gym, so it is important to more than one school.

The library is another much loved area, especially the cozy reading corner that features a gas fireplace and carpeted steps where children sit to hear stories. The climbing wall and other playground features are quite popular. Pre-school classes and Head Start share the west playground including the climbing equipment and tricycles and wagons.

Most important, says Patricia Martinez, is the multi-purpose room that is used for children's meals, programs and parent conferences. It is "a room of joy".[11]

Once the decision had been made to build Peakview School, the question arose of what to do with the old building that had started life about 1925 as Huerfano County High School, and had most recently been Walsenburg Middle School.

The red brick building was no longer needed as a school building. The classes transferring to Peakview School would make it possible for Washington School to accommodate the fourth, fifth and sixth grade classes. The seventh and eighth grade students would be placed in one wing of the west building on the John Mall High School campus. What would be done with the venerable old school in which so many residents of the community had spent their high school years? Some members of the school administration and the school board had long dreamed of having a regulation track. The track around the football field did not meet the specifications of the Colorado School Athletic Association, and the school district could not hold track meets in Walsenburg. To have enough land for the construction of a track, football field and spectator seating, and parking on the site of the current football field, would require the demolition of the three-story building. The school board quietly made plans for its demolition.

At an economic development meeting, Margaret Van Schoyck Gleisberg overheard two local men talking about a parking lot where Walsenburg Middle School stood. Suellen Levy, great-granddaughter of Alexander and Lillie Levy, and Edi Sheldon, daughter of Bill and Jeannette Faris Thach, also heard talk of the planned demolition of the school.

These women were outraged at the idea of demolishing this historic building and called a meeting to discuss what could be done to save it. They talked to Dave Marquez, Wayne Davis and others. Problems were encountered, but their research indicated that the school could be rehabilitated into a viable building that could be put to other uses.

At their first attempt to discuss the matter, School Superintendent Glenn Davis refused to talk with them. The group requested more time from the school district but were told they could not have more time. They contacted County Commissioner Oress DeHerrera, U. S. Congressman Scott McInnis and others. They visited Las Animas, Aguilar and Canon City, neighboring towns that were also attempting to save historic buildings scheduled for demolition.[12]

Another contact was with the State Historical Society. Here they learned that money was available for historic preservation, but that Huerfano County had only sought money twice — once for the Francisco Fort Museum in La Veta and once for the Huerfano County Courthouse. Huerfano County, they were told, would have an excellent chance at being awarded money. A formal organization called Save Our School was formed and, at last, a connection was established with Huerfano Re-1 School District that would allow time for possible uses for the building to be explored and for money to be obtained for the needed building assessment and feasibility studies.

Meetings of S.O.S. were held at the former union train depot, the Chamber of Commerce office, and a tourist information center. Many people expressed interest in the project, but those who were willing to commit time, money and effort were Gene and Margaret Gleisberg, Mary Jo and David Tesitor, Gretchen Sporleder Orr, Suellen Levy, Edi Sheldon, Jewel Krier Geiger and Betty Ridge. Others organizations, including the Walsenburg Woman's Club, helped greatly with mailings and getting public support.[13]

While all this was going on, another local entity had been making plans for expansion. The Spanish Peaks Public Library had been busily outgrowing its space for several years. Improvements had been made in recent years that had expanded the available space for children, but more space in the adult sections of the library just was not possible, and the demand for more books and more computer space kept growing.

The Board of Directors of the library began to seek grant money to fund building an addition to the 1952 building. Good grant writing brought in the money, but then the architect began to find problems with the existing building, which raised almost insurmountable barriers to the plans.

At this point the idea of using the first floor of the endangered red brick school building for the Spanish Peaks Public Library was advanced. The Friends of the Library organization became interested in the possibilities and went over the building from top to bottom. The organization, under the leadership of Jerry

Skrzynear, became excited about the project and decided to become involved with the Save Our School people.

The two groups approached the Huerfano County Historical Society for financial help for the initial studies. The Society is made up of members from both Walsenburg and La Veta. The aims of the two communities do not always coincide, but, in this instance, an agreement was reached, and HCHS agreed to sponsor the project. Its members remained helpful throughout. With HCHS signing on, grant money was obtained in the amount of $10,000 for the building assessment and $15,000 for a feasibility study.

The results of these studies were presented to the school board. A large community meeting was held at Peakview School, and the turnout clearly indicated the desire of many citizens to see the building saved rather than demolished for part of a sports complex. It was clear, however, that the school administration and the board were not yet convinced. While some citizens believed that since the building belonged to the people and since a viable plan to rehabilitate it was being offered, the school board should give the building to the Economic Development Corporation; the board did not see it that way.

Before things could reach a complete impasse, an unlikely newcomer entered the picture. The Colorado State Historical Society had long been involved in efforts to save historic school buildings in rural, southeastern Colorado but had met with little success. Now the Society decided to try a new approach. The Society offered $200,000 for the purchase of the school building.

The offer was enough to make the school board and administration consider the matter seriously, but their next step created another hurdle. They demanded $250,000 for the purchase of the school building and the gym built following the disastrous fire of 1975.

Of course, the library board and other groups did not have the larger sum, but, after further negotiations, the library board offered $225,000. The additional sum would come from the grant money the library had already received from other sources.

At last a deal was struck, and the red brick building became the property of the Economic Development Corporation who then deeded it to the Spanish Peaks Public Library.

The Master Plan for the library included the following goals:

1. An expanded children's area to provide space for story time and storage and more children's activities.
2. Increased shelving to relieve crowded shelves and to provide for all formats, books, videos, large print, over-sized books, etc.
3. Meet Americans with Disabilities Act.
4. Work space for staff and room for volunteers to sort, cover books, etc.
5. Preserve and rehabilitate the building to complement community, sustain long-term use, and be ecologically appropriate.
6. Necessary parking
7. A community anchor and destination.

Eventually enough grant money was obtained to enable the library to begin work on the massive task of preparing the old building for a new life. Sales have been held that allowed citizens to purchase old desks, books, and other usable items left behind by the school district.[14]

Now the story of a coal miner statue took a new turn. In 1983 School Superintendent Walter L. Way had made good on his promise to carve a statue of a coal miner to be placed in the triangle of land on Walsen Avenue near the United Church. Way tells the story.

> *My friend, Jake Pino, found a log in Gardner that was large enough to "fit" a miner. He hauled it to my home on Second Street and set it upright. Jake also volunteered to serve as a model. I had borrowed a miner's hat-with-lamp and a bucket, used for holding food and water, from a resident who told me about his son who had worn it, and who had been killed in a mine accident. A pick from a local hardware store completed the ensemble, and Jake, in typical working clothes, posed as I photographed him from all*

sides. The photos were scaled to create a 5 foot 9 inch figure sketched on the log, and carving began in September of 1983.

A chain saw helped in the removal of large chunks of wood, grinders with carbide bits were used to shape facial features, and chisels and gouges helped in creating the finer details of face, hands, and folds in the clothing. After sanding, the statue was covered with black walnut stain to give the appearance of bronze. a polyurethane finish was brushed on to preserve the miner who faced years of bright sunlight before the people of Walsenburg commissioned the bronzing of Mister Miner as a tribute to families of miners. This was truly a labor of love.[15]

As originally planned, the statue was installed in the Main Street Triangle, replacing Way's carving of an Indian which was moved to City Park on Seventh Street. For a number of years, the miner stood watch there, pick on his shoulder and lunch bucket in his hand. Wind and sunlight took its toll eventually, and the city decided to remove the figure. A nearby motel took it, and it stood there for another few years. When the motel owner also decided to get rid of the aging work, he called Betty Ridge and asked if the Walsenburg Mining Museum would like to have it. She said "Yes" and the miner was installed on his stump base in front of the museum located in the 1896 jail west of the courthouse. There he stood for many more years while wind and sunlight continued to wear away at the proud figure.

The members of the Board of Directors of the museum realized that it was only a matter of time until the wooden statue would be beyond saving. No one remembers exactly who first raised the idea of casting the miner in bronze. It was a scary idea because everyone knew that it would cost a great deal, but the members chose to explore the idea.

Board member Mary McIntyre undertook the task of contacting area sculptors to see what the possibilities were. Most artists resisted the idea of using the original statue. They preferred to sculpt a statue from the beginning, but the members knew that this would be too expensive. Besides, everyone liked the miner as he was. After many discussions, sculptor Nick Moffett of Pueblo West agreed to cast the original in bronze.

Dorothy Ree, chairman of the Board of Directors at the time, placed the item on the agenda at a regular board meeting. Relatively little discussion was held before the vote was taken. The board members unanimously voted to cast the miner in bronze.

At the annual luncheon honoring museum volunteers that spring, Richard and Betty Ridge got the fund-raising underway with a generous monetary gift. This gave heart to everyone that the funds could be raised, and the dream become reality.

The next matter to be decided was the base for the statue. The wooden miner had been carved from a single log and the base was simply several feet of the log. A base for the bronze statue would have to be considerably different.

Ultimately a large concrete square was built by the construction crew of Bill Reiners. It was located just in front of the museum in the same spot where the original statue had stood.

The concrete square would be faced with polished black granite slabs engraved with names of men who had worked in the mines. Family members or friends could have a name engraved for a donation of $100 to the museum. This sum would cover the cost of engraving each name and would pay for the very expensive black granite.

From that point on, museum fund-raising was concentrated on the statue. Regular fund-raisers included the August Ice Cream Social and the Christmas Bazaar.

In 2004 Margaret Gleisberg was chosen as chairman of the Board of Directors and they threw their considerable energies, full-time, into raising the money for the statue.

San Isabel Electric Company, in one of its many community service projects, agreed to remove the wooden miner from his base and transport him to the Moffet Studio in Pueblo West.

All members of the board gathered to watch the delicate task of cutting him loose, lifting him free with the San Isabel crane and placing him gently on a trailer. The greatest fear was that the aging statue would crumble away, but this did not happen.

With the statue in the hands of Nick Moffett, attention was now given to the matter of soliciting the names of miners for the base. Newspaper articles and a request form were printed in the *Huerfano World*, and before long, completed forms with names and the mines where men had worked, along with $100 donations, began arriving. Much of this activity happened by word of mouth with the descendant of one miner passing the opportunity on to another. Letters and donations came not only from Walsenburg and its surrounding area, but also from throughout the state and all over the nation.

After considering offers from several companies, the statue committee finally awarded the contract for the base to Classic Stone of Pueblo. The statue was completed and paid for, and it looked as if it might be possible to install and dedicate the statue in the fall of 2005. Soon, however, it became apparent that it would take longer for the black granite to be obtained. The company also needed at least forty-eight hours of above-freezing temperatures for the black panels to set properly when they were attached to the concrete base. Otherwise they might crack later on and, at the price of the black granite, the museum couldn't afford for that to happen. Soon after the first of the year the Board of Directors selected May 21, 2006, for the dedication of Mr. Miner, as he had come to be known.

Next came a time of nervously watching the weather reports for news of rising temperatures along with plans for the dedication ceremony.

Strong support for the project came from the Huerfano County commissioners: Oress DeHerrera, Roger Cain and Scott King. When replacing a broken window in the tower of the county-owned building proved to be more expensive than the museum could afford, the commissioners promptly had it replaced. They also agreed to install floodlights to light the statue at night. Throughout the project, the support of these men had been invaluable.

Walter Way, the sculptor of the original statue, was contacted and agreed to come to the dedication and to tell the visitors about the carving.

On May 8 the black granite panels with 179 names engraved were installed. On May 15 San Isabel workers brought Mr. Miner, swaddled in blue plastic, home and installed him on his base.

At the meeting of the Board of Directors that week, the question arose of what to do with the original wooden statue. Pieces had fallen off during transportation to Pueblo and the arms had been removed to facilitate making the molds for the bronze casting. The old statue could no longer be displayed, yet no member of the board wanted to see it cut up and thrown away. Once again Betty Ridge came to the rescue with an idea she had already researched. Why not bury the old statue in the Masonic Cemetery and install a memorial to represent all miners? The cemetery board not only agreed but also insisted that the spot be near the entrance where visitors would see it. The Board of Directors unanimously agreed to this proposal. Elaine Levy Lenzini, the granddaughter of Lillie Sporleder Levy, donated the black granite slab that honored Amelia Walsen, wife of Fred Walsen. Mr. Miner now has a "final resting place" in the Masonic Cemetery.

The morning of May 21, 2006, dawned clear, hot and slightly windy. By midmorning museum personnel were arriving to set up chairs, go over the program, and do all the other last minute tasks needed before the dedication ceremony in the afternoon.

Promptly at two o'clock the colors were presented by members of the VFW/American Legion and the national anthem was played by the Huerfano Winds, a small brass and wind ensemble of local musicians directed by Suellen Levy. Vocal music was provided by the Children's Chorale, also directed by Levy. A crowd of two to three hundred people filled the bleachers and chairs, while others sat on the grass of the courthouse lawn.

Scott D. King, county commissioner, made the welcoming address and Margaret Gleisberg, chairman of the Walsenburg Mining Museum Board of Directors, acknowledged the contributions of many people to the day's activities. Retired District Judge Albert Tomsic introduced the members of the Board of Directors. Carolyn Newman told the crowd about the history of coal mining in the county, and Mayor Edi Sheldon discussed the coming of the railroads to Walsenburg, and the importance of the role they played in the development of the town and county. County Commissioner Roger A. Cain told the story of the 1896 jail, and Walter Way related the story of his carving of the original statue. He introduced Jake Pino, who had been the model for the work. Two more short speeches concerning the Huerfano County Historical Society and the Walsenburg Mining Museum were offered.

At last County Commissioner Oress DeHerrera arose to dedicate the statue. He identified himself as a "coal camp kid", a person who had grown up in one of the many coal camps, and asked all in the audience who were "coal camp kids" to stand. About half the audience rose to the applause of everyone there.

Commissioner DeHerrera spoke the words of dedication. The three commissioners and Jake Pino then pulled away the wrappings that had shielded Mr. Miner from view.

The black granite panels with the carved names gleamed in the sunlight, and the proud face of the bronzed miner gazed out over the crowd that had come to welcome him.

In closing comments Margaret Gleisberg noted the presence of one man, John B. Meehan, age 94, who had actually worked in Toltec Mine in Huerfano County. Two women assisted the old man to rise from his wheelchair to accept the accolades of the audience.

To the playing of "National Anthem" by the Huerfano Winds, the flags were removed and the audience was invited to enter the museum and look around. The day for which so many had planned for, worked for, and contributed to was over and the results of all their work will stand for years to come to be enjoyed and appreciated by visitors to the museum and all of the residents of Walsenburg and Huerfano County.

A new spirit has come to Walsenburg. Good things are happening with schools, libraries, Main Street businesses, tourism and recreation. The gentle days of La Plaza de los Leones are gone. The turbulence of the mining days will come no more. It is hoped that the people will never again have to gather scrap metal and old rubber and send their sons and daughters to fight a global war.

More changes may come to the little crossroads town, but whatever changes come, the bronze miner will be seen striding out of Walsenburg's past with his eyes fixed on Walsenburg's future.

FOOTNOTES

Chapter One – La Plaza de los Leones

1. Vallejo papers.
2. Jackson, *Bits of Travel at Home,* "WA-HA-TOY-A," p. 158.
3. Vallejo papers.
4. Vallejo papers.
5. Delaney, "All Our Yesterdays," pp. 18-19.
6. Sporleder papers, "August Sporleder."
7. Ibid.

Chapter Two – The Pioneers

1. Sporleder Papers, "Miguel Leon and La Plaza de los Leones"
2. Ibid.
3. Ibid.
4. Vallejo Papers
5. Sporleder papers, "John David Albert."
6. Bauer, Ozment, Willard, *Colorado Postal History: the post offices,* p. 223.
7. Sporleder papers, "Henry Jones"
8. Sporleder papers, "John David Albert."
9. Interview with Elvera Cordova
10. Sporleder Papers, "Henry Jones"
11. Sporleder Papers, "August Sporleder"
12. Ibid.
13. Sporleder Papers, "Cornelius Hendren"
14. Ibid
15. Papers of Chuck and Nancy Hutchinson
16. Sporleder papers, "J. A. J. Valdez"
17. Ibid.
18. Sporleder Papers, "Benton Canon"
19. From research by George B. Ree and *Walsenburg World,* Dec. 9, 1892
20. Sporleder papers, "Charles Mazzone"
21. Notes from Benton Canon
22. Sporleder papers, "Charles Otto Unfug"
23. Ibid.
24. *Colorado Biography,* "Alexander Levy," p. 976.

Chapter Three – La Plaza Becomes Walsenburg

1. Sporleder Papers
2. Sporleder Papers, "The Georgia Colony"
3. Walker, *Pioneers of the Territory of Southern Colorado, Vol. II*, "The Antoine LaBrie family," pp. 61-62.
4. Ibid.
5. Byers, *Encyclopedia of Biography of Colorado*, p. 458.
6. Ordinances of the Town of Walsenburg.
7. Delaney, *All Our Yesterdays*, p. 14
8. Nardine, *In the Shadow of the Spanish Peaks*, p. 51
9. Ibid.
10. Delaney, *All Our Yesterdays*, pp. 21-22
11. Ibid.

Chapter Four – Coal

1. Vallejo papers
2. Ibid.
3. Griswold, *Rio Grande: Along the Rio Grande,* p. 62.
4. Vallejo papers
5. Ibid.
6. Ibid.
7. Ibid
8. Ibid
9. *Colorado Exchange,*"Wonderful Walsenburg."
10. Papanikolas, *Buried Unsung*, pp. 35-36.
11. Unpublished manuscript of Paul Krier
12. Ibid.

Chapter Five – The King of Huerfano County

1. McGovern and Guttridge, *The Great Coalfield War*, pp. 30-32
2. Beshoar, *Out of the Depths*, p. 7
3. *Cactus* newspaper, May 8, 1884, p. 1
4. Allison papers
5. Ibid.
6. Vallejo papers
7. Ibid.
8. McGovern and Guttridge, *The Great Coalfield War*, pp. 173-174
9. John Case Papers, "Report of Verdeckburg"
10. Ibid.

11. Ibid.
12. Ibid.
13. *Walsenburg World,*
14. Case papers, "Report of Verdeckburg"
15. Ibid.
16. Ibid.
17. Ibid.
18. Sinclair, postscript of *King Coal.*
19. *The Independent,* April 24, 1915, p. 1
20. Neelley vs. Farr, Colorado Supreme Court, April, 1916
21. Ibid.
22. Ibid.
23. Ibid.
24. Ibid.
25. *Walsenburg World,* June 22, 1916.
26. Beshoar, *Out of the Depths,* p 345

Chapter Six – Churches, Schools and Libraries

1. Delaney, *All Our Yesterdays,* p. 18
2. Ibid., p. 19
3. Ibid., p. 22
4. Ibid., p. 24
5. Ibid., pp. 41ff
6. Ibid. p. 59
7. Ree, Dorothy Rose and Carolyn Newman. "A Narrative History of the United Church of Walsenburg". 2004. p. 8
8. Ibid., p. 8
9. Elisha, Irene, *The Huerfano World,* March 1, 1984., p. 6.
10. Ibid.
11. Ibid.
12. Ibid
13. Ibid.
14. Davis, Alice. "History of the high school."
15. Elisha, Irene, *The Huerfano World,* March 1, 1984, p. 6
16. Ibid.
17. Ibid
18. *The World-Independent,* Feb. 19, 1934, p. 1.
19. *The World-Independent,* April 25-May 2, 1938, p. 1.
20. *The World-Independent,* June 1, 1928, pp. 1,5,8.
21. *The World-Independent,* Sept. 6, 1938, p. 1.
22. Martin, Clarence J., *The Star Journal,* Pueblo.
23. *The World-Independent,* Jan. 14, 1958.

24. Ree, Dorothy Rose, "An Informal History of the Huerfano County Library," unpublished manuscript, 2002, pp. 2-3.
25. Ibid.

Chapter Seven – War and Epidemic

1. Minutes of the Walsenburg City Council, May 5, 1915.
2. Ibid.
3. "A Short History of the Walsenburg Chamber of Commerce," pp. 5-6.
4. *The Independent*, Jan. 12, 1917, p. 1.
5. *The Independent*, Jan. 26, 1917, p.1.
6. *The Independent*, Feb. 9 and Feb. 16, 1917, p.1.
7. *The Independent*, April 6, 1917, p. 1.
8. *The Independent*, April 13, 1917, p. 1.
9. *The Independent*, April 20, 1917, p. 1.
10. *The Independent*, April 27, 1917, p. 1.
11. *The Independent*, May 11, 1917, p. 1.
12. *The Independent*, May 4, 1917, p. 1.
13. *The Independent*, May 11, 1917, p. 1.
14. "Short History of the Walsenburg Chamber of Commerce."
15. *The Independent*, May 4, 1917, p. 1.
16. *The Independent*, June 1, 1917, p. 1.
17. Ibid.
18. *The Independent*, Aug. 10, 1917, p.1.
19. *The Independent*, May 10, 1918, p. 1.
20. *The Independent*, April 20, 1917, p. 1.
21. *The Independent*, June 7, 1918, p. 1.
22. *The Independent*, June 28, 1918, p. 1.
23. *The Independent*, Nov. 22, 1918, p. 1.
24. *The Independent*, Nov. 29, 1918, p. 1.
25. *The Independent*, Dec. 27, 1918, p. 1.
26. Ree and Newman, *Narrative History of the United Church*, p. 16.
27. *The Independent*, Mar. 14, 1919, p. 1.
28. *The Independent*, July 11, 1919, p. 1.

Chapter Eight – The Quiet Twenties

1. *Walsenburg World*, Mar. 18, 1920, p. 1.
2. Ibid.
3. "Short History of the Walsenburg Chamber of Commerce."
4. *The Independent*, Nov. 11, 1921, p. 1.
5. *The Independent*, Mar. 22, 1922, p. 1.

6. *The Independent*, Aug. 14, 1923, p. 1.
7. Ibid.
8. Author's observation.
9. Ree, "An Informal History of the Huerfano County Public Library."
10. Personal interview by the author with Norma Lou Brunelli Murr.,
11. Mortimer, "Klan Politics in Colorado," *Journal of the West*, pp. 89-90.
12. *The Independent*, Sept. 27, 1927, p. 1.
13. Rees. "X','XX', and 'XXX': spy reports from the Colorado Fuel and Iron Company archives", *Colorado Historical Society*, Winter, 2001, pp. 28-41.
14. Ibid.
15. *The Independent*, Jan. 13, 1927, p. 1.

Chapter Nine – Dust and Depression

1. *The Independent*, Feb. 14, 1930, p. 1.
2. *The Independent*, Mar. 17, 1930, p. 1.
3. *The Independent*, June 3, 1930, p. 1.
4. *Walsenburg World*, June 24, 1930, p. 1.
5. Ibid, p. 3.
6. Personal interview by the author with Norma Lou Brunelli Murr.
7. *Walsenburg World*, July 15, 1930, p. 1.
8. *The Independent*, Sept. 12, 1930, p. 1.
9. *The Independent*, Oct. 3, 1930, p. 1.
10. *The World-Independent*, April 10, 1931, p. 1.
11. Ibid.
12. Ibid.
13. *The World-Independent*, May 8, 1931, p. 1.
14. *The World-Independent*, May 22, 1931, p. 1.
15. *The World-Independent*, Dec. 19, 1931, p. 1, and Feb. 5, 1932, p. 1.
16. *Walsenburg World*, Mar. 22, 1932, p. 1.
17. *Walsenburg World*, May 10, 1932, p. 1.
18. *The Independent*, July 22, 1932, p. 1.
19. *The Independent*, Nov. 11, 1932, p. 1.
20. *The Independent*, Oct. 27, 1933, p. 1.
21. *Walsenburg World*, April 27, 1933, p. 1.
22. *Walsenburg World*, May 19, 1922, p. 1.
23. *Walsenburg World*, May 23, 1933, p. 1.
24. *Walsenburg World*, May 30, 1933, p. 1.
25. *Walsenburg World*, June 15, 1933, p. 1.
26. *Walsenburg World*, Oct. 20, 1933, p. 1.
27. *Walsenburg World*, Oct. 27, 1933, p. 1.
28. *Walsenburg World*, Oct. 28, 1933, p. 1.

29. *Walsenburg World*, May 24, 1933, p. 1.
30. *Walsenburg World*, Dec. 19, 1933, p. 1.
31. *Walsenburg World*, Mar. 19, 1934, p. 1.
32. *Walsenburg World*, May 11, 1934, p. 1.
33. *Walsenburg World*, June 6, 1934, p. 1.
34. *Walsenburg World*, Aug. 6, 1937, p. 1.
35. *Walsenburg World*, Nov. 10, 1937, p. 1.
36. *Walsenburg World*, Dec. 9, 1937, p. 1.
37. *Walsenburg World*, Dec. 24, 1937, p. 1.
38. *Walsenburg World*, Jan. 4, 1938, p. 1.
39. *The Denver Post*, June 19, 1938.
40. *World-Independent*, July 22, 1938, p. 1.
41. *World-Independent*, Aug. 1, 1938, p. 1.
42. *Pueblo Chieftain*, May 25, 1938, p. 1.
43. *World-Independent*, June 5, 1939, p. 1.

Chapter Ten – War Comes to Walsenburg

1. *World-Independent*, Jan. 4, 5, 12, 18, 1940, p. 1.
2. *World-Independent*, Jan. 26, 30, 1940, p. 1.
3. *World-Independent*, April 8, 1940, p. 1.
4. *World-Independent*, May 24, 1940, p. 1.
5. *World-Independent*, June 28, July 3, 1940, p. 1.
6. *World-Independent*, Aug. 29, 1940, p. 1.
7. *World-Independent*, Jan. 23, 1941, p. 1.
8. *World-Independent*, Jan. 29, 1941, p. 1.
9. *World-Independent*, Feb. 17, 1941, p. 1.
10. *World-Independent*, Aug. 12, 1941, p. 1.
11. *World-Independent*, Dec. 9, 1941, p. 1.
12. *World-Independent*, Jan. 5, 1942, p. 1.
13. *World-Independent*, Jan. 7, 1941, p. 1.
14. *World-Independent*, January 1941 and 1942.
15. *World-Independent*, Jan. 7, 1941, p. 1.
16. *World-Independent*, June 9 and 15, 1942, p. 1.
17. *World-Independent*, July 14, 1942, p. 1.
18. *World-Independent*, Mar. 15, 1942, p. 1.
19. *World-Independent*, Mar. 26, 1943, p. 1.
20. *World-Independent*, April 19, 1943, p. 1.
21. *World-Independent*, April 20, 1943, p. 1.
22. *World-Independent*, June 21, 1943, p. 1.
23. *World-Independent*, Sept. 18, 1943, p. 1.
24. *World-Independent*, May 1, 1944, p. 1.

25. *World-Independent*, May 5, 1944, p. 1.
26. *World-Independent*, July 12, 1944, p. 1.
27. *World-Independent*, July 27, 1944, p. 1.
28. *World-Independent*, Aug. 10, 1944, p. 1.
29. *World-Independent*, Oct. 6, 1944, p. 1.
30. *World-Independent*, Oct. 13, 1944, p. 1.
31. *World-Independent*, Nov. 20, 1944, p. 1.
32. *World-Independent*, Jan. 3, 1945, p. 1.
33. *World-Independent*, Feb. 19, 1945, p. 1.
34. *World-Independent*, April 10, 1945, p. 1.
35. *World-Independent*, April 19, 1945, p. 1.
36. *World-Independent*, Oct. 21, 1948, p. 1.
37. *World-Independent*, Dec. 17, 1948, p. 1.

Chapter Eleven – Toward the End of the Century

1. *World-Independent*, Sept. 7, 1950, p. 1.
2. *World-Independent*, Feb. 21, 1952, p. 1.
3. *World-Independent*, Mar. 12, 1952, p. 1.
4. *World-Independent*, July 8 and July 20, 1953, p. 1.
5. *World-Independent*, Mar. 2, 1955, p. 1.
6. *World-Independent*, June 17, 1955, Special Edition, p. 1.
7. Personal interview by the author with Richard and Betty Ridge, 2006.
8. Ibid.
9. *World-Independent*, June 18, 1955, p. 1.
10. *World-Independent*, Jan. 4, 1956, p. 1.
11. Ibid.
12. *World-Independent*, Jan. 11, 1956, p. 1.
13. *World-Independent*, Jan. 20, 1956, p. 1.
14. *World-Independent*, Feb. 17, 1956, p. 1.
15. *World-Independent*, Feb. 21, 1956, p. 1.
16. *World-Independent*, July 5, 1955, p. 1.
17. *World-Independent*, Sept. 22, 1955, p. 1.
18. *World-Independent*, Oct. 17, 1956, p. 1.
19. *World-Independent*, May 1, 1957, p. 1.
20. *World-Independent*, Oct. 31, 1957, p. 1.
21. *Huerfano World*, Feb. 7, 1958, p. 1.
22. *Huerfano World*, Nov. 5, 1959, p. 1.
23. *Huerfano World*, various papers throughout 1961.
24. *Huerfano World*, April 6, 1961, p. 1.
25. *Huerfano World*, June 14, 1962, p. 1.
26. *Huerfano World*, Dec. 5, 1963, p. 1.

27. *Walsenburg Independent,* July 30, 1964, p. 1.

28. *Huerfano World,* July 21, 1966, p. 1.

29. *Huerfano World,* Aug. 25, 1966, p. 1.

30. *Huerfano World,* August and September, 1966.

31. *Huerfano World,* July 25, 1968, p. 1.

32. *Huerfano World,* Feb. 27, 1969, p. 1.

33. *Huerfano World,* Aug. 28, 1969, p. 1.

34. Personal interview by the author with Elaine Lenzini, 2006.

35. *Huerfano World,* Feb. 12, 1970, p. 1.

36. *Huerfano World,* Oct., Nov. and Dec. 1970.

37. *Huerfano World,* Jan 21, 1971, p. 1.

38. *Huerfano World,* Aug. 26, 1971, p. 1.

39. *Huerfano World,* Oct. 28, 1971, p. 1.

40. *Huerfano World,* Dec. 16, 1971, p. 1.

41. *Huerfano World,* Feb. 17, 1972, p. 1.

42. *Huerfano World,* Mar. 9, 16, May 25, 1972, p. 1.

43. *Huerfano World,* Mar. 16, 1972, p. 1.

44. *Huerfano World,* May 25, 1972, p. 1.

45. *Huerfano World,* June 29, 1972, p. 1.

46. *Huerfano World,* July 6, 1972, p. 1.

47. *Huerfano World,* Nov. 30, 1972, p. 1.

48. *Huerfano World,* Feb. 8, 1973, p. 1.

49. *Huerfano World,* July 12, 1973, p. 1.

50. *Huerfano World,* May and June, 1973.

51. *Huerfano World,* July 12, 1973, p. 1.

52. *Huerfano World,* Nov. 15, 1973, p. 1.

53. *Huerfano World,* Mar. 7, 1974, p. 1.

54. *Huerfano World,* July 11, 1974, p. 1.

55. Ibid.

56. *Huerfano World,* Oct. 19, 1974, p. 1.

57. *Huerfano World,* Nov. 11, 1974, p. 1.

58. *Huerfano World,* Oct. 23, 1974, p. 1.

59. *Huerfano World,* July 22, 1976, p. 1.

60. *Huerfano World,* Sept. 16, 1976, p. 1.

61. *Huerfano World,* Mar. 24 and 31, 1977, p. 1.

62. *Huerfano World,* April 13, 1978, p. 7.

63. *Huerfano World,* Oct. 5, 1978, p. 1.

64. *Huerfano World,* Sept. 20, 1979, p. 1.

65. *Huerfano World,* Jan. 24, 1980, p. 1.

66. *Huerfano World,* Mar. 20, 1980, p. 1.

67. *Huerfano World,* June 19, 1980, to Jan. 15, 1981.

68. *Huerfano World,* Mar. 28, 1981, p. 1.

69. *Huerfano World*, June 17, 1982, p. 1.
70. *Huerfano World*, May 26, 1983, p. 1.
71. *Huerfano World*, Mar. 15, 1984, p. 1.
72. *Huerfano World*, July 26, 1984, p. 1.
73. *Huerfano World*, Jan. 1983, various papers.
74. *Huerfano World*, April 11, 985, p. 1.
75. *Huerfano World*, May 2 and 9, 1985, p. 1.
76. *Huerfano World*, July 11, 1985, p. 1.
77. *Huerfano World*, Dec. 12, 1985, p. 1.
78. *Huerfano World*, Mar. 1, 1986, p. 1.
79. *Huerfano World*, April 10, 1986, p. 1.
80. *Huerfano World*, Feb. 5, 1987, p. 1.
81. *Huerfano World*, Mar. 12, April 22 and May 7, 1987.
82. *Huerfano World*, July 2, 1987, p. 1.
83. *Huerfano World*, Aug. 6, 1987, p. 1.
84. *Huerfano World*, Dec. 1, 1988, and May 4, 1989.
85. *Huerfano World*, Mar. 23, 1989, p. 1.
86. *Huerfano World*, June 1, 1989, p. 1.
87. *Huerfano World*, Nov. 9, 1989, p. 1.
88. *Huerfano World*, Feb. 7, 1991, p. 1.
89. *Huerfano World*, Aug. 7 and Nov. 7, 1991.
90. *Huerfano World*, Sept. 5, Oct. 31, 1991, Jan. 9, 1992.
91. *Huerfano World*, April 30, 1992, p. 1.
92. *Huerfano World*, April 8, 1993, p. 1.
93. *Huerfano World*, July 22, 1993, p. 1.
94. *Huerfano World*, Oct. 30, 1997
95. *Huerfano World*, Oct. 30 and Nov. 3, 1997.
96. *Huerfano World*, June 10, 1999
97. *Huerfano World*, Nov. 5, 1998

Chapter Twelve – Into the Twenty-First Century

1. *Huerfano World*, Jan. 6, 2000, p. 1.
2. *Huerfano World*, May 18, 2000, p. 1.
3. *Huerfano World*, Jan. 27, 2000, and Oct. 25, 2001.
4. *Huerfano World*, June 1, 2000, p. 1.
5. *Huerfano World*, various papers in 2000-2001.
6. Personal interview by the author with Marti Henderson, businesswoman, April 20, 2006.
7. Personal interview by the author with Maurice Brau, former mayor and city councilman, April 12, 2006.

8. Personal interview by the author with Glenn Davis, former superintendent of Huerfano Re-1 School District, April 11, 2006.

9. Ibid.

10. Personal interview by the author with Patricia L. Martinez, principal of Peakview School, 2006.

11. Ibid.

12. Personal interview by the author with Margaret Gleisberg, president of the Walsenburg Mining Museum Board of Directors, April 13, 2006.

13. Ibid.

14. Personal interview by the author with Monica Kirby, Spanish Peaks Library Director, April 20, 2006.

15. Way, "The Story of Mister Miner," a speech.

Appendix A
Mayors of Walsenburg

The Town of Walsenburg was established in 1873 and was governed by a Board of Trustees. The first trustees were Fred Walsen, Joseph Bourcy, John Albert, Jose Rafael Esquibel, and Carmel Martin, with Walsen as head trustee. It is not entirely clear when the town began to have elections and to elect a mayor and other officers. In the early years, town trustees and mayors were elected in April for a one-year term. In later years, they were elected in November for two-year terms.

This mayor list was compiled from mayor's signatures on ordinances and from newspaper stories.

Some forty-one ordinances were passed by the Board of Trustees before one was signed by a mayor. The ordinances of the town are signed by the mayor, or mayor pro-tem, in some cases and by the city clerk in other cases. It is possible that some mayors were elected and served out a term without any ordinances being passed. One source lists a mayor in 1884 and another in 1885, but their names do not appear in the ordinance books.

1884 Cornelius Downing Hendren
1885 J. A. J. Valdes
1886 Charles Mazzone (This is the first mayor to have signed an ordinance.)
1887 Charles Unfug
1888 L. D. Baird
1889 Charles Unfug

1889 – 1890 T. F. Martin
1890 T.L. Creesy
1891 Charles O. Unfug
1892 J.A.J. Valdes
1893 Horace D. Wheeler
1894 – 1895 Fred E. Cowing
1896 – 1897 Theo Grantham
1898 J. P. Kearns
1899 Dr. T. D. Baird
1900 George Dick
1901 Dr. T. D. Baird
1902 George Dick
1903 – 1914 James B. Dick
1915 F. E. Cowing (March)
1915 T. D. Baird (August)
1916 T. D. Baird (March)
1916 Adolph Unfug (also March)
1916 – 1917 John J. Kirkpatrick (November)
1918 – 1920 C. Victor Mazzone
1920 – 1923 James W. Sears
1923 – 1924 H. D. Mustain
1925 – 1926 John J. Pritchard
1927 – 1933 A. J. Merritt
1933 – 1935 G. R. Mallett
1935 – 1937 Leighton H. Kirkpatrick
1937 – 1938 S. Julian Lamme
1939 – 1941 Andrew C. Schafer, Jr.
1941 – 1943 Dr. G. R. Mallett
1943 – 1944 Herman Mazzone (Appointed to fill out unexpired term of Dr. Mallett, who moved to Denver.)

1945   Joe Mosco, Jr. (Became mayor in a controversial action of a new city council following a tie vote in the election and lots of confusion before Mosco was finally chosen by the Colorado State Supreme Court.)

1945 – 1948   James B. Dick, Jr.

1948 – 1951   Joe Mosco, Jr.

1951 – 1954   George Turner (Elected to replace Joe Mosco, Jr.)

1955 – 1959   Donald D. Haney (Defeated George Turner in the election.)

1959 – 1963   Ethel Stacy

1963 – 1965   Joel R. Chambers

1965 – 1968   Joe Mosco, Jr.

1968 – 1969   John Geiger (Resigned.)

1969 – 1971   Derito Bonicelli (Appointed to fulfill Geiger's term and then was elected to a full term.)

1971 – 1975   Leo Maes

1975 – 1977   Robert Hemphill

1977 – 1983   Leo Maes

1983 – 1987   Betty Ridge

1987 – 1989   Tom Powell

1989 – 1991   Joan Crump (Died in office.)

1991 – 1992   Ray Sandoval (Mayor pro tem, interim replacement.)

1993 – 1999   Jay Crook

2000 – 2001   Fred Rodriguez

2002 – 2005   Maurice Brau

2006 – 2009   Edith Sheldon

2010 – 2011   Bruce Quintana

2012 –   Larry Patrick

Appendix B
Walsenburg Businesses

Neelley-Caldwell Hardware Co.

Schafer Packing Co.

Andrew C. Schafer, Sr. and his sons Andrew and William. Supply beef products to many areas. Located south of Walsenburg. Wholesale meat to restaurants, etc. plus Schafer's Market.

Opera House Café

Snodgrass Food Co.

Star Drug Company

Sporleder Selling Co.

Unfug Trading Co.

Walsenburg Mercantile Co.

Walsenburg Electrical Supply Co.

Walsenburg Creamery – Frank S. Mauro. Products included Mountain Gold butter, which was sold in many towns. Milk, cream and ice cream also processed and delivered.

Wayt Bros. Lumber Co.

Walsenburg Bottling Works – L. H. Kirkpatrick

Fox Theatre – Paul Krier

Bernstein's Dept. Store

Royal Beer Tavern, next to Klein Hotel. Tom Hobeika, Prop (1937)

Dr. F. W.Schafer, Chiropractor

San Isabel Liquor Store

Dick Abstract and Investment Co.

Stiglich Shoe Repairing

Mazzone Opera House

Walsenburg Livery Barn, W. N. Houser, Prop., Oscar Joyner, Mgr. Telephone Connections with Klein Hotel

John P. Kearns, Real Estate

New Meat Market, A. J. Sanchez, Prop.

Walsenburg Livery Barn, J. W. Stewart, Prop. 1916

First National Bank – Received its charter in 1903. Board of Directors was composed of Fred O.Roof, George Dick, James B. Dick, J. J. Pritchard and Jefferson B. Farr.

Guaranty State Bank, founded in 1909 by Paul Frohlich, Charles Agnes, G. R. Moore and Tim M. Hudson. Merged with First National later.

Baxter and Kearns Hardware and Trading Co.

Joe Mosco and Sons Grocery Store. Later became the Arts and Crafts Shop of Vinzie Mosco Scarafiotti.

Bibliography

BOOKS

Beshoar, Barron B., *Out of the Depths: The Story of John R. Lawson, a Labor Leader*. The Colorado Labor Historical Council of the Denver Trades and Labor Assembly. 1942, 372 p., biblio.

Byers, William N., *Encyclopedia of Biography of Colorado: History of Colorado*. Chicago, The Century Publishing and Engraving Company, 1901.

Bauer, William H.; Ozment, James L.; Willard, John H.; *Colorado Postal History: the Post Offices*, J. B. Publishing Co., c 1971.

Colorado Biography, *Portrait and Biographical Record of the State of Colorado*, Chapman Publishing Company, Chicago, 1899, illus. 1492 p.

Delaney, Howard L., *All Our Yesterdays, the Story of St. Mary Parish*, Walsenburg, Colorado. (No publishing data), 42 p., illus.

Griswold, P.R. "Bob", *Rio Grande: Along the Rio Grande*. Boulder, Talbot House Publication Services, c. 1986, illus. biblio.

Jackson, Helen Hunt, *Bits of Travel at Home*. Boston, Roberts Brothers, 1878.

Martelle, Scott, *Blood Passion: The Ludlow Massacre and Class War in the American West*. New Brunswick, NJ., Rutgers University Press, 2007, 266 p., illus., biblio.

McGovern, George S. and Leonard F. Guttridge, *The Great Coalfield War,* Boulder, Colorado, University Press of Colorado, c. 1996, 1972. 383 p. illus., biblio.

Nardine, Henry,. *In the Shadow of the Spanish Peaks; a History of Huerfano County, Colorado.* (no publishing data), c. revised 1988. 188 p. illus.

Papanikolas, Zeese, *Buried Unsung: Louis Tikas and the Ludlow Massacre*, University of Nebraska Press, c. 1982. 331 p. biblio., illus., biblio.

Ree, Dorothy Rose and Carolyn Newman, *A Narrative History of the United Church of Walsenburg.* 2004. 80 p., appendices.

Sinclair, Upton, *King Coal.* New York, Bantam Books, c. 1917, 1984, 1994, 430 p.

Southern Colorado Auxiliary of the Territorial Daughters of Colorado, *Pioneers of the Territory of Southern Colorado, Vol. II.* c. 1980, 156 p., illus.

NEWSPAPERS AND OTHER PERIODICALS

Colorado Exchange newspaper
Huerfano Cactus and *Yucca* newspapers
Huerfano World newspaper 1961-2006
Independent newspaper 1913-1931
Journal of the West, Vol. 15 (1976), pp. 76-101
Pueblo Chieftain and *Star Journal* newspapers
Walsenburg World newspaper 1904-1914
World-Independent newspaper 1930-1960

DOCUMENTS

Allison, Archibald, *Allison Papers*, WH739, Western History Collection, The Denver Public Library.

Case, John, *John Case Papers*, WH67, Western History Collection, The Denver Public Library.

Hutchinson, Chuck and Nancy, "Hendren Papers."

Krier, Paul, "Memories of Walsenburg", unpublished manuscript

Minutes of City Council Meetings of Walsenburg, CO.

Ordinances of the City of Walsenburg.

Ree, Dorothy Rose, "An Informal History of the Huerfano County Library," published document.

"A Short History of the Walsenburg Chamber of Commerce", unpublished manuscript.

Sporleder, Louis Bernhardt, "Family Papers", WH916, Western History Collection, The Denver Public Library.

Vallejo, Edmund, "The Seventh Street Massacre,", manuscript.

Vallejo, Frances Atencio Nelson, notebooks and other documents.

INTERVIEWS

Brau, Maurice
Davis, Glenn
Cordova, Elvera
Geiger, Jewel Krier
Gleisberg, Margaret Van Schoyck
Lenzini, Elaine Levy
Henderson, Marti
Kirby, Monica
Martinez, Patricia L.
Murr, Norma Lou Brunelli
Sporleder, Gerry
Summers, Dan Unfug
Tressell, Marian

DOROTHY ANNE ROSE REE

Dorothy was a retired librarian from John Mall High School, in Walsenburg, Colorado.

She received a B.A. in English, Speech, and Drama from Eastern New Mexico University, in 1952; an M.A. in English and History from Eastern New Mexico University, in 1956; an M.A. in Librarianship from University of Denver, in 1970.

She served as chair of the Walsenburg Mining Museum Board of Trustees, as docent for the Museum, and was a member of the Huerfano County Historical Society.

She was co-author of *A Narrative History of the United Church of Walsenburg* and wrote the history of the local library. She also wrote for the local newspaper.

Dorothy died October 17, 2006, leaving her husband, George Ben Ree.

INDEX

B